Sport—Commerce—Culture

Toby Miller
General Editor

Vol. 11

PETER LANG
New York • Washington, D.C./Baltimore • Bern
Frankfurt am Main • Berlin • Brussels • Vienna • Oxford

David L. Andrews

Sport—Commerce—Culture
Essays on Sport in Late Capitalist America

PETER LANG
New York • Washington, D.C./Baltimore • Bern
Frankfurt am Main • Berlin • Brussels • Vienna • Oxford

Library of Congress Cataloging-in-Publication Data

Andrews, David L.
Sport—commerce—culture: essays on sport in late
capitalist America / David L. Andrews.
p. cm. — (Popular culture and everyday life; v. 11)
Includes bibliographical references and index.
1. Sports—United States—Marketing. 2. Sports—Economic aspects—
United States. 3. Sports—Social aspects—United States. I. Title.
II. Series: Popular culture & everyday life; v. 11.
GV716.A55   338.4'7796'0973—dc22   2005023198
ISBN 0-8204-7438-X
ISSN 1529-2428

Bibliographic information published by **Die Deutsche Bibliothek**.
Die Deutsche Bibliothek lists this publication in the "Deutsche
Nationalbibliografie"; detailed bibliographic data is available
on the Internet at http://dnb.ddb.de/.

Cover design by Sophie Boorsch Appel

The paper in this book meets the guidelines for permanence and durability
of the Committee on Production Guidelines for Book Longevity
of the Council of Library Resources.

© 2006 Peter Lang Publishing, Inc., New York
29 Broadway, New York, NY 10006
www.peterlang.com

Printed in the United States of America

This book is dedicated to the enduring memory of Kieran McGinnity.

CONTENTS

ACKNOWLEDGMENTS

This book has been a long time in the making. Although its failings and oversights are attributable to no one other than myself, this book should be considered a collaborative endeavor, in the truest sense of the term: numerous people and institutions have encouraged and supported me over the past fifteen years or so, and thereby contributed to this summative work coming to fruition. Uppermost, my parents, June and Peter Andrews, need to be thanked for their love, unceasing selflessness, and understated—though unerringly apposite—guidance. I am not entirely sure how to repay them, other than by expressing my profound gratitude and love. John W. Loy was instrumental in my going to study at the University of Illinois and became, and has remained, an important influence on my life. Similarly, Ralph C. Wilcox provided me with my first *proper* job (with apologies to all my previous employers up to that point) at the University of Memphis, wherein he created an uniquely supportive climate designed to facilitate the growth of junior faculty. At the University of Maryland, Jane E. Clark should be applauded for countering the general trend within higher education by actively encouraging—as opposed to paying administrative lip service to—new forms and expressions of interdisciplinarity within her truly expansive vision of kinesiology. Also at Maryland, Mike Silk has been the epitome of the encouraging friend and colleague, as well as being someone responsible for creating a stimulating, and truly rewarding, working environment. Despite the significant influence of the aforementioned, the truth of the matter is that this project would not have even been muted were it not for the enthusiastic encouragement of the series editor, Toby Miller. Equally,

Damon Zucca and Lisa Dillon, at Peter Lang, have proved to be calming, patient, and supportive influences. Of course, there are countless others who have contributed, in various ways, to my intellectual, professional, and indeed personal development, and who are thus implicated, to greater and lesser degrees, in this project. The following is almost certainly an incomplete list of those people to whom I feel most indebted (with apologies in anticipation of the glaring omissions that will no doubt come to light): John Amis, Alan Bairner, Toni Bruce, Ben Carrington, Jay Coakley, C. L. Cole, Jim Denison, Norman Denzin, Michele Donnelly, Eric Dunning, Michael Friedman, Grant Farred, Mike Giardina, James Gillett, Richard Giulianotti, Andy Grainger, Lawrence Grossberg, Jean Harvey, Cynthia Hasbrook, Michelle Helstein, Jeremy Howell, Amy Hribar, the late and greatly missed Alan Ingham, Steve Jackson, Douglas Kellner, Samantha King, Mary McDonald, Jim McKay, Joseph Maguire, Pirkko Markula, Sonya Michel, Josh Newman, Dave Nurse, Robert Pitter, Genevieve Rail, Steve Redhead, Davy Rees, Gareth Rees, Roger Rees, Bob Rinehart, George Ritzer, David Rowe, Trevor Slack, Nancy Spencer, Jennifer Sterling, Lisa Swanson, Mary Tate-Evans, Nancy Theberge, Darren Treasure, Lee Vander Velden, Steve Wagg, Tony Walker, Belinda Wheaton, Ryan White, Brian Wilson, and Detlev Zwick. Last, and definitely not least, I have to acknowledge the debt of love and gratitude I owe to Lisa, Frankie, and Freya, without whom none of this would have been realized, and with whom all is put in its rightful place.

PERMISSIONS

The majority of the essays in this collection have appeared, in earlier iterations, within prior publications. However, many of these pieces have been revised for this volume, although the extent of revisions ranges from the extensive to the minimal. As a result, I secured formal permissions for using those works that formed the bases of various chapters, the details of which are as follows. In addition, where chapters have been inspired by previous works (and therefore do not require formal permission for publication), I wanted to acknowledge the origins of my present position.

Chapter 1 represents a revision and updating of "A Propos de la NBA." In *L'aventure des «Grands» Hommes. Etudes sur L'histoire du Basket-Ball,* edited by F. Archambault, L. Artiaga and P.-Y. Frey, 271–92. Limoges, France: University of Limoges Press, 2003.

Chapter 2 was previously published as "Speaking the 'Universal Language of Entertainment': News Corporation, Culture and the Global Sport Media Economy." In *Critical Readings: Sport, Culture and the Media,* edited by D. Rowe, 99–128. Berkshire, England: Open University Press, 2003.

Chapter 3 represents a revision and updating of a co-authored piece with Josh Newman and Andrew Grainger titled "Even Better Than the Real Thing? The XFL and Football's Future." *Football Studies* 6, no. 2 (2003).

Chapter 4 was previously published as "Feminizing Olympic Reality: Preliminary Dispatches from Baudrillard's Atlanta." *International Review for the Sociology of Sport* 33, no. 1 (1998): 5–18.

Chapter 5 is a newly conceived chapter inspired by collaborations with Steven Jackson ("Introduction: Sport Celebrities, Public Culture, and Private Experience." In *Sport Stars: The Cultural Politics of Sport Celebrity,* edited by D.L. Andrews and S.J. Jackson, 1–19. London: Routledge, 2001), and C.L. Cole ("America's New Son: Tiger Woods and America's Multiculturalism." *Cultural Studies: A Research Annual* 5 [2000]: 107–22).

Chapter 6 represents a revision of "Contextualizing Suburban Soccer: Consumer Culture, Lifesyle Differentiation, and Suburban America." *Culture, Sport, Society* (now *Sport in Society: http://www.tandf.co.uk*) 2, no. 3 (1999): 31–53.

Chapter 7 was previously published as a co-authored piece with Michael Friedman and Michael Silk titled "Sport and the Façade of Redevelopment in the Post-industrial City." *Sociology of Sport Journal* 21, no. 2 (2004): 119–39.

Chapter 8 is a newly conceived chapter inspired by the following collaboration with Michael Silk "Beyond a Boundary? Sport, Transnational Advertising, and the Reimagining of National Culture." *Journal of Sport & Social Issues* 25, no. 2 (2001): 180–201.

The conclusion represents a revision of "Dead or Alive? Sports History in the Late Capitalist Moment." *Sporting Traditions: Journal of the Australian Society for Sports History* 16, no. 1 (1999): 73–85.

Introduction

SITUATING SPORT

At the beginning of any academic discussion of sport it is common practice to define the central term. As a point of departure for this project, I feel compelled to offer a brief rejoinder to this convention. In short, I would contend that there is no guaranteed or essential manifestation, experience or, indeed, definition of sport. Although physically based competitive activities are a feature of virtually all human civilizations, the popular myth of sport as a fixed and immutable category is little more than a pervasive, if compelling, fiction. Sport should instead be used as a necessarily malleable collective noun suggesting the diversity and complexity of what are temporally and spatially contingent expressions of physical culture. In Cashmore's terms, sports are fluid and ever changing "products of cultural endeavors, enterprises that have been manufactured in particular kinds of historical and social circumstances" (2000, p. vii). So, rather than seeking to develop some universal definition of sport, a more productive interpretive strategy is to locate particular sport forms and experiences in the socio-historical context within which they came to exist and operate.

This project, like countless others within the cultural studies of sport, is prompted by the work of C. Wright Mills, whose "sociological imagination" represents one of the more compelling statements on the importance of context to the practice of critical sociological inquiry (Mills, 1959). Mills realized the need to anchor any examination of social existence within the historical moment and conditions that frame it. In forwarding this approach Mills invoked the work of Karl Marx: "What Marx called the 'principle of historical specificity' refers, first, to a guide-line: any given society is to be understood in terms of the specific period in which it exists" (Mills, 1959, p. 149). The concept of the sociological imagination took off from this historical materialist premise and sought to develop the type of social inquiry that would allow analysts to "see it whole" (Mills, 1959, p. 153). As Mills famously stated, "The sociological imagination enables us to grasp history and biography and the relations between the two within society. That is its task and its promise" (1959, p. 6).

Marx's "dialectical version" (Rigby, 1998, p. 184) of the base and superstructure model—wherein elements of society interact in a two-way relation, characterized by mutual constitution and influence—had a significant influence on Mills's thought. Marx's dialectic materialism (c.f. Callinicos, 1983, pp. 58–64; Ritzer, 1988, pp. 18–20), itself an amalgam of Hegel's dialectic and Feuerbach's materialist understandings, asserted that human consciousness and practice was the product of an engagement with material social reality. The corollary was a new social condition produced by this interaction. According to this "ontological dialectic" (Miliband, 1983, p. 122) individual actions and consciousness are no longer reduced to being the effects of a dominant economic order as a more deterministic reading of Marx would assert. Instead, within the context of the web of societal constraints faced according to one's social and historical location, individual agents possess a degree of autonomy in shaping their life experiences. Marx's dialecticism is most famously expressed in the following quotation from *The Eighteenth Brumaire of Louis Napoleon:*

> Men [*sic*] make their own history, but they do not make it just as they please; they do not make it under circumstances chosen by themselves, but under circumstances directly encountered, given, and transmitted from the past. The tradition of all the dead generations weighs like a nightmare on the brain of the living. (Marx, 1977a, p. 300)

In 53 words Marx captures the constitutive interdependency of the structure-agency relation, linking individuals and the society in which they are located and which, through their actions, they help to form. This understanding is not only applicable to individual actions, for the same holds true for the relation between society and larger formations of individual agents (collective practices, institutions, and organizations). So, following Marx's ontological dialecticism, it could be argued that people make their own working, leisure, political, religious, and indeed sporting lives, but not in the conditions of their own choosing. They do so under the constraints and opportunities of their particular social location, which their working, leisure, political, religious, and sporting lives reproduce or challenge.

While by no means universally Marxist in terms of theoretical and/or political underpinnings, there would seem to be a widespread consensus among the sociology of sport community regarding the need to comprehend fully a sporting practice's necessary interrelation with the social formation in which it is located. While some may engage in a form of willing suspension of cynicism when viewing or attending a sporting event, in the academic sphere sport has been *outed* as the labyrinthine and multifaceted social institution that it is. According to Jarvie and Maguire, there has been:

a transcendence of a general belief that sport and leisure were somewhat autonomous or separate from society or politics or problems of social development . . . [which] gave rise to a growing recognition that sport and leisure were far too complex to be viewed as simple products of voluntary behaviour or totally autonomous entities. (Jarvie & Maguire, 1994, p. 2)

Or, as Sage outlined:

Sport is a set of social practices and relations that are structured by the culture in which they exist, and any adequate account of sport must be rooted in an understanding of its location within society. The essence of sport is to be found within the nature of its relationship to the broader stream of societal forces of which it is a part. Thus, a real necessity for everyone trying to understand the sociocultural role of sport in American society is to approach sport relationally, always asking, "What are the interconnections of sport to other aspects of American society?" (Sage, 1998, p. 14)

Arguably the most explicit and influential sport-focused elaboration of Marx's cultural dialecticism came within Richard Gruneau's critical analysis of modern sport, *Class, Sports and Social Development*. Informed by the work of Karl Marx, Thorstein Veblen, Antonio Gramsci, Anthony Giddens, and Raymond Williams, Gruneau sought to transcend the varieties of empiricism, idealism, and vulgar Marxism that shackled the early development of the sociology of sport. Gruneau interrogated sport as a cultural practice that neither "transcends the society that produces it nor is a simple mirror reflection" (Critcher, 1986, pp. 335). Further illustrating the dialecticism implicit within it, Gruneau's approach is expressed by the fact that sport is seen as created by society, but is correspondingly one way in which social beings are able to maintain and develop a sense of themselves. Sport is at the same time constitutive of the boundaries framing social experience, and a forum for the manufacturing of individual lives:

play, games, and sports ought to be seen as constitutive social practices whose meanings, metaphoric qualities, and regulatory structures are indissolubly connected to the making and remaking of ourselves as agents (individual and collective) in society. To put the matter another way, rather than view any feature of play, games, and sports as some sort of transhistorical essence, need, or transcendent metaphysical form, or rather than see them as activities simply reducible to a "separate" material reality, I am opting for a view where play, games, and sports are all regarded as irreducibly constitutive of our social being. They are, in differing ways, all forms of social practice. As a result, even their "essential" or formal qualities cannot be conceived of independently of the organizing principles, expectations, conflicts, and disappointments that define lived social experience at any given historical moment. . . .

We will have to be more sensitive to the dialectical relationships between socially structured possibilities and human agency. In other words, we must struggle to avoid one-sided considerations of players as voluntary agents acting in the absence of constraining structures and of structures which do not allow for the creative and transformative capacities of players. (Gruneau, 1983, pp. 50–51)

Although utilizing somewhat different terminology, within his expansive *Football: A Sociology of the Global Game,* Richard Giulianotti is equally explicit with regard to his dialectic underpinnings:

> Football and other kinds of sporting practice are not "dependent" on the wider society: they are instead influenced by and influential upon the broader social context. . . . My position throughout the book, therefore, is that the social aspects of football only become meaningful when located within their historical and cultural context. Football is neither dependent upon nor isolated from the influences of that wider milieu; instead, a relative autonomy exists in the relationship between the two. (Giulianotti, 1999, p. xv)

Gruneau and Giulianotti are by no means alone. They are merely part of a slew of likeminded sport researchers (c.f. Birrell & McDonald, 2000; Carrington, 2000; Cole, 1996; Cole & Andrews, 2000; Howell & Ingham, 2001; Ingham, 1985; Maguire, 2000; Miller, 2001; Miller, Lawrence, McKay, & Rowe, 2001; Rowe, 1995; Silk, 2002; Tomlinson, 1999) whose collective contribution has conclusively affirmed the importance of a dialectic sensibility. As Ritzer (1988, p. 135) reminds us, with sport as with any other experiential domain "one component of social life cannot be studied in isolation from the rest."

This project is primarily concerned with illuminating the manner, and effects, of sport's dialectic relation to the commercial structures and rhythms that form the fulcrum of consumer capitalism within the contemporary United States (heretofore referred to as either the US or America). Of course, the use of the noun *America* throughout this book, and specifically in its subtitle, requires a degree of qualification. In an analogous vein to the position advanced by Lafrance, I am uncomfortable with the self-centering, and self-aggrandizing propensities of the American appellation that, whether advertently or otherwise, advances the "truly 'imaginary' character of a national imagination that views the United States of America as the only America that matters" (Lafrance, 1998, p. 136). While acknowledging its problematic assumptions, it is evident that America—the exclusive noun–and American–the exclusive adjective–liberally punctuate a variety of sporting contexts and discourses, in a manner which infuses both the national culture, and its constitutively allied sport culture, with a palpable sense of exceptionalism and ingrained superiority (Markovits & Hellerman, 2001). So, while not wishing to further this form of linguistic imperialism, this project illuminates—and thereby encourages the problematizing of–the normalized and normalizing position of American rhetoric within the US sporting vernacular.

Returning to the dialectic nature of the sport-society relation, cultural practices, such as sport, are produced from specific socio-historic contexts, they are also actively engaged in the ongoing constitution of the conditions out of which they emerge; they are "always constituted with and constitutive of a larger context of relationships" (Grossberg, 1997a, p. 257). Thus, contemporary American sport culture must be considered as both a product, and producer, of the social formation (contemporary American society) in which it is situated. Mindful of such an understanding, in a broad sense, this discussion is concerned with "forging connections" (Grossberg, 1992, p. 54) between sport and the multiplicity of forces, relations, and effects (economic, political, social, cultural, and technological) associated with the contemporary American context, described as the moment, or condition, of "late capitalism" (Jameson, 1991). The prevailing sport forms of both pre-industrial and industrial eras were both a "product of historical conditions . . . and are fully applicable only to and under those conditions" (Marx, 1977b, p. 355); the maturation of nation state-based capitalism in Western Europe and North America, during the second half of the nineteenth century, was accompanied by the emergence of institutionalized sport as—at least partially—an agent of social control for the urban industrial masses. By codifying sporting practice (regulated participation) and sanctioning cathartic release (mass spectatorship), the patrician-industrialist power bloc ensured that sport helped constrain working bodies to the demands and discipline of the industrial workplace, while simultaneously contributing to the commercialization of urban leisure culture (Butsch, 1990). As characterized by Harry Braverman, the noted labor historian:

> the filling of the time away from the job also becomes dependent upon the market, which develops to an enormous degree those passive amusements, entertainments, and spectacles that suit the restricted circumstances of the city and are offered as substitutes for life itself. Since they become the means of filling all the hours of "free" time, they flow profusely from corporate institutions which have transformed every means of entertainment and "sport" into a production process for the enlargement of capital. (Braverman, 1998, p. 279)

Thus, within the modern industrial era, institutionalized sport became an emergent site of "surveillance, spectacle, and profit" within the newly defined realm of "free" time (Miller & McHoul, 1998, p. 61).

Despite a few examples of sport's commercialization in the US before the industrial era (for example, in the promotional activities of colonial taverns, c.f. Struna, 1996), many sport organizations and institutions continued to outwardly resist the lure of capitalist economic forces well into the twentieth century (some undoubtedly conditioned by residues of de Coubertin-esque idealism). Sport in this sense remained a "semiautonomous sphere of culture" (Jameson, 1991, p. 48), only *somewhat* removed from the practices and pressures of the marketplace. After World War II, however, the intensification of corporate-based consumer capitalism accelerated the "infiltration" (Habermas, 1979) of market forces into almost every facet of human existence, including sport. Corporate capitalism's inexorable appropriation of sport culture replaced the amateur(ish) volunteerism of official "Old Boy" sporting values with the scientific business principles and rationalities espoused by "men and women of the Corporation" (McKay & Miller, 1991, p. 86). These new values infiltrated sport via "modern forms of domination, such as 'business administration,' and techniques of manipulation, such as market research and advertising" (Bourdieu, 1998, p. 35). Sport was thereafter effectively and efficiently reorganized in accordance with corporate commercial structures and logics which routinely placed economic (profit maximization) ahead of sporting (utility maximization) imperatives: sport, to invoke an oft cited cliché, became *big business*.

In the second half of the twentieth century, sport was conclusively—and, apparently, irreversibly—integrated into the commercial maelstrom of the dominant consumer capitalist order, such that presently "complex industrial processes and relations . . . together produce sport as one of the world's largest economic enterprises" (Rowe, 1995, p. 115). Contemporary sporting institutions and *bodies* (sport organizations, events, leagues, teams, athletes, etc.) thus became enmeshed with the structures, values, and directives of late capitalist culture: Put simply, a conjuncture within which "everything . . . has become cultural; and culture has equally become economic or commodity oriented." (Jameson, 1998, p. 73). Within this context:

> spectator sports have emerged as the correlative to a society that is replacing manual labor with automation and machines, and requires consumption and appropriation of spectacles to reproduce consumer society. The present-day era also sees the expansion of a service sector and highly differentiated entertainment industry, of which sports are a key part. (Kellner, 2002, p. 66)

Of course, many sporting entities (such as Major League Baseball [MLB], the National Basketball Association [NBA], the National Football League [NFL], the National Hockey League [NHL], and their respective franchises) originated as professional, commercially oriented ventures. However, until relatively recently, most had historically occupied a space at the periphery of the commercial marketplace, with utility maximization (sporting performance) routinely taking precedence over—frequently to the exclusion of—profit maximization (financial performance). The commercialization and commodification of sport—what Walsh and Giulianotti referred to as "the ongoing process . . . of translating the social meaning of a practice or object into purely financial terms" (2001, p. 55)—reached a heightened level of intensity with the advancement of the profit-driven corporation as the naturalized, and largely unquestioned, model of societal organization:

> The history of modern capitalism is the corporatization of social life worlds once under communal and normative control. Education, health, leisure and sport, marriage, child-rearing, work, community life, welfare (the traditional infrastructures of publics) lose their relative cultural autonomy to a formal dependency upon bureaucratic organizations, professional experts, and the imperial decisions of invisible executives. (Alt, 1983, p. 98)

The sporting response to the broader reorganization of social existence—what Alt referred to as the "social hegemony" (1983, p. 98) of corporatization—has been manifest in the emergence of the "corporate sport" modality, against which established and new sporting entities are measured (McKay & Miller, 1991). This normalized, and indeed normalizing, blueprint for commercial sport organizations (Andrews, 1999) privileges, to varying degrees and in varying intensities, the following structural and processual elements: profit-driven executive control and management hierarchies; cartelized ownership and franchized organizational structures;

rational (re)location of teams and venues; the entertainment-driven mass mediation of sporting spectacles; the reconfiguring of sport spectacles and spaces as sponsorship vehicles for advancing corporate visibility; the cultural management of the sport entity as a network of merchandizable brands and embodied sub-brands; the differentiation of sport-related revenue streams and consumption opportunities; and, the advancement of marketing and promotional strategies aimed at both consolidating core, and expanding new, sport consumer constituencies.

The forces responsible for the congealing corporate sport hegemon came from both internal and external points of origin. In terms of the former, and with varying degrees of willingness (recognizing its commercial potential) or reluctance (capitulating to its inevitability), many sport administrators simply acquiesced to what was perceived to be an unrelenting corporatist tide. Thus, a corporatizing wave spread across the sporting landscape, vanguarded by a new generation of executives, whose overriding goal was to manage sport products in such a ways as to maximize profit within the increasingly competitive leisure marketplace (Butsch, 1990; McKay & Miller, 1991).

The reorganization of sport in accordance to the strictures of economic rationality was also informed by externally grounded influences. Sport's latent, and largely underexploited, commercial potential was clearly vulnerable to corporate colonization. The recognition that, within an ostensibly consumption-based economy, ownership of a commercial enterprise invoking a level of popularity and loyalty exceeding far "beyond most other experiences" (Miller, Lawrence, McKay, & Rowe, 2001, p. 1), made sport an attractive proposition for institutional and individual investors alike (many of whom, in previous generations, may have involved themselves in sport more for the social benefits accrued from what they perceived to be a form of community-based altruism, than any expectation of commercial gain). So, through a series of institutional takeovers by various corporate interests (from traditional manufacturing and, more recently, from the burgeoning financial, mass media, and high-technology sectors) outmoded organizational sporting sensibilities have largely been replaced by the profit-driven rationalities of corporate managerialism (with varying degrees of sporting and/or financial success). This is particularly evident at the franchise/team level, where the corporate appropriation and reorganization of sport's storied institutions regularly invokes the disdain of the sporting public.

Sport's internally and externally driven corporate restructuring had the effect of positioning it more centrally within American commercial life. Moreover, sport's aggressive commercialization became an exemplar of the "culturalization of economics" (Rowe, 1999, p. 70) fuelling the late capitalist condition. As Jameson (1991, p. xxi) reiterated, in a manner which speaks to the processual dualism associated with the corporate sport modality (the commercialization of sport/sportization of commerce), the "*cultural* and the *economic,* thereby collapse back into one another and say the same thing in an eclipse of the distinction between base and superstructure." If sport institutions were ever an organic element of civic life—however, nominally and symbolically—romanticized allusions to the public *ownership* of sport were categorically repudiated by the corporatist colonization and revisionism that transformed sport into an unapologetic vehicle for the investment and advancement of private capital. It is in this sense that the Super Bowl has come to be understood, even celebrated as the "annual midwinter festival of athleticism and commercialism" (Elliott, 2003, p. C4), and NASCAR gratefully described by Tom Higgins, CEO of NASCAR corporate sponsor, Best Western, as a "business opportunity cleverly disguised as a sport" (Marketplace, 2004).

Since late capitalism's culturally inflected regime of accumulation is prefigured on the operationalizing of the mass media (simultaneously as both core product and process), the corporatization of sport has become inextricably tied to the rhythms and regimes of an expanding media-industrial complex. As Rowe observed, "sport and the sports media, as cultural goods par excellence, are clearly a central element in a larger process (or set of processes) that is reshaping society and culture" (1999, p. 67). So, the relentless rise of commercial television in the post-World War II era—as a major conduit to both the *commercialization of culture,* and the associated *culturalization of the economy*—has revolutionized the sport economy; escalating fees from the selling of broadcast rights and media sponsorships having become, for many professional sports, teams, and events, the single most important source of revenue generation (Bellamy, 1998).

Equally, a new order of entertainment-oriented corporate leviathans (McChesney, 1997)—many of whose organizational histories betrayed origins in the material mass manufacturing past: the newly fused media conglomerate, NBC Universal, is still parented by General Electric, while Viacom's lineage can be traced back to that symbol of American manufacturing, Westinghouse—have come to rely upon sports as an invaluable source of programming content across the breadth of their multi-platform domains (i.e., network and cable television, radio, Internet, film studio, newspaper, and magazine outlets). The principal revenue stream for the commercial media derives from audiences generated (either in terms of television viewers, radio listeners, web page visitors, or magazine readers etc.), which are subsequently sold, as de facto commodities, to advertisers (Grossberg, Wartella, & Whitney, 1998). For this reason, audience size, in terms of quantity and quality, assumes critical importance. Of course, increased advertising revenue is not the only perceived benefit of televising popular sport spectacles, they also represent a priceless opportunity for promoting the network's other programming (particularly new shows) to otherwise unimaginable percentages of the national populace. In the cutthroat world of primetime television, this entrée into audience consciousness can have important effects on establishing the popularity (and hence longevity) of new programming, thereby affecting the profitability of entire networks.

Within this commercially driven media universe, sport's historically and culturally entrenched popular appeal (in terms of audience quantity: sport's ability to deliver a sizeable audience) has elevated it to such an extent that the clamor for the exclusive rights to broadcast sporting mega-events (Roche, 2000) generates inflation-inducing bidding wars: NBC invested $3.55 billion for television rights to the 3 Summer and 2 Winter Olympiads between 2000 and 2008 (Real, 1998);

broadcast rights for the NFL's Super Bowl also represent a significant part of the shared $17.6 billion eight-year contract signed by the NFL and ABC/ESPN, CBS, and Fox in 1998. Having effectively purchased the American population's attention, it is subsequently leased for exorbitant sums to corporate advertisers, usually resulting in sizeable broadcaster profits, despite the magnitude of the initial investment. Even regular sport programming—often with seemingly modest audiences in terms of volume—are lucrative media properties, largely because of the level of interest generated among the 18–34-year-old male viewers/consumers prized by corporate advertisers (audience quality: sport's ability to deliver high concentrations of the *right* audience). While we may be seduced into thinking that media outlets are providing a public service by satiating the nation's appetite for sport, the cold reality is:

> The media have no inherent interest in sport. It is merely a means for profit making. . . . For TV and radio, sport gets consumers in front of their sets to hear and see commercials; in effect, TV and radio rent their viewers' and listeners' attention. (Sage, 1990, p. 123)

For this reason, and as Jary lamented, there exists an "increasing tendency for sport organizations in particular to become indirectly controlled or monopolized by media organizations and/or major advertisers" (Jary, 1999, p. 120). Indeed, for many commentators, contemporary sport culture can only be understood in light of its collusive linkages with the media industry, thus references to "mediasport" (Wenner, 1998), the "sports/media complex" (Jhally, 1989), or the "sport-business-TV nexus" (Rowe, 1996, p. 565), all of which corroborates Real's identification of the "institutional alignment of sports and media in the context of late capitalism" (Real, 1998, p. 15). Or, as perhaps best described by Kellner, contemporary "sports . . . merge sports into media spectacle . . . and attest to the commodification of all aspects of life in the media and consumer society" (2002, p. 66). Such is the focus, both individually and collectively, of the essays brought together within this book.

Chapter 1 focuses on the NBA as an exemplar of the late capitalist sport organization, in that it has seamlessly blurred the boundaries between sport, media, and entertainment sectors. The NBA's metamorphosis into a mass media entertainment empire has pivoted on the league's ability to create multi-platform popular media spectacles around which its ancillary sectors (and, indeed, revenue streams) have propagated. In this manner, the NBA can certainly be likened to the Disney Corporation, in that mass media are harnessed as the NBA's principal mechanism, and primary source, of capital accumulation. Consequently, Bryman's (1999) concept of Disneyization—specifically the interrelated processes of theming, dedifferentiation of consumption, merchandising, and emotional labor—are examined and explicated within the empirical context of the NBA. This leads to a discussion of the aggressive globalization of the NBA spectacle which has, perhaps unlike Disney in this case, contributed to the recent internationalization of the league's player personnel; thus furthering the resonance of the league within the global cultural marketplace.

Looking from the other side of the sport-media complex, Chapter 2 examines the commercially driven rationale underpinning News Corporation's (the global media behemoth headed by Rupert Murdoch) extensive and aggressive forays into the global sport landscape. In seeking to harness the public's interest in sport as a means of building audiences for its fledgling network and satellite television interests, News Corporation has not only transformed sport's economic landscape (through its willingness to pay inflated sums for broadcast rights to sporting events), it has changed the modus operandi for global media giants seeking to, more efficiently and effectively, control sport media products, and thereby capitalize upon the popularity of sport (through its propensity for either purchasing or creating sport leagues, teams, and stadia, and inserting them into News Corporation's vertically integrated corporate structure). Murdoch thus led the commercially induced charge responsible for reducing sport to being little more, or indeed less, than a source of mass media content.

Developing on issues pertaining to the sport-media complex, Chapter 3 explicates the corollary of what occurs when sporting and media entertainment interests share the responsibility, or perhaps more appropriately the blame, for the conception of new sport forms. Focused on the short-lived XFL professional football league, the discussion demonstrates how this fusion of professional wrestling's (the World Wrestling Federation) populist sensibilities and network television's (NBC) commercial avarice, led to the instantiation (if only for one season) of what was an illuminating statement on what has come to be the hegemonic union of sporting and entertainment universes.

As evidenced in the reasons for the XFL's rapid demise, even the most august and revered aspects of contemporary sport culture—such as the Olympic Games—have become incorporated into the sportainment hegemon. Thus, Chapter 4 illuminates the commercial imperatives prompting NBC's molding of Olympic Games coverage into primetime network entertainment, and the attendant advancement of traditionally feminine codes within, and through, the content and structure of its Olympic broadcasts. Focusing specifically on NBC's coverage of the 1996 Atlanta Olympic Games, the analysis demonstrates how the potentialities of an increased female participant presence in the Olympic spectacle was devalued by the manner in which NBC portrayed women as fetishized hyperfeminine objects of production, and essentialized, hypersensitive subjects of consumption. In doing so, NBC, and by appropriation, the Olympic Games themselves, constructed a regressively gendered reality that confirmed, as it further normalized, the inequalities implicit within the contemporary gender order.

Turning to the embodied spectacles proliferating within today's [sport] celebrity culture, Chapter 5 engages the complementary yet contrasting commercially mediated personas of Michael Jordan and Tiger Woods as a means of divining the public representation, authorization, and experience of race and racial difference in contemporary America. Keying on the central role played by Nike in nurturing their celebrity identities, the discussion illustrates how Jordan came to function as a signifier of an atypical African American-ness, which displaced the attributes stereotypically associated with African American males onto other Black bodies. Although Woods entered the mainstream consciousness as the heir to Jordan's All-(African) American mantle, he was soon molded into America's multicultural *everyman:* a figure whose self-evident, but tantalizingly indistinct, multi-ethnicity allowed him to become the property of all and sundry within commercial America's compelling, if spurious, multicultural vision of itself. Thus, Jordan and Woods act as public individuals—seemingly progressive embodiments of American racial advancement—whose very presence, in actuality, flames the very racial stigmas and prejudices their celebrated existence suggests have been superseded.

Chapter 6 turns the focus onto the interrelationship between sport, social class, and space, through an analysis of the American suburban soccer phenomenon. Although seemingly more distanced from the imperatives of contemporary commercial culture than the empirical sporting worlds discussed in previous chapters, this examination contextualizes the suburban soccer field (understood in Bourdieuian and vernacular notions of the term) as an important constitutive element of the innately competitive, socially differentiating, and highly stylized lifestyle projects, through which individuals (and, indeed, families) engage in the socially sanctioned forms of consumption that conspicuously express their membership of what is a highly valorized middle class culture. In other words, soccer presently enunciates the dominant codes of suburban existence through what is a seemingly natural, un-self conscious vehicle of cultural expression and social organization.

Moving from suburban to urban spaces and concerns, Chapter 7 interrogates the cultural and economic derivations, and implications, of the sport-based spectacularization of many urban environments in the US. Through recourse to the instructive example of Baltimore (and, particularly, the definitive Oriole Park at Camden Yards complex), this analysis elucidates the practices and procedures whereby cities have utilized professional sport venues and facilities as anchoring, both physically and symbolically, components of broader urban redevelopment policies. More importantly perhaps, it assesses the consequences of such strategic policy initiatives—particularly concerning the gathering and distribution of tax revenues—for city inhabitants, many of whom are neither served by, nor serve in meaningful any capacity, at these cathedrals of sporting consumption.

Broadening the spatial focus of analysis even more, Chapter 8 illuminates the strategies used by major corporations (many, such as Coca-Cola, McDonald's, and Nike, American in their *origin*) pertaining to the fact that securing an expansive and profitable global presence necessitates negotiating within the language of the local. Sport frequently acts as a *de facto* cultural shorthand for local differences and identifications. Hence, this discussion examines the reimagining of the local, specifically through sport-inflected advertising and marketing campaigns, that has become the prevailing mechanism whereby transnational corporations entities seek to engage and constitute local markets.

Finally, this collection of essays focused on various aspects of sport's relation to the late capitalist American condition concludes with the—not entirely frivolous—

assertion that the commercial dictates propelling the tenor of contemporary existence have, in a Fukuayaman sense, led to the rejection of anything other than minor variants on the theme of sport as a corporately structured and commercially compelled cultural arena: Any other models of sporting existence being cast to the margins of cultural existence, from where they are destined to perish in a mass media-disregarded anonymity. Thus, in terms of being an organically evolving, dynamic, social institution, sport has reached the end of its "natural" life (it is, now, resigned to being terminally overdetermined by the cyclically regenerating, if largely minor and cosmetic, variants responsible for the characteristic perpetual dynamism of consumer capitalism). The practices of socio-cultural excavation and contextualization advanced within this book thus evince a strategy through which it may be possible to identify, and hopefully intervene into, the creeping politico-economic inertia and cultural banality which pervades—to the point of asphyxiating replication—contemporary sport culture. For, the derivations, manifestations, and implications of the hypercommercial sport cultures that can, at times, transfix and temporarily transform many of our lives, need to be regularly and rigorously interrogated (rather than uncritically absorbed). It is this viscerally seductive and seemingly benign rendering of physical culture which normalizes, as it naturalizes, many of the practices and ideologies that encourage not only the uncritical acceptance of late capitalist sport, but also, and more profoundly, the unquestioning acquiescence to the late capitalist order in general.

1

THE WONDERFUL WORLD OF THE NBA

Perhaps more than any other American sporting entity, the National Basketball Association (NBA) has, within a truly global context, successfully blurred the boundaries between the sport, media, and entertainment industries. As renowned cultural critic Douglas Kellner noted, "professional basketball has emerged . . . as the game that best symbolizes the contemporary sports/entertainment colossus" (2002, p. 66). This observation can be empirically tested by the simplest of anthropological challenges: try existing for one day, anywhere on the planet where people congregate in reasonable numbers, without being confronted with some representation of the NBA, either televisual or material. The increasingly demanding nature of this invitation attests to the remarkable transformation experienced by the NBA over the past twenty years. Having been a chronically troubled sporting entity, the league was molded into a vibrant marketing and entertainment company at the core of the American sporting landscape, from where it was aggressively and successfully propelled into the global cultural economy. Thus, a new sporting form was conceived: a fantastical market-driven hybrid of sport and entertainment, owing more in terms of production values, content, and global aspirations, to the *Wonderful World of Disney* than to the *Wide World of Sports*.

The NBA occupies a strange and instructive place in American sporting culture. It is not the historically anointed national pastime that is Major League Baseball (MLB), nor the focal point of the popular sporting imaginary that the National Football League (NFL) has become. Nevertheless, there is a case to be made for the NBA being the most representatively American of the major sporting leagues, in that it exists and operates in a manner most closely attuned to the broader forces and constraints that shape contemporary American life. Differently put, the necessarily interrelated processes of mass mediation, commercialization, and globalization presently constituting the terrain upon which American culture is experienced are perhaps nowhere better illustrated or experienced than within the machinations of the NBA.

It would not seem unreasonable to assert that the NBA can only be fully understood as both a constituted and constitutive element of the late capitalist forces associated with the postmodern condition (c.f. Harvey, 1989; Jameson, 1991, 1998) within which television acts as a principal *mechanism* and *source* of capital accumulation within developed economies. Most sporting entities, including the NBA, are willing participants in the media sport feeding frenzy. There are countless examples whereby popular sport leagues have been willingly manipulated by commercial media outlets in pursuance of the audience demographic most desirable to their corporate advertisers. Moreover, sport franchises, and even entire leagues, have been commandeered by, and integrated into, transnational media corporations seeking to vertically integrate their entertainment economy empires (Andrews, 1999; Herman & McChesney, 1997). Indeed, the domineering cultural and economic presence of hypercommercial and hypermediated sport spectacles effectively nullifies the perceived viability of alternatives to the commercially mediated sport model. Most sport organizations assert themselves as brazenly commercial enterprises, and make no pretense as to the cardinal importance of delivering entertaining products designed to engage the largest audience possible, and thereby maximize profits (Andrews, 2001).

So how does the NBA relate to this late capitalist sport-media complex? Quite simply the league has, for more than a decade, been lauded as an exemplar of how a professional sport organization *should* be run. While formed in 1949, the concerted commercial spectacularization of the NBA can be traced to its struggle against, and eventual merger with, the rival American Basketball Association (ABA) during the period 1967–1976. As an upstart competitor, the ABA sought to define itself against the rather staid and unimaginative image of the NBA. This was achieved through the adoption of strategies drawn from the burgeoning sport marketing industry. In other words, the ABA sought to incorporate elements that would render basketball a more entertaining spectacle. These included the introduction, use, and/or encouragement of: the three-point shot; a no foul-out rule; a suitably patriotic red, white, and blue colored basketball; a less strategically constrained and more expressive style of play; a Slam Dunk Contest as a feature of the league's All-Star Games; and a greater emphasis on player celebrityhood (Pluto, 1991). Despite these innovations, and what was widely viewed as an excellent standard of play, virtually from the outset the ABA lost the battle with the more established NBA for the attention of the American public. Predictably, therefore, in 1976, and under mounting financial pressure, the ABA folded, leading to four franchises joining the NBA for the 1976–1977 season: the Denver Nuggets, the San Antonio Spurs, the Indiana Pacers, and the New York Nets.

While the NBA proved victorious in the struggle with the ABA, the newly expanded league was certainly not in a position to rest on its laurels. Evidently, questions as to the feasibility of the American market supporting two national basketball leagues had been conclusively answered in the negative. Serious doubt remained as to whether the NBA was itself a viable sporting enterprise. In the years immediately following the NBA-ABA merger, the NBA was at an all-time low in terms of its symbolic and economic value (Charles Grantham, former executive director of the NBA Player's Association, quoted in Voisin, 1991, p. F1). The league's problems came to a head during the 1980–81 season when only 7 of the NBA's 23 franchises made a profit, average game attendance totaled 10,021 or about 58 percent of the league's arenas, and the total league attendance dropped by over a million from the previous year (Swift, 1991a, p. 78). Such were the NBA's problems that the league's commissioner, David Stern, later admitted the goal at this time "was to get through the day. Then we expanded it to the week" (quoted in Heisler, 1993, p. C10).

The NBA's problems at the time have been attributed to the widespread view that the league was too regional, too black, and drug-infested (Cole & Andrews, 1996). The NBA's perceived regionalism can be attributed to the erratic presence of games on national network television. For instance, the CBS network only showed the concluding game of the 1980 NBA Finals between the Los Angeles Lakers and the Boston Celtics on a tape delay, presumably after regularly scheduled primetime programming. The tendency for the coverage of NBA games to be mostly local meant that the league as a whole made a negligible impact on the national psyche, and its suitability for television was even questioned (Blount, 1979). Another core feature of the NBA "image crisis" (Cady, 1979) at this time was the domineering presence of African American athletes, and the racist pathologies that had historically been ascribed to black masculinity, and which were now engaged within the context of professional basketball coverage. This can be illustrated by the following racially coded diatribe from one *New York Times* reporter:

> The level of play throughout the NBA is under attack. "Selfishness" is seen to be rampant. Players are disdaining defense, complaining that their salaries aren't astronomical enough, demanding to be traded to some team where they will fit in, or where everyone will fit around them. . . . One problem in the NBA today is conflict of interest. Among players on the same team there is disagreement as to who should be shooting. Among players on opposing teams there is agreement that everyone's main interest is shooting. (Blount, 1979, p. 4)

Within the mass media, and thereby helping to constitute the American public's perception of the league, the problems of the NBA were regularly attributed to the playing styles and personal sensibilities supposedly brought to the game by African American players. Indeed, such was the virulence of this accusatory racism, that even players such as Kareem Abdul-Jabbar and Julius Erving, who dominated the league, were habitually labeled as lazy, lacking motivation, irresponsible, flashy, selfish, and overpaid (see Blount, 1979; Cady, 1979; Moran, 1979). Leading on from this point, the popular media used the specter of drug abuse within the league as evidence of the pathological depravity of the African American men who dominated, and were thus threatening the very existence of, the NBA and, again by inference, that of the American nation as a whole. Hence, according to the prevailing climate within the American racial formation, the reactionary conflation of racial identity with criminal deviance meant that the NBA was perceived as being too drug infested simply because it was too black (Cole & Andrews, 1996; Kiersh, 1992).

From the nadir of the early 1980s, within little more than a decade the NBA could legitimately be described as "an innovative, multifaceted, billion-dollar global marketing and entertainment company whose future literally knows no bounds" (Swift, 1991a, p. 77). There are, of course, many reasons for this stunning metamorphosis. However, arguably the single most important factor has been the influence of David Stern, who, since February 1984 has acted as the league's commissioner. Stern may be considered a sporting visionary, because he understood the cultural logics driving contemporary capitalism to which any sport was compelled to become attuned in order to survive.

In approaching the NBA as a brand located within the highly competitive entertainment industry, Stern assumed the position of de facto brand manager for the NBA. As such, his brief was to reframe the NBA brand into an exhilarating and exciting sport entertainment offering played by talented, fun-loving, and charismatic individuals. In acting as "captain of consciousness" (Ewen, 1976) for the NBA, Stern designed highly visible proactive responses to the league's perceived problems. These included the installation of an accusatory anti-drug policy, the establishment of collective bargaining between owners and players, and the subsequent enforcement of a salary cap (Staudohar, 1989). Equally importantly, Stern oversaw an aggressive restructuring of the NBA from an archaic professional sport industry focusing on the league's properties and administration, to a multifaceted marketing and entertainment conglomerate incorporating over 20 divisions, including NBA Properties, NBA Entertainment, NBA International, and NBA Ventures. Arguably the most important aspects of the NBA's reformative resuscitation derived from securing increased television exposure on the major networks.

As the 1980s unfolded, television exposure (either through direct broadcast coverage, highlight display, or elaborative commentary) became the single most important agent in the transformation of this once aberrant sporting league into a leading exemplar of "the high-flying entertainment-media-sports industry" (Marantz, 1997, p. 14). Until the 1989–1990 season, this was realized through an intensified relationship with the incumbent broadcaster, CBS. However, the mutually reinforcing and only recently interrupted relationship with NBC (which broadcast the league on network television between 1990–1991 and 2001–2002 for a combined $3.1 billion), was perhaps most responsible for the advancement of the NBA as a popular media spectacle. However, from 2002–2003, the league switched its network broadcasters to Disney's ABC networks, which paid $2.4 billion for a 6-year contract to show a significantly reduced number of games on ABC's main national network, but with expanded coverage on ESPN, the cable component of the Disney/ABC sport television behemoth (the NBA is also shown on TNT through a separate 6-year $2.2 billion contract, which also began in 2002–2003). The NBA's move from NBC to ABC/ESPN/TNT speaks to significant changes in the contemporary media environment. Dick Ebersol, chairman of NBC Universal Sports and Olympics, ruefully reflected on the loss of one of NBC's prized sport broadcasting assets:

> For the first time a major sports property has largely migrated from network to cable, where the dual revenue streams of subscriber fees and advertising can support the escalating costs of broadcast sports rights. . . . In the future, it will become almost impossible for broadcast television sports to match the power of those "sub" fees, which are unique to the cable world. (Ebersol, quoted in Isidore, 2002)

Thus, while terrestrial network ratings may decline in relative terms, Stern ensured a balance of national exposure and increased revenue from the dual platform delivery of the NBA to the US home audience. In addition, by developing in-house promotional programs, commercials, pre-recorded videocassettes, and even a 24-hour cable channel (NBA TV) Stern further immersed the NBA within the "all engulfing dynamic of [televisual] promotion" (Wernick, 1991, p. 185) which had come to dominate contemporary American culture. In doing so, the NBA has become the quintessential exemplar of the late capitalist tendency to merge sport forms into media spectacles (Tomlinson, 2002).

One of David Stern's more significant insights centered on his recognition of sport's, and particularly the NBA's, potential for being used as a vehicle for successfully building a (multi-platform) mass-media-oriented entertainment empire. Today, and certainly within the American sporting context dominated by swaths of sport marketing executives, this is a normalized assumption. However, in the early 1990s, such brazen sporting commercialization was still likely to upset the conservative sensibilities of the sporting world. Within this context, David Stern's unfettered celebration of the similarities between the NBA and the Disney Corporation can almost be seen as a prophetic challenge to the rest of the sport industry:

> They have theme parks . . . and we have theme parks. Only we call them arenas. They have characters: Mickey Mouse, Goofy. Our characters are named Magic and Michael [Jordan]. Disney sells apparel; we sell apparel. They make home videos; we make home videos. (David Stern, quoted in Swift, 1991a, p. 84)

Stern dismantled the boundaries between professional sport and media entertainment, effectively defying anyone to think of sport as anything but a form of popular entertainment. More than any other professional sports league, the NBA is aligned with and attuned to the corporations that dominate the entertainment market place. As Stern later admitted, "We're saying, 'What's Disney doing? What's Time-Warner doing?'" (quoted in Weir, 1993, p. 1A).

Akin to Disney, AOL-Time Warner, Viacom, and News Corporation, the NBA has enthusiastically embraced the circuits and manifestations of mediated promotion that drive consumer capitalism (Wernick, 1991). Through the circulation of televised game coverage, televised promotions, the 24-hour NBA TV cable channel, pre-recorded videocassettes, books, magazines, computer games, and an extensive array of licensed sports apparel, the NBA is delivered to a now-expectant American populace. In this way, the NBA has been transformed into a multifaceted media entertainment enterprise with the game of basketball as its intertextual core. Returning to Braverman (1998), the NBA has effectively been transformed into an entertainment-based spectacle whose very existence, like that of any other capitalist enterprise, is premeditated on the search for ever-more-expanding returns from capital investment. So, while World Wrestling Entertainment's Vince McMahon may be lauded (or in some circles vilified) for being the original architect of now pervasive the sport-entertainment hybrid (see Atkinson, 2002), David Stern's more covert, yet arguably more influential, steering of a traditional sport league into entertainment economy places him, and the NBA, at the vanguard of this trend.

As a means of understanding the processes of the NBA's evolution from sport to sport-entertainment, it is instructive to consider Bryman's theorization of the Disneyization of society. He writes:

> Disneyization is depicted as a process by which the principles of the Disney theme parks dominate more and more sectors of society. It is presented as comprising four aspects: theming, dedifferentiation of consumption, merchandising, and emotional labour. (Bryman, 1999, p. 25)

Over the last two decades or so, the NBA has been rendered a virtual Disney theme park, inasmuch as it is structured, oriented, and experienced according to the processual logic identified by Bryman as the core aspects of Disneyization. For instance, in terms of theming, the NBA represents a complex economy of branded commodity-signs (those pertaining to the league itself, its franchises, and perhaps most importantly its cultural economy of superstar players) from which the consumer is encouraged to derive a positive and consistent sensory experience (Goldman & Papson, 1996; Klein, 1999). The theming of the NBA reached its most explicit expression in a joint venture between the NBA and Hard Rock Café that resulted in the opening of the NBA Café, a restaurant at the Universal Studios theme park in Orlando, Florida, and the evident corollary of a collision/fusion between entertainment universes. Leading on from the overarching commercial logic of theming, Bryman's notions of dedifferentiated consumption and merchandising are aspects of the Disneyization process equally in evidence within the context of the NBA. In Bryman's terms, dedifferentiated consumption:

> denotes simply the general trend whereby the forms of consumption associated with different institutional spheres become interlocked with each other and increasingly difficult to distinguish. (Bryman, 1999, p. 33)

In this regard, it is possible to distinguish how the NBA is implicated in numerous multifaceted, yet seemingly coherent, spaces of consumption. Indeed, it would be possible to characterize NBA stadia as themed cathedrals of consumption (Ritzer, 1999), offering numerous points of consumption (the actual game itself, restaurants, shops, museums, etc.), which collectively contribute to the total NBA experience. Perhaps even more insidiously, and again following the lead of the Disney Corporation, the NBA's aggressive merchandising practices now mean the league, its franchises, and players can be experienced in multifarious commodified forms, the most obvious being through engagement with NBA televised game coverage, televised promotions, pre-recorded videocassettes, books, magazines, computer games, and an extensive array of related sports apparel. In Debord's oft-cited, but in this case most appropriate words, the various ways through which the NBA can be experienced (or consumed) thus exemplify the "historical moment at which the commodity completes its colonization of social life . . . commodities are now all there is to see; the world we see is the world of the commodity" (Debord, 1994, p. 25).

While each is insightful and relevant, Bryman's identification of emotional labor is perhaps the most salient element of Disneyization (Bryman, 1999) in regard to the evolution of the NBA as a commercial sport spectacle. The phenomenon of emotional labor refers to highly contrived and rehearsed practices whereby service workers express what are perceived to be socially desired expressions and behaviors, during the course of interactions with the consuming public (Bryman, 1999). Within the theme park context, manifestations of emotional labor are readily apparent in the willing smiles and demeanors of service workers. Although somewhat less obvious, high profile sport leagues similarly seek to ensure that the embodied representations of their organization (in this case, playing personnel) exhibit what are perceived to be commercially desirable personas. Unlike in the Disney scenario, the NBA's personalities do not have to be uniformly wholesome (although some are); they simply need to project an identifiable character that would interpellate (Althusser, 1971) the subjectivities of commercially viable swathes of the consuming populace. Hence the NBA marketing machine has been responsible for the manufacture of a phantasmagorical world of commodity-signed personal narratives and identities: triumphs and tragedies; successes and failures; heroes and villains. As the noted sociologist Gary Alan Fine identified:

> What sports needs, and what the N.B.A. has very successfully developed . . . is a coterie of players that fans can relate to. Not just Magic Johnson the player, but Magic Johnson the person. Not just Larry Bird the player, but Larry Bird the person. Even if we don't know them, we feel we know them. (quoted in Voisin, 1991, p. F1)

The very essence of basketball lent itself to the reengineering of the NBA into a manufacturer of personality cults. It is an extremely telegenic sport, inasmuch as the "The athlete's face—and emotions—aren't shielded by a helmet as it is in football" (longtime Deputy Commissioner of the NBA, Russ Granik, quoted in Moore, 1994, p. 1B).

Evidently, David Stern and the rest of the NBA executives possessed sufficient cultural awareness to realize the importance of celebrity within an age dominated and defined by "the personal, the intimate, and the individual" (Marshall, 1997, pp. xiii). As a consequence, during the early to mid-1980s, Larry Bird's whiteness and Magic Johnson's disarming black smile and style were consciously mobilized in the remodeling of the NBA into a racially ambiguous—and thereby accessible to mainstream American sensibilities—popular cultural space (Cole & Andrews, 1996). Bird and Magic came to represent, however spuriously and un-representatively, the public *face* of this cosmetically managed NBA.

However, it was Michael Jordan's imaged identity which was to play an even more instrumental role in what could be described as the racial disassemblage of the NBA into a viable commercial product (Andrews, 2001). Through the mutually reinforcing narrative strategies engaged by the NBA, Nike, and a multitude of other corporate interests, Jordan was constructed as a racially neutered (hence, non-threatening), popular representation of black male athleticism. Thus, Jordan's imaged identity harnessed and nurtured the racially acceptable semiotic space initiated by the Bird-Johnson dyad, and ushered in an even more lucrative era of popular acceptance for the NBA. Ironically, although Jordan had a colossal impact on rescuing the NBA from its ghettoized image, his dominance of the NBA as a signifying system is based upon, and indeed perpetuates, a regressive racial logic that has returned to haunt the league. Jordan was generally positioned as a wholly virtuous and wholesome figure; an atypical African American male, whose very existence reinforced the pejorative rhetoric that dominated popular perceptions of African American males. So, while rendering the NBA accessible to primetime American audiences, the precise commodification of Jordan's blackness reinforced historically grounded perceptions of "good" and "bad" blacks (Boyd, 1997; Wilson, 1997). As Jordan's playing career reached its latter stages, and particularly during his many interrupted retirements, the NBA became a compelling microcosm of the American nation as a whole. The racial paranoia and insecurity that pervades popular discourse so depicted the very presence of young African American players (Chris Webber, Isaiah Rider, and Allen Iverson, to name three) who, for various reasons, did not exude the Rockwellian flair of Jordan, as threatening the stability of the NBA, just as the perceived criminal, sexual, and moral irresponsibility of the young urban African American male threatened American society as a whole (Reeves & Campbell, 1994). Indeed, Burwell notably castigated an:

> entire generation of slammin', jammin', no jump-shooting, fundamentally unsound kids who have bought into the NBA's and Madison Avenue's shallow MTV-generated marketing of the game. People with no soul for the essence of the game turned the poetry into gangster rap. (Burwell, 1993, p. 3C)

While the search for the next Jordan (an imperious African American player whose countenance massages rather than challenges America's racial anxieties) continues, ironically, but perhaps not surprisingly within the late capitalist context, numerous commercial interests have also sought to engage, and thereby capitalize upon, what is considered to be the resistant and oppositional tendencies exhibited among America's youth cultures (Smith & Clurman, 1997). Specifically, the NBA's seemingly endless supply of African American "anti-Jordans" are cast by the promotional messages emanating from shoe, fast food, and mobile phone companies alike as seductive frames from which to engage the sensibilities of predominantly white American youth. As Goldman and Papson identified, these "signifying practices speak volumes about colonizing the culture of the hood to fuel bourgeois conceits and pretensions about authenticity" (1996, p. 42). They are compelling examples of what Dyer-Witheford described as "market-racism" (1999, p. 10). Therefore the NBA ultimately fails as a potentially rich site for the assertion of culturally and politically progressive representations of African American masculinity, because it merely reinforces historically grounded discourses of acceptable and unacceptable blackness (Carrington, 2000; 2001) in a manner which draws further parallels to the more reactionary outpourings of the Disney Corporation (Giroux, 1994).

Although an explicitly American artifact in terms of its origin, as with other forms of late capitalist American popular culture (once again the comparison with the Disney Corporation is instructive), the league, its franchises, and players, have become touchstones of contemporaneous processes and experiences of globalization. According to Albrow (1996), we are presently ensconced in the "global age," wherein specific political, economic, technological, and cultural forces have resulted in ever-increasing conditions and experiences of "complex connectivity" linking disparately situated peoples and institutions around the globe in relations of mutual interconnection and interdependence (Tomlinson, 1999, p. 2). While not an exclusively economic phenomenon, it would be true to say that in one sense, "Globalization is about the organization of production and the exploitation of markets on a world scale" (Robins, 1991, p. 25). The contemporaneous manifestations of globalization are merely the latest phase in a process of economic expansion initiated by the rise of merchant capitalism in the seventeenth century, which has seen the space of capitalism distended from the bounded confines of national, regional, and imperial structures to the unbounded global domain. Whereas the earliest phases in the process of commodity globalization were prompted by the economic impulses of Western European colonial/industrial expansion, the new culturally oriented economic globalization—what Hall (1991, p. 27) calls the rise of a global mass culture—has been influenced greatly by the interconnected technological, capital, and media flows emanating from the US.

At least since the advent of the talking picture, and in a concerted fashion since the spread of television technology in the decades after the Second World War, the various manifestations of America's commercial- and media-oriented culture have increasingly made their presence felt on the world stage. As Kellner indicated, American popular culture is "exported to the entire world" and invades "cultures all over the world, producing new forms of the *global popular*" (Kellner, 1995, p. 5). Although some contend that the global export of American commercial culture is part of a concerted and contrived process of American cultural imperialism, it would appear its primary impetus is economic. Instances of cultural homogenization may result from the seemingly unfettered global flow of American cultural products; this was not necessarily the primary intention, but perhaps an unavoidable by-product.

Certainly the NBA's global expansion, which only began in earnest during the mid to late 1980s, was primarily motivated by economic imperatives. As the twentieth century drew to a close, the US market became saturated by NBA programming and products, effectively foretelling an impending period of economic stagnation for the league, as manifest in a flattening of annual percentage growth rates in game attendance, television audience, and retail sales figures. The insecurities inherent within capitalist modes of accumulation demand ever-increasing rates of economic growth as evidence of continued corporate vitality, so the NBA, like Coca-Cola, Disney, and McDonald's before it, and at roughly the same time as Nike, turned its covetous gaze to the largely untapped consumers living beyond the bounds of the US. As Stern admitted, since there are "250 million potential NBA fans in the U.S., and there are 5 billion outside the U.S. . . . We like those numbers" (quoted in Comte, 1993, p. 42). Thus, he continued, "Global development is a certainty—with or without us" (quoted in Heisler, 1991, p. C1).

Driven more by economic necessity than some proselytizing zeal for the game of basketball, during the early 1990s the league added a new armature, NBA International (presently the International Group within the NBA Properties division), to its organizational structure. NBA International's responsibilities are partially devolved to regional offices through which, among other responsibilities, national television and licensed merchandising agreements are negotiated. Following steady expansion, there are presently 11 NBA regional offices worldwide, situated in Paris, Geneva, London, Barcelona, Melbourne, Hong Kong, Mexico City, Miami (serving Latin American markets), Taiwan, Tokyo, and Toronto. Peopled with specialists in business, marketing, and international relations, the various NBA regional offices use television as the primary vehicle for engaging, and indeed constituting, overseas markets. Television coverage acts as a seductive mechanism for thrusting the game, its franchises, and, perhaps most importantly, its major stars, into the minds of the global youth identified as the primary overseas market for the NBA brand. Television exposure, in turn, is expected to stimulate consumer demand for NBA licensed merchandise. In order to secure the broadest reach in its coverage, NBA International frequently levies minimal television rights fees (depending on the economic wherewithal of the nation in question) to national broadcasters. The aim is to increase these fees once the game has been established as an important component of local programming.

It would be difficult to argue against the success of the NBA's global televisual expansion, since during the 2002–2003 season, the league was televised in 212 countries, in 48 languages, by 148 different broadcasters (Anon, 2002). In order to corroborate the NBA's presence in overseas markets, the league has organized regular and preseason games in Japan and Mexico; reigning NBA champions have taken part in the McDonald's World Club Championship tournament; and leading players act as NBA international ambassadors to far-flung outposts. Most conspicuously, while never recreating the near-hysterical worldwide media exposure that enveloped the original "Dream Team" at the 1992 Barcelona Olympics (Wenner, 1994), Team USA's collection of NBA notables habitually represents the most celebrated participants at Olympic, World, and Pan-American tournaments. Designed to encourage more active overseas consumer involvement in the NBA experience, the league also organizes numerous participatory programs and events throughout the world. Despite the success of this array of promotional circuses, the NBA hierarchy has until relatively recently displayed little interest in locating NBA franchises farther afield. According to Dave Checketts, onetime president of the New York Knicks, during the early 1990s the league's global intentions were "to keep going [expanding overseas] . . . not for the purpose of selling teams, but to enhance licensing and TV packages" (quoted in Moore, 1992, p. 1B). In the intervening decade or so, something has plainly changed, for now David Stern has admitted "I think it's fair to say my successor will in fact be looking to expand into Europe as the infrastructure improves and teams begin to grow. The issue to me is not travel. . . . It's the infrastructure and fan support" (quoted in Denberg, 2003, p. 10D).

What Checketts plainly did not foresee, but what Stern was responding to, is the stupendous internationalization of NBA playing personnel over the past decade, which has radically altered the popular engagement with the NBA around the globe. The NBA's early phases of global marketing keyed on the essentially American nature of the brand. As one NBA administrator stated, "People in other countries . . . like the N.B.A. because they want the American look and the American image. And that's what they get with the N.B.A. . . . Americana, a piece of America" (Josh Rosenfeld, then the NBA's Director of International Public Relations, quoted in Andrews, 1997). Today, within many countries, the NBA's residual Americanness is frequently conjoined with local interest derived from the presence of their local players in the league. As was the league's stated intent, as well as generating broadcast fees and licensed merchandising revenues, the multifaceted globalization of the NBA as a mediated spectacle has spurred countless aspirants to seek the rewards and acclaim derived from playing in the strongest basketball league in the world. As Michael Jordan commented:

> You need to commend David Stern [for] the expansion and globalization of basketball. . . . David expanded it to where European players understood the competition and the glamour that came along with it and to experience playing against the best [*sic*]. (quoted in Wilbon, 2003, p. D1)

Especially in the early years of basketball talent migration into the US, many foreign players failed to make the NBA grade. Recently, however, the number of players from Europe, Africa, South America, and Asia playing within the NBA has increased significantly, such that one commentator opined that "When the NBA comes to Europe, for many it will simply be a case of coming home" (Stark, 2002, p. C8).

Indications of the NBA's recent internationalization can be gathered from numerous sources: in the 2002 NBA draft, 5 of the first 16 players drafted were from outside the US (including the number one pick, Yao Ming of China); during the 2002–2003 season, NBA rosters included 66 foreign players from 34 different countries (a figure that had risen 200 percent since the 1996–1997 season); 27 of the league's 29 teams had at least one foreign player and 11 teams had foreign players in their starting lineups; and 6 foreign players played in the 2003 All-Star Game (Stark, 2002; Weingarten, 2002; Wilbon, 2003). With players such as Steve Nash (Canada), John Amaechi (England), Tony Parker (France), Ruben Boumtje-Boumtje (Cameroon), Dirk Nowitzki (Germany), and Pau Gasol (Spain) plying their trade to such effect in the NBA, it is clear why the NBA (and associated corporate concerns) should see the marketing potential of engaging those who follow their home-grown NBA heroes from afar (Fisher, 2003). As Andrew Messick, senior vice president of the NBA's international division identified:

> we're now entering an era of self-perpetuation. . . . Kids in Germany looking up to . . . Dirk Nowitzki . . . are now dreaming of playing in the NBA. That didn't necessarily happen before. Some of those kids will actually make the league, and they'll in turn bring another generation of fans. (quoted in Fisher, 2003, p. A1)

Without question, the emblematic figure in this regard is Yao Ming, who provided the NBA with a high profile Chinese icon to be used to lure some of China's 1.2 billion consumers to the NBA marketplace. To this end, the NBA initiated a website written in Chinese characters (www.nba.com/china), and provides NBA coverage to no less than 12 Chinese telecasters (Anon, 2002). With suitable understatement, the NBA's Messick declared, "Yao Ming is not the first great international player we've had, but he is a very exciting international player, one that represents a very important country for us . . . China in particular, but really all of Asia are definitely areas of growing focus for us" (quoted in Fisher, 2003, p. A1).

Interestingly, the NBA's internationalization has provided the opportunity for some paranoid introspection concerning the state of American basketball, much of which is steeped in the racist rhetoric that resides just below the surface of the NBA spectacle. This sentiment came to a head after the 2002 World Basketball Championships, where the US team lost to Argentina, Yugoslavia, and Spain, and finished sixth. As one observer summarized:

> The NBA is signing foreign players left and right for the same reason the NHL brought them in before: they're better. It's not just that Americans have gotten complacent, though that's part of the story, as budding American stars worry more about sneaker contracts and slam dunks than basic skills such as passing. Over the past decade, the NBA has allowed high-schoolers and non-college graduates to go directly to the pros; the result has been an influx of immature players who lack basic skills and coaching. (Stark, 2002, p. C8)

As within much popular basketball discourse, phrases pertaining to the questioning of a player's fundamental skill level, work ethic, and maturity are patent euphemisms for the pernicious manner through which African American youth are regularly pathologized within popular ideologies. This process of covert racial stigmatization was even more evident within a newspaper debate focused on the merits of drafting either an American or foreign player. In the words of the proponent for foreign players:

> I'd draft a good foreign player over a good American player. Nothing against the red, white and blue, but I'll take the work ethic and maturity of foreign players over American players any day. . . . It's the attitude that "you owe me," the image they get of themselves from every leech around them telling how great they are. And when they have a pro coach telling them to drop the 'tude and start working harder, they pout and rebel. You don't find that with foreign players. They are grateful for a chance to pursue a career they would never have dreamed possible. It's why they work and they rarely complain. Give me a guy like that anytime. (Higgins & Tillery, 2003, p. C12)

This diatribe captures the disgruntlement expressed by those dismayed by what is considered to be American youth's—and African American youth in particular—rejection of the delayed gratification demanded by the American Dream mythos (Nixon, 1984). As for the eponymous foreigner, in familiar conceited and self-righteous nationalistic tones, he is lauded for acknowledging the debt owed to the American experience. Evidently historically entrenched social hierarchies fit neatly into the rhetoric of the global-local media entertainment order; so much for the *Wonderful World of the NBA*.

2

A COG IN THE GLOBAL
MEDIA MACHINE

Given its propensity for inspiring the interest and adulation of the global masses, it is easy to see why sport has become a prized asset for global telecommunications corporations. Media giants such as Disney, General Electric, News Corporation, and Viacom routinely insert sporting spectacles into their program schedules, which allows them to benefit from, and indeed cultivate, sport's established popularity through increased viewership and advertising revenue. While News Corporation's pioneering sport media strategies are widely acknowledged, among the academic ranks they are generally only discussed as part of broader projects (see Cashmore, 2000; Harvey, Law, & Cantelon, 2001; Herman & McChesney, 1997; Miller, Lawrence, McKay, & Rowe, 2001; Shawcross, 1997). So, in order to examine the position and influence of televised sport within the global media entertainment economy, this discussion focuses on the paradigmatic strategies through which News Corporation appropriated sporting content as a means to penetrate worldwide television media markets, both terrestrial and satellite.

Perhaps more than any other media industry hierarch, Rupert Murdoch, News Corporation's longtime Chairman and CEO, has both recognized and productively mobilized sport's utility within the media entertainment economy. For this he has garnered a welter of criticism from individuals and institutions troubled by such explicit commercialization of the sport domain. Much to his detractors' ire, Murdoch has forged a brazenly dispassionate contract with sport, which he describes as the "universal language of entertainment" (Murdoch, 1998). Such criticism seems only to motivate Murdoch's competitive instincts (Shawcross, 1997);

the result is News Corporation's truly boundless sporting reach and influence, which has radically altered the global sport landscape (see Pierce, 1995; Rofe, 1999; Rowe & McKay, 1999). Indeed, News Corporation's acquisitional and diversified sport strategizing has created a web of sport-media interdependencies which are bewildering in their complexity and scope (Andrews, 2003).

Sport has not always been a staple of News Corporation's media strategizing, which originated in a much more conventional fashion with Murdoch's inheritance of two regional Australian newspapers (the *Adelaide News* and the *Brisbane Courier-Mail*), following his father's death in 1952 (for a detailed discussion of Murdoch's life, and especially the circumstances surrounding his inheritance and the early years at the helm of News Corporation, see Shawcross, 1997). Through a series of increasingly audacious acquisitions beginning in Australia then moving into New Zealand, the UK, and the US, News Corporation fashioned vast print media holdings that presently number more than 130 separate properties (for more comprehensive listings of News Corporation's labyrinthine media properties, see Barker, 1997; Harvey, et al., 2001; Herman & McChesney, 1997; News Corporation, 2004a). However, News Corporation only became a "main player in the global media system" (Herman & McChesney, 1997) with its incursion into the American movie and television industry. Specifically, the purchase of a 50 percent stake in the struggling Twentieth Century Fox film and television studio, for $325 million in 1985, proved a key initiative (News Corporation later bought the remaining 50 percent to gain complete control of the studio). The acquisition of Twentieth Century Fox provided News Corporation with an established brand identity within the American television market, extensive production facilities, and a vast library of media content, all of which helped realize Murdoch's goal of creating a fourth national television network to challenge the media oligopoly of ABC, CBS, NBC. To this end, Fox Television Incorporated was founded in May 1985 with the $2 billion purchase from Metromedia of television stations in the major US television markets (New York, Los Angeles, Chicago, Washington, Houston, and Dallas). Fox Television's subsequent purchases, including the acquisition of 10 television stations resulting from the Chris-Craft Industries takeover in 2001, brought the number of News Corporation's US television station holdings to 33, by some distance the greatest rate of ownership among the US television network organizations. In a remarkably short time, and primarily through a financially aggressive business plan, the upstart Fox network built a national organizational structure and market presence to rival its more established competitors.

As was no doubt the rationale behind the initial investment, Twentieth Century Fox provided the facilities required for the production of the original network programming (supplemented by content drawn from Twentieth Century Fox's film library) required by the fledgling national network to help consummate its schedule. Predictably, and to the chagrin of many, Murdoch introduced his unapologetically populist production values—honed as they were in the highly competitive tabloid newspaper business—to network audiences. With scant regard for television's educative and informative potential, Fox originated a repetitious menu of entertainment-oriented programming, targeted at the lowest common denominators of popular sensibilities, and aimed at generating sizeable advertising revenues through the maximization of audience share. So, Fox Television signaled its arrival with an unrelenting diet of bawdy situation comedies, titillating teen dramas, irreverent cartoons, and tabloidic telejournalism, shows such as *In Living Color, Beverly Hills 90210,* and *The Simpsons,* initiated a lowbrow revolution that is still being played out within the national network environment.

Having secured a foothold in the all-important American network television market, Murdoch expanded his ambitions to the colonization of new media, specifically cable and satellite platforms, that emerged from the global spread of both new telecommunications technologies and the widespread instantiation of media deregulation and privatization policies during the 1980s and 1990s (Barker, 1997; Fairchild, 1999). Despite not owning a controlling interest in a cable or satellite delivery system within the American context (not, that is, until the recent purchase of DirecTV, the leading satellite television company in the US), News Corporation made a concerted effort to assert itself within the new media universe, through the establishment of channels such as the Fox News Channel, FX, the Fox Movie Channel, the various regional Fox Sports Channels, Fox Sports World, and the recently sold Fox Family Channel. Such new media innovations were not limited to the US, however, as News Corporation embarked on a truly global satellite television expansion. This process included substantial investment in satellite delivery systems and channels in, among others, the UK (BSkyB), Australian (Foxtel), Japanese (JSkyB), Indian (Zee TV), New Zealand (Sky), German (Vox), and Asian (Star TV) media markets. All of these combined to create a whole greater than the sum of its parts: A truly global television complex that makes up an important part of News Corporation's self-described "constellation of media businesses" (News Corporation, 2004a).

Within half a century of his initial inheritance, Murdoch oversaw the transformation of News Corporation from a regional Australian print media concern to an economically and culturally imposing global media leviathan, rivaling, and in some cases surpassing, the financial might, sectoral diversity, and geographical reach of Time Warner, Disney, and Viacom. In purely financial terms, News Corporation is presently one of the most significant media companies in the world, with assets in 2004 of US$73.7 billion, annual revenues of US$29.4 billion, and net annual profits of $2.3 billion. Of the company's 2004 earnings, $5.2 billion (17.7%) was derived from filmed entertainment, $5.0 billion (17%) from the television sector, $3.4 billion (11.6%) from newspapers, $2.5 billion (8.5%) from cable network programming, $1.3 billion (4.4%) from book publishing, $979 million (3.3%) from magazines and inserts, and $862 million (2.9%) from other sources. With regard to the geographic distribution of News Corporation's total revenue generation, $20.2 billion (68.7%) derived from the US, $6.5 billion (22.1%) from the UK and Europe, and $2.6 billion (8.8%) from Australasia (News Corporation, 2004b). The corollary of News Corporation's expansionist, acquisitional, and innovative strategizing has thus been the establishment of a truly global multimedia empire, incorporating nine media formats, spanning six continents, and purportedly reaching two thirds of the world's population (Barker, 1997; Herman & McChesney, 1997).

Before delving into the—not inconsiderable—role played by sport in News Corporation's ascent to the exclusive brethren of the global media oligopoly, it is worth, however briefly, considering the unique properties and opportunities sport offers the mass communications industry in general. Sport, described by Rowe as "the regulated expression of physical culture" (1995, p. 104), can be considered a unique form of mass entertainment due to: its explicit telegenic physicality (conjoined as it is with an implicit eroticism); its innate competitive structure (which demands empathy-inducing personal narrativizing); its potential for generating visceral excitement (created by the uncertainty, real or imagined, surrounding the outcomes of sporting contests); its nurturing of deep-rooted personal identifications and loyalties (the strength of which corporate brand managers can only dream); its relatively straightforward and inexpensive production demands (especially compared with equivalent programming lasting more than two hours); and—no doubt as a confluence of many of the aforementioned factors—its continued widespread popularity, and specifically its rare ability to attract high concentrations of 18–34-year-old male consumers, the demographic traditionally most prized by corporate advertisers (Bellamy, 1998; Dunning, 1999; Giulianotti, 2002; Herman & McChesney, 1997; Miller, et al., 2001; Sugden & Tomlinson, 1994). It is precisely these properties and opportunities which News Corporation and other media concerns have sought to capitalize upon, quite literally, within their sport programming. Thus, News Corporation's multifaceted investment in sport rights and properties exemplifies an economically driven rational pragmatism, with little or no sentiment for the traditions or protocols of sport culture.

Of all the global media corporations, News Corporation has demonstrated the most concerted incorporation of sport into its business model. As Rowe noted, "There is no one in the media world who has a greater commitment to the commercial exploitation of sport than Murdoch" (1999, p. 191). Murdoch has been unambiguous in his identification of sport's unique televisual qualities and their role in constructing a global media entertainment empire. His most revealing pronouncements came in his 1996 speech at News Corporation's annual meeting in Adelaide:

> Sport absolutely overpowers film and everything else in the entertainment genre. . . . Football, of all sports, is number one . . . Sport will remain very important and we will be investing in and acquiring long-term rights . . . We have the long-term rights in most countries to major sporting events and we will be doing in Asia what we intend to do elsewhere in the world, that is, use sports as a "battering ram" and a lead offering in all our pay television operations. (quoted in Milliken, 1996, p. 28)

At the heart of Murdoch's corporate media philosophy is the steadfast belief that "sports programming commands unparalleled viewer loyalty in all markets" (Murdoch, 1996), and can therefore be used as a "battering ram" to penetrate media markets more effectively, and indeed more rapidly, than any other entertainment genre. This point has been corroborated by Peter Chernin, News Corporation President and COO, when identifying movies and live sport programming as the pivotal elements in their "worldwide TV ventures. . . . And sports is the more important" (quoted in Bruck, 1997, p. 826). Interestingly, however, while News Corporation is liable to charges of advancing a globally uniform process regarding the use of sport to penetrate national television markets, any global homogenization concerns are tempered by the nation-specific sporting content used to actually engage the local audience. As Murdoch himself outlined:

> You would be very wrong to forget that what people want to watch in their own country is basically local programming, local language, local culture . . . I learned that many, many years ago in Australia, when I was loading up . . . with good American programs and we'd get beat with second-rate Australian ones. (quoted in Schmidt, 2001, p. 79)

Thus, News Corporation can be considered an archetypal transnational media operation, in that it operates seamlessly within the language of the local, simultaneously, in multiple locations (Dirlik, 1996; Morley & Robins, 1995).

News Corporation's first and arguably most financially consequential use of sport as a (local) media "battering ram" came with British Sky Broadcasting's (BSkyB) securing of the television broadcast rights for the English Premier League (EPL) in 1992. In 1990, News Corporation obtained a 50 percent stake in the newly formed BSkyB, following the merger of Murdoch's Sky Television with its chief rival in the UK satellite broadcasting market, British Satellite Broadcasting. The financial struggle that led up to the merger resulted in News Corporation incurring massive losses, which threatened the parent company's very existence. As a pay television service, BSkyB's long-term profitability, indeed its immediate viability, was dependent upon the attraction of significant numbers of subscribers (from whom BSkyB would derive significant subscription revenues, and whom they could also use as a justification for levying premium advertising rates). This conundrum was solved in 1992 with BSkyB's signing of a £304 million, five-year deal for exclusive broadcast rights to the newly established EPL, with the deal representing a staggering 600 percent increase over the previous broadcast rights contract. BSkyB executives felt the EPL to be "the only sport that was clearly capable of attracting significant numbers of new customers to satellite TV," and their assumption proved correct (Williams, 1994, p. 387). Within a year of signing the EPL contract, BSkyB subscribers doubled to approximately 3 million, effectively guaranteeing its future and, to all intents and purposes, that of News Corporation as a whole (Lefton & Warner, 2001).

Having identified the EPL as its "jewel in the crown" (Arundel & Roche, 1998, p. 73), BSkyB moved quickly to quash any competitors by agreeing to pay £670 million for a four-year deal when its original contract ended in 1997, followed by successive contract renewals for 2001–2003 (£1.1 billion), and 2004–2006 (£1.024 billion). Over the past decade BSkyB's relationship with the EPL has resulted in these two commercial entities becoming synonymous with each other: "Sky without football would be like Unilever without Persil or Mars without chocolate bars" (Anon, 2000a, p. 28). Moreover, BSkyB recognized the audience potential of other sporting contests, and subsequently embarked on a relentless pursuit of Britain's most coveted sporting events, including most of the English national soccer team's games, the English cricket team's test matches, many major rugby union games, rugby league in its entirety, and the Ryder Cup (see Arundel & Roche, 1998). This allowed Murdoch to boast, as early as 1996, that "Sky Sports has a lock on many of the commanding heights of British sport" (1996). As a consequence, by the dawn of the twenty-first century, BSkyB's *sportcentric* strategies had come to play an important role in securing more than 20 percent of homes in the UK as subscribers, thereby establishing the satellite broadcaster as a fixture within the British broadcasting landscape (Lefton & Warner, 2001).

In an effort to encourage sport's migration to pay television platforms on a truly global scale, the BSkyB/EPL scenario has been replicated across numerous national media and sporting contexts, with News Corporation's local satellite subsidiary securing the broadcast rights to the sporting entities that most resonate with local audiences. News Corporation has also adopted a similar sport-centered approach when building the brand identity and presence of its Fox Television terrestrial network in the US. At the vanguard of this network building process was the four-year $1.58 billion contract signed with the NFL in December 1993, for broadcasting rights to National Football Conference (NFC) games. Justifying the vastly inflated sum, proffered in an ultimately successful bid to deter his more established and fiscally conservative competitors, Murdoch later conceded:

> We put that $380 million a year on the table to help build Fox. We didn't do it so some quarterback can make another half million a year. . . . That's just a by-product. What we did, we did selfishly, to build the network. It was a selfish business decision. (quoted in Pierce, 1995, p. 182)

Selfish it may have been; effective it most definitely was. Through the regular Sunday NFC schedule and the Thanksgiving Day game, as well as NFC play-off games, and the rotational broadcasting of the Super Bowl spectacle, Fox's investment provided significant opportunities for magnifying the network's national visibility, elevating direct advertising revenues, and enhancing opportunities for network programming promotions. Fox's relationship with the NFC thus proved hugely influential in establishing and defining its network identity within the American popular consciousness. It also alerted television executives to that which they had long suspected, that the NFL represents "the most reliable programming on television. . . . Football on television is the closest thing to essential, network-defining programming" (Carter, 1998, p. C1).

Having aligned with the NFL to such great effect, predictably, Fox was at the forefront of negotiations for the renewal of the contract, and in early 1998 Fox ($4.4 billion) joined with ABC/ESPN ($9.2 billion) and CBS ($4.0 billion) in signing an eight-year $17.6 billion (or $2.2 billion annually) contract for NFL television rights. By this time, Fox, in conjunction with NBC and ESPN, was also in the midst of a five-year $1.7 billion contract (1996–2000) for the television broadcasting rights to MLB (it should also be noted that Fox controlled the television broadcast rights to the NHL for 1995–1999, but decided not to renew the contract due to disappointing television ratings). This experience proved successful enough for Fox subsequently to sign a $2.5 billion contract with MLB to be the sole broadcaster of every All-Star, play-off, and World Series game for the period 2001–2006. According to David Hill, Fox Sports Group Chairman and CEO, the "worthwhile" nature of this latest MLB contract can be measured in a number of ways, one of which speaks as much to the season's continuation into "sweeps," one of the twice-yearly auditing periods for television ratings, as it does to the game's residual popularity:

> The playoffs are in a great time of the year, just prior to November sweeps, and they are really an ideal platform for the entertainment boys to launch their wares. . . . Add in the fact that they rate and the country focuses on the sport alone during that time of year, and we think it's an incredible property. (Quoted in McAvoy, 2001, p. 26)

As well as dominating the national network delivery of the game, Fox has utilized MLB as a crucial aspect of its cable television strategizing. News Corporation initially developed a significant sporting presence within the US cable market by setting up the Fox Sports channel in 1993. Nine regional cable sports networks were subsequently purchased in 1996, providing the groundwork for the innovative Fox Sports Net, a network of 22 regionally based cable sports channels linked by the national nightly highlight show *Fox Sports News* and other nationally aired programming, but also incorporating a large proportion of regionally focused sports coverage. Fox Sports Net presently controls the local cable television rights to an overwhelming majority of US-based MLB, NBA, and NHL teams, placing it in a significantly stronger position than ABC's more established, but less regionally flexible, ESPN and ESPN2 cable sports channels. Indeed, such is its vigorous good health that one commentator referred to the "8,000-pound gorilla that Fox Sports Net has become" (Rofe, 1999, p. 24). Clearly, baseball has, and continues, to play an important role in establishing the Fox Sports Net network of regional cable channels, which currently broadcasts more than 2,000 regular MLB games per season, as part of the benefit derived from purchasing the local cable rights to 26 of the league's 30 teams. Fox and its affiliates have also come to dominate the local free-to-air delivery of baseball games, now controlling the rights to 15 teams. Fox's increased control over the platforms through which baseball television coverage is delivered to the American public has allowed it to facilitate the continuing migration of baseball from free-to-air to cable television (McAvoy, 2001). This strategy effectively necessitates the inclusion of the regional Fox Sports Net channel in local cable program packages, even those owned by News Corporation's media adversaries. Through its procurement of national, local, and cable rights, Fox effectively commandeered baseball coverage to the same extent that NBC has come to dominate, and indeed define itself through, its

Olympic scheduling (c.f. Andrews, 1998). In effect, Fox has fabricated a televisual "baseball monopoly" (McAvoy, 2001).

Having secured broadcasting rights to two of the more established American sport properties, Fox subsequently turned its attention to NASCAR, the sporting phenomenon of the last decade (Hagstrom, 1998; Hamilton, 1996). Hoping to benefit from the sport's growing popularity (NASCAR rose to being the second rated sport on television, behind only the NFL), Fox joined with NBC and TNT in signing a $2.4 billion television rights contract for NASCAR's Winston Cup and Busch Series races for the period 2001–2008. As David Hill admitted:

> The key to our interest, was very simple. . . . In a world of fragmented entertainment choices where everything is slipping, you look at NASCAR and the ratings for the sport over the last five years have remained pretty static. What that means in this day and age is you had an increasing and very loyal fan base. . . . To us, life is a gamble and we took a bet, but we think it's a pretty safe bet. I think NASCAR can get much bigger than what is now, if it's on every week and people get used to it. From a ratings standpoint, I don't think it's anywhere near maxed out. (Quoted in Schlosser, 2001, p. 18)

The NASCAR contract was prompted by the same network building impulses that underpinned Fox's initial relationship with the NFL. However, now the network could benefit from its earlier investment by directing, through strategic promotions, its established NFL audience to its new NASCAR offering. Within contemporary commercial culture, television programming represents a site for numerous promotional opportunities which, if successfully presented, become linked in a "chain of mutual reference and implication" (Wernick, 1991, p. 187). As an example, Fox used its broadcasting of the 2002 Super Bowl as a forum for promoting its first half season of NASCAR coverage on Fox and cable channel FX, and to announce the debut of its new cable outlet, the Speed Channel (the relaunched version of Speedvision, which Fox purchased in July 2001).

With the NFL, MLB, and NASCAR in the Fox television portfolio, it is clear to see why Murdoch has become such an important figure within the American sport economy (and, as will be evidenced later, in the broader global sport economy). He successfully identified, cultivated, and capitalized on, televised sport content as the core product within the new information-based mode of production, so emblematic of late capitalist economies (Jameson, 1991; Poster, 1990). In addition to crafting the hegemonic blueprint for sport media strategizing, Murdoch has practiced a financially aggressive modus operandi, which "inflates cost and undercuts competitive balance" (Miller, 1999, p. 32). Thus, both substantively and economically, he has thrust News Corporation to the vanguard of the global sport media economy, while forever changing the global sport landscape. For this, Murdoch's power and influence cannot be underestimated. As NBC Sports chairman Dick Ebersol commented in response to Murdoch's repeat ranking at the top of the *Sporting News Power 100,* the annual list of the top 100 most powerful people in sports, "It isn't even remotely a race. You could make him Nos. 1 through 5" (Knisley, 1998, p. 16).

According to then Co-Chief Operating Officer, Chase Carey, News Corporation's "entry into sports [is] driven by a belief that sports and live events are going to play a more and more important role in television" (quoted in Rofe, 1999, p. 24). Such an assertion explains why News Corporation has increasingly looked beyond the mere securing of television broadcasting rights in its desire to exert influence over the sport media economy. In short, News Corporation's goal has been to centralize ownership, and therefore control, over the various revenue-generating nodes of the sport entertainment commodity chain, with the ultimate aim of creating a vertically integrated and globally encompassing sport media network (c.f. Castells, 1996; Gereffi & Korzeniewicz, 1994). The process of vertical integration is prompted by the desire to manage the market uncertainties that accompany a corporation's reliance on external units for core products and services. Hence, vertically integrating a corporation represents a process of internalization, whereby "The planning unit takes over the source of supply or the outlet; a transaction that is subject to bargaining over prices and amounts is thus replaced with a transfer within the planning unit" (Galbraith, 1985, p. 28). The market uncertainties implicit within the sport media economy—particularly the imponderables surrounding the periodic and increasingly hyper-inflationary bidding wars for broadcasting rights—no doubt galvanized News Corporation's vertical integration agenda:

> We are really content providers. We look upon ourselves as a creative company [that] owns newspapers, books, whatever . . . but to ensure their distribution and also to ensure that no one has a choke hold on us . . . we'd like to be vertically integrated from the moment of creation right through to the moment of delivery into the home. (Murdoch, quoted in Schmidt, 2001, pp. 78–79)

News Corporation is well advanced in this process, being, alongside Disney, Viacom, and Time Warner, a primary "player in the vertical integration game" (Stotlar, 2000, p. 2).

Having invested in the ownership of numerous broadcast platforms and channels, News Corporation subsequently turned to the procurement of the actual sport entities (leagues, teams, and stadia) from which programming content is derived, and the controlled predictability of vertical integration realized. The basic rationale is that "buying sports properties is cheaper than renting—and it heads off the competition" (Rofe, 1999, p. 24). In more specific terms, this provides a position of ascendancy within the television rights fees scramble (indeed, the purchasing or establishment of sport leagues relinquishes the need to bid for television rights, while the ownership of sport teams puts media corporations in the advantageous position of negotiating with themselves). The mammoth financial outlay required for the purchase of sporting properties is offset by numerous other opportunities for direct revenue generation. Sport programming is customarily attractive to advertisers; it offers significant opportunities for intra- and cross-network promotion; and, its popularity allows networks to increase the rates paid by cable systems for carrying their channels. The control afforded by sport property ownership also provides networks with the ability to generate significant revenue from the "migration" of game coverage to lucrative pay-per-view television platforms. Despite his purported indifference toward sport (Bruck, 1997; Pierce, 1995), it is thus clear why Murdoch would consider sport property ownership to be vital in his grand global design for News Corporation.

Murdoch's initial steps toward vertically integrating his sport media empire came within the parochial domain of Australian Rugby League (ARL). Despite the global reach of News Corporation's various armatures, within the Australian media landscape Murdoch has struggled for preeminence with his media mogul rival, Kerry Packer (see Rowe & McKay, 1999). Nowhere was Packer's presence more apparent than within the Australian televised sport marketplace, wherein his terrestrial Nine Network had successfully commercialized and spectacularized cricket and ARL coverage (Miller, et al., 2001). In the mid-1990s, Packer ventured into the pay television domain in a collaborative venture with the telecommunications company, Optus Vision, which secured the pay television broadcasting rights to both the ARL and the Australian Football League (AFL). This latter development troubled Murdoch, since he was acutely aware of the need for popular programming content for his new Foxtel pay television network. Thus, Packer's commandeering of Australia's two most popular football codes compelled Murdoch into the production of Foxtel's own sporting content. As a consequence, in April 1995 News Corporation embarked on a AUS$500 million undertaking aimed at establishing the Super League, a rival to the ARL, comprising teams made up of elite players prized away—by large financial inducements—from the ARL. Super League's subsequent poaching of player and coaching talent did not go unchallenged, yet the ARL's counter-offers (bankrolled by Packer and Optus Vision) were generally declined, and legal action seeking to prohibit individuals' breaking existing ARL contracts proved unsuccessful. So, in March 1997, the Super League commenced in direct competition to the ARL.

Due to the perceived dilution of both rugby league products, and the groundswell of public criticism deriving from the public and legal wrangling between these adversarial sport media coalitions, both the ARL and Super League fared poorly in terms of game attendance and television viewership. Given the economic impracticability of rival leagues competing for a diminishing spectatorship, in December 1997 the inevitable ensued, with an ARL-Super League merger to form the National Rugby League (NRL), owned in equal partnership between the Murdoch and Packer camps (Rowe, 1997; Rowe & McKay, 1999). The NRL debuted in 1998 as a 20-team competition, a figure that was reduced to 14 by 2000 due to the slew of team closures and mergers stimulated by the market rationalities of the corporate media concerns running the league. So, despite a mammoth financial outlay for a half share in the merged league, and the public relations debacle ensuing from the perceived hypercommercial corruption of the game in Australia, the NRL scenario once again evidenced Murdoch's conscienceless and ruthless "determination to secure whatever corporate advantage he can, regardless of the cultural or commercial obstacles" (Hiltzik, 1997). In this case, corporate advantage accrued from the ability to control, even if in partnership, a pivotal source of televised sport content.

The Australian Super League initiative was but one element—albeit the keystone—of News Corporation's broader goal of developing a globally integrated rugby league competition incorporating contests within and between clubs in the northern and southern hemispheres (Denham, 2000; Falcous, 1998). In order to facilitate this, in 1995, News Corporation gained control of the British Rugby Football League (RFL) with the signing of a five-year £87 million contract; the financial details of this deal bound the RFL's clubs' very survival to Murdoch's corporate strategizing (Denham, 2000). Put crudely, News Corporation purchased a controlling interest in a 100-year-old sport culture, ingrained in the working class history and experience of northern England, and transformed it from a financially troubled and poorly administered sport into a financially stable media production unit. BSkyB, effectively the RFL's owners and administrators, soon set about changing the culture of the game through the execution of a divisional restructuring, the implementation of aggressive management and marketing initiatives, and even the institution of American-style team names like the Bradford Bulls, the Wigan Warriors, and the Halifax Blue Sox (Arundel & Roche, 1998; Kelner, 1996). Perhaps the most radical change to rugby league culture came with the switching of the playing season from winter to summer, as dictated by the corporate exigencies of British and Australian media markets. In terms of the former, the British Super League's (the new name for the RFL) summer scheduling meant it would not clash with English Premier League soccer, BSkyB's prize possession within a British broadcasting rights context. With regard to the latter, News Corporation hoped close season contests between Australian and British teams (realized by the alignment of playing seasons) would add an unmatched international dimension, and thereby enhanced brand equity, to Foxtel's Australian Super League coverage. In this way, as Falcous noted, "British Rugby League had been used as a tool in a broader global struggle" (1998, p. 8).

In instances where News Corporation has been confronted with sport organizations and cultures wherein league ownership or new league development was neither feasible nor even admissible, Murdoch has turned his attention to the ownership of professional teams as a means of exercising control over the sport media economy. However, his ambition of owning a high profile NFL franchise within a major US television market was stifled by the league's prohibition on corporate ownership of league franchises. According to NFL Commissioner Paul Tagliabue, a media corporation's involvement in the league "would present a conflict of interest in competitive situations" over rights fees negotiations. "We always want our interests to have but one interest. That might be compromised" (Heath & Farhi, 1998, p. A1). With such restrictions in place, Murdoch turned to America's other major professional sports. Most notably, in March 1998, and after protracted negotiations with MLB, Fox purchased the entire Los Angeles Dodgers organization for $311 million. Thus, Murdoch commandeered "one of the great brand names in America in a world where brand names are increasingly important" (Peter Chernin, News Corporation's president, quoted in Heath & Farhi, 1998, p. A1). The relationship proved less than satisfactory from virtually every conceivable standpoint, prompting the 2004 sale of the franchise to Frank McCourt, a real-estate developer, for $430 million. However, the deal, engineered as part of McCourt's takeover, saw Fox Entertainment (a News Corporation subsidiary) retaining the broadcast rights to Dodgers' games. This was arguably the primary reason for the purchase of the franchise to begin with.

Through its relationship with the Dodgers (initially as owner, and subsequently as contracted broadcaster), Fox Entertainment purchased a high profile presence in one of the largest US television markets by being able to offer a marquee programming attraction to the local viewing audience. The fact that information on the Dodgers was, during their time of ownership, located within the "cable" section of the News Corporation website, is illustrative of the purely instrumental value Murdoch places on sport. It certainly vindicated Miller's observation that:

> "software" is what media empires call the teams they own. Fans may see the Los Angeles Dodgers or the New York Knicks as home teams with illustrious histories, but the new breed of owners—Rupert Murdoch's News Corp., Time Warner, Disney, Cablevision, Comcast—view them as content, programming fodder for the insatiable beast called television. (Miller, 1999, p. 23)

Fox's position in the Los Angeles market is likely to be strengthened by Murdoch's stated intention to exercise his option to purchase 40 percent of the Los Angeles Kings and 10 percent of the Los Angeles Lakers; both clauses associated with his 40 percent investment in the team's new arena, the Staples Center, in April 1998. Also in 1998, Fox Entertainment gained another foothold in the American sports franchise market with the 40 percent interest in both the New York Knicks and the New York Rangers (and, incidentally, the Madison Square Gardens arena), acquired as part of News Corporation's purchase of a 40 percent share in Rainbow Media Holdings, a Cablevision subsidiary.

As evidenced by NFL ownership restrictions, Murdoch's acquisitional impulses have had to be flexible (in both sporting and geographic terms) in order to gain the broad landscape of broadcast rights he ultimately covets. Thus his audacious, and ultimately unsuccessful, £623 million bid for the English Premier League's most prized asset, Manchester United, came as no surprise to many sport media industry observers. The bid was ultimately blocked by the British government's Mergers and Monopolies Commission (MMC) in April 1999 (Walsh & Brown, 1999), the rationale for the denial centering on the anticipated deleterious effects on competition in the broadcast sport industry arising from the competitive advantage BSkyB would command—as owners of the most popular and high profile EPL club—when negotiating for the league's television rights. Murdoch consequently changed tack and has, through stealth as opposed to brute force, sought to garner influence over the future destination of English Premier League television rights. To this end, BSkyB embarked on a "buying spree" of up to 9.9 percent (the maximum percentage allowed for ownership in multiple clubs) of shares in individual clubs, with Manchester United, Manchester City, Leeds, Chelsea and Sunderland all added to its football portfolio, thereby strengthening BSkyB's position in the scramble for EPL television rights (Cassy & Finch, 1999).

Having outlined the various levels of its engagement with sport as part of realizing its goal of vertical integration, it becomes evident that News Corporation is simultaneously part of a horizontal web of competing, yet collaborating, companies within the contemporary media industry (Auletta, 1997). This new industrial order, referred to by the Japanese as a *keiretsu,* is based on intricate networks of cross-company alliances and investments, which protect and strengthen the position of the conjoined mega-corporations while simultaneously restricting the ability of external competitors to challenge their ascendancy: "While the companies continue to do battle with one another, however, they increasingly collaborate, and the result is a horizontal web of joint partnerships. . . . These companies join forces for various reasons. They do so to avoid competition" (Auletta, 1997, p. 227). Thus, News Corporation's various collaborative ventures within the sport media economy include associations with a number of its fiercest competitors. These include the alliance with Kerry Packer over the Foxtel and NRL ventures; collaborations with rival American networks for shares of the broadcast rights of premium sports properties (like that of NBC with regard to televising NASCAR, and that of ABC and CBS with regard to televising the NFL); the convoluted web of relations involved in News Corporation's interest in Rainbow Media Holdings, the Cablevision subsidiary owners of the New York Knicks, New York Rangers, and Madison Square Garden, which is also part owned by General Electric; and perhaps the most unlikely collaboration of all, the ESPN Star Sports partnership in Asia, which brings together News Corporation and Disney, in what has proved to be a highly successful venture. Evidently, unlike the Ford Corporation during its pre–World War II war heyday, the vertical integration celebrated by Murdoch cannot be viewed in rigid monolithic terms (Castells, 1996; Harvey, 1989). Each unit within News Corporation's vertically integrated structure relies, to varying degrees, on horizontal relations developed with its market competitors. Hence, in Auletta's (1997) terms, News Corporation could be said to exemplify a new order within the media entertainment industry—a sport media *keiretsu*—dependent upon horizontal peer networking, in order to share the risks and responsibilities of, yet continue to derive the benefits from, a vertically integrated organizational structure.

Although virtually impossible to assess with any degree of certitude, the commonly accepted estimate is that News Corporation's satellite television platforms reach 66 percent of global households owning a television (Stotlar, 2000). With such a multi-channeled global television footprint, the cross fertilization of sport programming has become yet another lucrative option for News Corporation. For instance, BSkyB feeds of EPL soccer represent a staple of the Fox Soccer Channel's (previously Fox Sports World) offerings in the US, with live games on Saturday and Sunday mornings also available to pay-per-view satellite systems. Similarly, Star Sports broadcasts Australia's NRL Telstra Premiership games across the Asian continent from Hong Kong to India. Evidently, the once implausible suggestion that News Corporation may one day "be able to offer any game, any where, any time of day" is in no longer as far-fetched as it initially seemed (Heath & Farhi, 1998, p. A1). Moreover, this scenario illustrates the promotional potentialities offered by media corporations who interlace sport within a broader business network (Maguire, 1999; Miller, et al., 2001): A game involving Manchester United (of which News Corporation owns a 9.9% share), is framed to the world by the hyperbolic rhetoric of the BSkyB commentary team, and no doubt favorably reported upon by News Corporation's various national newspaper properties. Thus the circuit of intra-organization marketing and promotion is complete.

Despite its burgeoning global media architecture, all is not rosy in the News Corporation garden. Most pertinently, there is a growing body of evidence to suggest that, within the ever-fragmenting American media market in particular, live television coverage of major sporting events is failing to maintain audience ratings. If this is indeed the case, then News Corporation's strategically inflated investments in television broadcasting rights in particular, and other sport properties in general, have little chance of making significant returns. Certainly, this prognosis has been vindicated by News Corporation's restructuring of its television contracts, through a "one-time abnormal charge" of $909 million in February 2002. This payment—divided between the NFL (who received $387 million), NASCAR ($297 million), and MLB ($225 million)—allowed News Corporation to adjust (or "write down," to use the industry parlance) its future television contract payments, based on the anticipated advertising revenues derived from projected viewing figures:

> The severe downturn in sports related advertising during the second half of calendar 2001, the lack of any sustained advertising rebound subsequent to September 11th and the reduction of forecasted long-term advertising growth rates all resulted in a reduction of our projections of direct revenues from these contracts. (News Corporation, 2002, p. 6)

In other words, News Corporation admitted its overpayment on these contracts and sought to redress this with the $909 million "abnormal charge," in order that future NFL, NASCAR, and MLB coverage would be in a position to contribute toward—rather than deplete—the quarterly and annual earnings statements from which public companies derive their market share value. As indicated in the statement, News Corporation attributes some of the revenue decline to the post-September 11th economic downturn; however, some analysts view it as the most vivid manifestation of a long-term trend: "This time there appears to be an across-the-board write-down of major sports and a walk away from major sports" (Neal Pilson, sports television consultant and former president of CBS Sports, quoted in Mullen, 2002, p. 33).

> In certain quarters, the death knell is already being rung for major professional sport, so long dependent on television revenues as a means of financing its own inflationary economy: Sports could well have a lot less income in the future. They're going to

have to look for corporate support at a very basic level if they're not getting it from media. . . . The media companies are almost certainly to blame for it. They put the money up, and because their business models haven't worked out the clubs, which are used to a certain level of income, are going to suffer. (O'Riordan, 2002, p. 3)

Whether or not such doom-laden forecasts are realized, News Corporation may well have discovered the future of televised sport, through the resuscitation of the "trash sports" genre of television entertainment prevalent in the 1970s (Rinehart, 1998). This came to the fore with the "Celebrity Boxing" special, aired in March 2002 on the Fox network. Pitting B-list, faded celebrities against each other in crassly themed bouts (e.g., *The Partridge Family*'s Danny Bonaduce against *The Brady Bunch*'s Barry Williams; and troubled ice skater Tonya Harding against Clinton paramour Paula Jones) the primetime special easily outdrew Fox's regular sport and general entertainment programming. Equally importantly, the broadcast attracted major sponsors, such as Chevrolet, McDonald's, and VoiceStream Communications (Anon, 2002, p. 16; Carter, 2002), and led to a slew of duplicative and replicative programming across network and cable outlets.

Of course, the popularity of such novelty programming will probably be fleeting. Nevertheless, its ability to grab the public's attention—even momentarily—does offer network executives a vindication of recent initiatives designed to broaden sport's appeal through the advancement of what noted *New York Times* columnist Robert Lipsyte described as "sportainment" (1996), a commercial cultural form through which the narratives and aesthetics of mainstream entertainment genres have increasingly commandeered the production of televised sporting events. Doubtless, Murdoch and News Corporation will be at the vanguard of such initiatives, for their corporate investment in sport is such that they are compelled to cultivate its broadest appeal. As Tracy Dolgin, president of Fox Sports Net, revealed in relation to NASCAR coverage:

We have some tricks up our sleeve to try to Foxify it . . . We're not only going to appeal to the hard core NASCAR fans, but we're going to try and reach out to the moderate fans and bring them in, trying not to alienate the serious fans at the same time. (quoted in Schlosser, 2001, p. 18)

Whether or not the process of "Foxification" is a good thing for sport per se is immaterial since, as has been demonstrated throughout this discussion, News Corporation's rational pragmatism approaches sport as nothing more than a "cog in the machine" of global media capitalism (Miller, 1999, p. 32). Periodic component modification, and even replacement, are merely part of the process of ensuring the machine runs as efficiently and productively as possible.

3

THAT'S SPORTAINMENT!

Perhaps the most distinctive element of the late capitalist order can be discerned from the intensifying convergence of various facets of social existence. As Jameson noted, the late capitalist condition is marked by a "dedifferentiation of fields" (Jameson, 1998, p. 73) such that the once perceived—but never in actuality real-ized—clear distinctions between cultural, political, economic, and even spiritual life have become blurred. This is evident within a contemporary US context liber-ally punctuated by the presence of corporatized universities, market-driven public health initiatives, commercially driven religious institutions, and even faith guided polities. Sport—whether acknowledged or not—has long been subject to such sec-toral indivisibility:

> the processes involved in the formation of modern sport were not just *disciplinary*, they also simultaneously worked to *commodify* sport. Just as the standardization of sport according to the regulation of time, space and conduct, provided a method of social control through the regulation of popular culture, it also produced a spectacle that could be sold to spectators through admission fees. In this way sport was part of a broader process of commercialisation of popular culture from the end of the nine-teenth century. (Brookes, 2002, p. 9)

The social, political, and economic forces of industrialization clearly aided and abetted the mass industrialization of sport culture, just as media- and information-based post-industrial forces have facilitated sport's post-industrialization. How-ever, although regularly used to describe popular music, film, television, and fashion sectors, sport has rarely been identified or addressed as a culture industry. This is most perplexing since, perhaps more than anything else, within today's mass media driven economy, professional sport organizations are "brazenly commercial enterprises, that make no pretense as to the paramount importance of delivering *entertaining* products designed to maximize profit margins" (Andrews, 2001, p. 154, italics added).

Contemporary sport culture routinely exudes the "profit making" focus and "rationalized organizational procedures" exhibited by the more readily accepted forms of industrialized mass culture (Negus, 1997, p. 77). If popularity is any indication, then certainly sport can be considered a legitimate culture industry, in that it represents a lucrative site for the accumulation of capital via the manufacture of popular practices and pleasures for mass audiences. Moreover, as Bell and Campbell noted, "Its drama, its personalities and its worldwide appeal mean sport is the new Hollywood" (Bell & Campbell, 1999, p. 22). In all likelihood, this observation is even more insightful than the author's original intention. Not only has sport matched Hollywood in terms of its cultural and economic influence as a "dream factory" for the consuming masses (Powdermaker, 1950), like the film industry during the 1930s and 1940s; sport in the late twentieth and early twenty-first centuries could be considered the emblematic cultural industry of its time.

In his informative overview, Hesmondhalgh (2002) posits sport at the periphery of the core culture industries (advertising, broadcast media, film, Internet, music, and various forms of publishing). He precludes live sport contests and events (whether consumed *in situ* or via media broadcasts) from membership of this core group due to their innately unpredictable character, which distances them from the highly regulative and predictive practices of truly industrialized mass cultural production. Far from being designed and produced for maximum entertainment, and thereby maximum revenue generation, sport is "fundamentally competitive, whereas symbol making isn't. Texts tend to be more scripted or scored than sport, which is essentially improvised around a set of competitive rules" (Hesmondhalgh, 2002, p. 13). Evidently, such thinking fails to consider the manner in which sport has been transformed by the dictates of a corporate capitalist order propelled by commercial media. This is most graphically illustrated in the conclusive conflation of sporting and mass mediated entertainment universes in the past few decades:

> There was a time when the thought of comparing professional wrestling and the NFL, NBA, or major college sporting events was unthinkable. The lines of distinction were simply too clear. Wrestling was staged. Rivalries were created then hyped. What transpired outside of the ring was every bit a part of the show as what went on in it. It was entertainment pure and simple. *Real* sports were something entirely different. They were serious. It was the game that mattered. But there is little difference between today's professional, and increasingly, college sporting events and an ECW or WWF event. . . . To describe an NBA or NFL game or the Final Four as a "sporting event" is no longer accurate. These events are entertainment extravaganzas, subject to all the promotional and marketing gimmicks of a three ring circus. . . . Today,

sport is packaged, merchandised, and marketed as entertainment. It is more about money, television ratings, advertising rates, and corporate sky boxes than it is about sport. (Gerdy, 2002, pp. 25, 26)

While romanticizing sport's "real" past, Gerdy's characterization of "sportainment society" (2002, p. 30) nonetheless points to the "seductively consumerist union of commerce, sport and television" (Rowe, 1996, p. 566) that has come to dominate, and indeed define, contemporary sport culture.

The fusion of sport and entertainment domains is, according to Hall (2002), a logical convergence derived from sport's evolution into a commercial product operating within the highly competitive leisure marketplace, and the entertainment economy's perpetual need to harness the emotions (and discretionary incomes) of the consuming masses:

> Sport alone is no longer the opiate of the masses. Professional sports have responded with their interpretation of market demands and the competition they face for the audience's attention and money. That response is "sportainment"—the merging of sport and entertainment.
>
> Sportainment is a marketplace reaction to increasing popular demand for greater human excellence and more escape plus the desire spectators have to feel the experience. Professional sport can no longer hold its audience with promises of greater human accomplishments, and entertainment has no new escape or feeling. Sportainment is the combined result of separate realities that no longer meet our audiences' expectations. (Hall, 2002, p. 23)

Hence, sportainment: "where athletic performance is merely an element used to give a sense of 'real-life drama' to staged spectacle. It is the equivalent of a TV movie that purports to be 'based on a true story'" (Lipsyte, 1996, p. 10). Sportainment has become both the anticipated form and the intended corollary of mass mediated sport spectacularization.

The blurring of sport and entertainment economies reached its apogee—or, as some suggested, its nadir—with the fleeting presence of an upstart 8-team professional football league, the XFL, on US television screens in the spring of 2001:

> It wasn't the Xtreme Football League or the X-rated Football League, although those were dual implications of the ubiquitous twenty-fourth letter, which the American public had come to recognize as the default signpost for "aggressive." No, this was just XFL. (Forrest, 2002, p. 9)

While only in operation for a single season, this innovatively structured and produced professional football league provided an exaggerated, but nonetheless illuminating, statement on the forces and relationships underlying the sportainment phenomenon. Rather than an ephemeral and inconsequential sporting anomaly, as some chided (Fendrich, 2001c; Forrest, 2002; McNulty, 2001), the XFL represents a fertile site for examining the commercial media production values which have, arguably, become the principal motor (to use a metaphor drawn from popular economic rhetoric) for professional sport's development in general. For, as Anderson fore-warned in regard to the XFL's television coverage, "don't think you're watching football. You're just watching programming" (Anderson, 2001, p. D1).

Born of the creative minds of the WWF (World Wrestling Federation, since re-named World Wrestling Entertainment) professional wrestling empire, and largely facilitated through the broadcast and financial endorsement of the NBC television network, the XFL was ostensibly a radical morphing of hyper-dramatized production values and sporting content. According to Brookes, the XFL "used many of the presentational methods familiar from wrestling (building up soap opera storylines around interpersonal conflicts, etc.), while at the same time maintaining the integrity of the sport" (2002, p. 13). The contentiousness of Brookes' last point aside for the present, the XFL clearly can only be understood as an ultimately misguided outgrowth of the WWF's expansionist impulses.

Up until the mid-1980s, professional wrestling in the US was comprised of a loose aggregate of regionally bounded wrestling associations, many of which pro-duced popular television programming for local affiliates. As such, the sport was characterized by a fragmented regionality that, while holding considerable local resonance, effectively limited the WWF's geographic reach. On acquiring the WWF from his father in 1983, Vince McMahon Jr. embarked on an ambitious growth strategy for both his organization and professional wrestling in general. At the forefront of McMahon's expansionist agenda was the acquisition of compet-ing professional wrestling organizations. Seduced by the WWF's acquisitional pull, the 20 regional promoters operating in 1984 had shrunk to fewer than 5 in 1989 (Assael & Mooneyham, 2002). In buying out their main competitors, the WWF forged an effective monopoly within the professional wrestling industry and thereby gained control over a widening network of venues and television mar-kets. In effect, McMahon's "take-no-prisoners business style" (Zaleski et al., 2002, p. 44) resulted in the nationalization of the WWF. In taking his version of profes-sional wrestling to a national (and, ultimately, a global) audience, McMahon stirred the interest of corporate advertisers seeking to engage particular youth and male consumer demographics. Thus, the WWF benefited from significant in-creases in advertising revenue, which McMahon subsequently reinvested into ele-vating the production values of WWF programming in order to produce the "best television product," through which it came to dominate the professional wrestling industry (Sheldon Goldberg, quoted in *Bodyslam!*).

During the 1980s the WWF also benefited from, and indeed helped to nurture, the expanding cable television universe. While the development of pay and cable television began during the 1950s (Mullen, 1999), deregulation during the Reagan administration permitted extensive growth within this media sector. The matura-tion of the cable medium brought with it a need for a broadening range of content that could be offered across the platform's ever-expanding array of channels (Segal, 1994). As a result, emerging cable outlets were soon in need of inexpensive con-tent that could, nonetheless, draw viewers and attract relatively high ratings, some-thing that sport was seen to provide. Cable thus offered the necessary growth medium for the WWF to infiltrate American homes, while wrestling provided cable television with commercially viable content around which they could build their network brands. According to Eric Bischoff, onetime president of erstwhile WWF/WWE rival World Championship Wrestling (WCW) and professional wrestling personality:

> God bless cable television . . . that's all I can say. I might be doing something else for a living right now if it wasn't for cable. When cable was growing and expanding, wrestling was one of the things that really helped cable gain an audience. (Quoted in *Bodyslam!*).

A further mass-media relationship which paid dividends for the WWF was the creation of *Saturday Night Main Event,* a wrestling program developed during the late-1980s for the NBC network. Rather than air re-runs of the popular sketch-comedy *Saturday Night Live,* NBC executive Dick Ebersol chose to fill *SNL's* time slot with the WWF on a tri-weekly basis. *Saturday Night Main Event* soon became the centerpiece of the WWF's cable and network programming, with many of the more-marketed storylines transpiring during the NBC broadcasts. Moreover, the show's ratings success, and the relationship developed between the organizations' executives, laid the groundwork for the financial and creative collaboration between the WWF and NBC that spawned the XFL (Forrest, 2002).

Despite increases in attendance, viewership, and revenue generation during the 1990s, the WWF steadily began to face increasing criticism over the scripted, non-authentic nature of its core product, the wrestling spectacle. Throughout the 1980s, the league had been averse to admitting that the wrestling was scripted. Still, the more popular wrestlers of the era were widely acknowledged to be the better actors and personalities rather than the more skilled athletes (Webley, 1986). During the 1990s, however, McMahon and his wrestlers became increasingly willing to admit that the wrestling under their name was indeed simulated. As McMahon now trumpets: "We were the first promoters to say that this is not a sport; never has been a sport. It's really entertainment. It's sports entertainment" (quoted in *Bodyslam!*). The WWF's newfound openness on the issue of sporting inauthenticity signaled the beginning of a shift in promotional emphasis; that is, the WWF had moved away from accentuating sporting elements in favor of producing ever more entertaining spectacles. As a result, by the end of the 1990s, the WWF had become "one of the most powerful and influential entertainment companies in existence" (Rider, 2000, p. 8D), generating $356.7 million in annual sales, with yearly profits greater than $70 million (Brady, 2000). Most of this money was a result of widespread merchandising and sales from the corporation's various live, cable, and pay-per-view events. In an ironic twist, the WWF was recently forced to change its name to World Wrestling Entertainment (WWE). The change—mandated after a successful lawsuit filed by the similarly acronymed World Wildlife Fund—was, however, deemed a positive opportunity by the organization's executives (Finnigin, 2002). As Linda McMahon, Vince McMahon Jr.'s wife and the current CEO of WWE, stated: "Our new name puts the emphasis on the 'E' for entertainment, what our company does best" (Finnigin, 2002, p. 12).

The XFL emerged from the WWF empire at a time when the company's fiscal and cultural status had scaled new heights and penetrated new markets, making it one of the world's leading sports-entertainment corporations (Atkinson, 2002). By the end of 2000, the WWF's stock was trading at a high; the WWF brand was expanding through new ventures such as a just-opened restaurant in New York's Times Square; and the cable television ratings for WWF programming were at a peak. While company boss McMahon had always expressed an interest in entering the football business, various obstructions had continually precluded these aspirations being realized (he made unsuccessful attempts to buy the Canadian Football League and an NFL franchise). The XFL, however, provided McMahon with another vehicle for advancing his successful, if formulaic, approach to the production, delivery, and marketing of *sports entertainment*. In doing so, he could augment the close relationship between the WWF and the demographic that comprised the primary market for both professional wrestling and the NFL. The intention was to draw young adult males away from the NFL to the WWF, through a football forum, the XFL, which pointed to the staid irrelevance of the NFL.

Following a press conference on February 3, 2000, announcing the creation of the XFL, McMahon received a reaffirming phone call from Dick Ebersol, the head of NBC Sports. In it he proclaimed, "Vince, don't do anything TV-wise until we talk" (Heath, 2000, p. D01). For McMahon, this signaled the resurrection of a crucial relationship between the WWF and the network that had vaulted his organization into the upper echelons of America's most powerful entertainment entities. The renewal of their partnership presented mutually beneficial and timely opportunities for each organization. NBC's involvement gave the XFL the financial backing to pursue the personnel, property, and advertising necessary to start the league. While the WWF invested roughly $110 million in the new league, Ebersol and NBC Sports provided an estimated additional $100 million dollars over the (anticipated) first two years of the XFL's existence, "chump change compared with the annual $150 to $200 million in losses the network would incur if it were airing NFL games" (Manly, 2001, p. E8). Conversely, NBC eagerly jumped on board with ambitions of regaining a generationally engaging football product following the loss of pivotal NFL television rights to rival networks FOX, ABC, and CBS in 1997 (Stewart, 2000). In this way, NBC's investment in the XFL was prompted by the same motivations underpinning their inauguration of the Gravity Games as an alternative to the NFL. Though referring to the Gravity Games, Ruibal (1999) identifies NBC's motivation for investing in the XFL:

> Instead of running dead air or Lassie reruns, the Peacock Network is attacking the soft underbelly of the NFL: boys ages 10 to 17. Some of them don't care about the NFL—yet. They like football when they play it on a video game, but their favorite TV sport is pro wrestling. . . . That demographic niche also happens to be the Holy Grail of marketing: Snickers-munching, Pringles-crunching, Gatorade-sucking, acne-wary consumers who have yet to form life-long brand preferences. (Ruibal, 1999, p. 12C)

Hence, like the WWF, NBC sought to question the relevance of the NFL spectacle to the male youth and young adult markets, and thereby undermine the ratings and profits of rival networks, through advancing programming with values and aesthetics that seemed to clash with the sporting mainstream.

The primary goal of the XFL business plan was to achieve at least a 4.5 rating for NBC's primetime Saturday night slot during the spring of 2001 (Cafardo, 2000). Although modest, such ratings would ensure the financial stability necessary to continue league operations during the inaugural season. The initial response was favorable beyond expectations, as the XFL's debut broadcast on NBC drew an unexpectedly high overnight rating of 9.5 with a 17 share. A rating of 10.2 for men 18 to 34 was better than the 9.5 average for ABC's *Monday Night Football* during the previous NFL season, and better than the 8.2 rating garnered by Major League Baseball's World Series on the Fox Network ("54 million watch XFL," 2001). Not only did the program win the time slot, but viewers tuned in at twice the rate XFL and NBC executives had hoped for ("Ratings for XFL plummet," 2001). NBC's cable broadcast partners were equally successful. Cable networks TNN and UPN had joined the broadcasting line-up in late 2000, giving the league three televisual platforms for delivering their product (Doyle, 2001). UPN's first telecast drew a high rating of 3.1, and TNN's first XFL game drew an equally impressive 2.4 ("XFL helps UPN ratings surge," 2001).

With the conjoined cultural appeal of football and professional wrestling as a selling point, the XFL seemed destined to break the cycle of failed challenges to the NFL American football monopoly. However, the morphing of WWF-style marketing with American football's mass appeal, under the direction of NBC producers, created a skeptical response from many commentators even before the league started play. Most of the critiques were directed at new rules conjured up by McMahon and NBC, the overtly sexual sideshow of XFL cheerleaders, and the personalities directly and indirectly associated with NBC telecasts. Control over the XFL was essentially divided between McMahon and the WWF, NBC Sports, and Ebersol's production crew. While broadcast logistics were largely left to Ebersol and NBC, McMahon and the WWF were responsible for shaping the structure of the league (including decisions on team location and names: Birmingham Thunderbolts, Chicago Enforcers, Las Vegas Outlaws, Los Angeles Xtreme, Memphis Maniax, New York-New Jersey Hitmen, Orlando Rage, and the San Jose Demons); formulating suitably modified rules of the game; creating the personalities nurtured within and through game broadcasts; and advancing a league-wide mantra of the importance of on-site entertainment. It was hardly surprising, therefore, that the league's in-stadium aesthetic closely resembled that of the WWF. Certainly parallels between the XFL and WWF were intentional, as XFL Executive Vice President Billy Hicks stated before the start of league play:

> ticket holders in stadiums would see a display that includes pyrotechnics, loud music, and big video screens—just like the WWF. On the tube, viewers will get all that plus video clips about the players and cheerleaders, also shades of the WWF (Reeves, 2000).

On-site, the XFL adhered to the pre-established models set forth by the WWF. At the same time, Ebersol and NBC strived to deploy the latest broadcast technologies to ensure that the XFL would be "football like you've never seen it. With microphones all over the field, cameras peeking into huddles, and interviews with players right after a big run or a sack, the new league aim[ed] to take TV viewers where they [had not] gone before" (Fendrich, 2001a). NBC's broadcast method hence both contributed to, and was shaped by, the XFL's overt "sportainment" countenance. Prying camera narratives were only one production element contributing to the visceral voyeurism of the XFL experience. Again echoing the WWF, fan involvement was a core component of the XFL entertainment package. As McMahon himself alluded, "The NFL has forgotten about the fans. What we're doing is respecting the fans, giving them more than their money's worth and bringing them closer to the game" (Fisher, 2001, p. B1). Indeed, the centrality of the fan experience—both live and televisual—in shaping XFL production values was underscored by the importance of audience involvement. As the Marketing Manager for the Memphis Maniax (personal communication) stated, "Similar to what the WWF does with their live events, we want the crowd to feel as though they are part of the show."

Despite the seemingly suffocating presence of the NFL, XFL executives held fast to the notion that there was room in the American sport/entertainment marketplace for a new professional football league. As league president Basil Devito stated, "It's simple. Nobody owns it. Nobody owns football" (quoted in Gano, 2000, p. 1). League executives made a concerted effort to suggest the XFL as the "anti-NFL" (Jenkins, 2000) by integrating rule changes, seemingly taboo sexual content, innovative camera angles, and "involved" narrative during live games and telecasts. Both functionally and symbolically, Vince McMahon and other executives from the XFL took great measures to position the emerging league against the existing one. NBC Sports Chairman Ebersol explained in January 2001, "Right now we are selling the differences between us and traditional football. We're tinkering with the game and trying to get some of the duller elements out" (quoted in "XFL on TV aims to be different," 2001, p. 3D). Though often disparaging in the comparisons, the media certainly recognized the differences. Sportswriter Thomas Heath described the XFL as the "Un-FL, featuring fewer rules, less choreography, no superstars but attitude to spare" (2001, p. D1). Certainly, on the field, XFL promoters promised a game that was faster, harder hitting and more viewer-friendly than the NFL (Reeves, 2000). Meanwhile, NBC promised a televisual experience unlike anything previously offered in American football: "cameras in the locker rooms at half time, microphones on the sideline, cozy cheerleaders, and [Minnesota governor and former WWF wrestler] Jesse Ventura . . . as the tasteless TV analyst" (Anderson, 2001, p. D1). The in-stadium, television-friendly spectacle that McMahon had created featured player introductions, sideline interviews during play, pyrotechnics galore, the integration of personalities from the WWF, and inordinate coverage of the XFL cheerleaders, all of which occupied at least equal billing to football content itself (Forrest, 2002). To this end, one commentator argued, "football has little to do with the made-for-TV XFL, which is more about provocatively clad cheerleaders and trash-talk than touchdowns and tackles. The action on the field was little more than a sideshow" (McNulty, 2001, p. C6). A further report succinctly evinced the WWF edict infiltrating the XFL by describing NBC's XFL telecasts as "the perfect marriage between sex and violence . . . you're pretty much on the playing field with these pumped-up bozos and their bimbo mascots" (Robbins-Mullin, 2001, p. B3).

A final component of the XFL spectacle, also modeled after the WWF, was the fabrication of celebrity figures as an integral part of NBC's XFL broadcasts. Over the past two decades, the WWF brand and its pantheon of "superstars," have emerged as serious commercial entities within both the American sporting and entertainment landscapes. As testament to the strength of the WWF brand: two of its "celebrities" have each produced *New York Times* best-selling autobiographies; WWF superstar The Rock, despite minimal cinematic experience, has crafted a moderately successful (as measured in terms of box office revenue) film career; and, when a WWF personality is on the cover of *TV Guide*, copies reportedly "fly off newsstands so fast they have to be reordered" (Stoeltje, 1999, p. 1). Seeking to manufacture its own constellation of celebrity sub-brands, the XFL crudely created characters like "Touchdown" Tommy Maddox and Rod "He Hate Me" Smart and disseminated them through television and print promotions. This process of instant celebritization was necessary, since the players had little or no recognition among the general public, with the exception of a few high-profile figures who had underperformed in the NFL (e.g., former Heisman Trophy winner Rashaan Salaam). Typically, XFL participants were drawn from the anonymous ranks of undrafted college, former NFL, CFL, or Arena League players (Smart, who became the league's most recognizable [anti-]hero in the guise of "He Hate Me" was an undrafted college player from Western Kentucky). McMahon's choice of personalities to narrate XFL action also exemplified his commitment to bringing wrestling values and approaches to a football product. Taped scenes and live appearances of WWF "superstars" such as The Rock and "Stone Cold" Steve Austin became important elements of XFL broadcasts, and the XFL employed the services of WWF personalities such as Ventura, Jim Ross, and Jerry "The King" Lawler in further attempts to appeal to the wrestling-oriented consumer (Forrest, 2002).

Superficially, the XFL seemed a more than adept unification of the perceived strengths of the NFL—violence, warlike combat, and visceral intensity—and the spectacular essence of the WWF—violence, hyper-masculinity, and anti-tradition insolence (c.f. Atkinson, 2002; Trujillo, 1995). As one journalist argued prior to the start of play, the new league would succeed because "America loves football and young America loves wrestling" (Cafardo, 2000, p. C8). However, by the XFL's second week, the NBC share had fallen to 4.6, as more than half of the viewers from the first game switched over or switched off ("Ratings for XFL plummet," 2001). Decreasing viewership during the course of each game signaled further bad news: as in the first week, each 30-minute measure indicated more and more viewers were changing the channel (Fendrich, 2001b, 2001c). In week three, the drop-off was significant as the NBC share fell to 3.1 (Fendrich, 2001d). Bob Reardon, the XFL's Vice President of Sales, stated that, owing to the dismal ratings, the league was going to have to give away free advertising for the week 5 broadcast (Westhead, 2001). NBC's cable partners, UPN and TNN, were experiencing the same rate of decline in viewers, and by the end of the season, ratings had reached abysmal lows on all three networks ("XFL ratings falling fast," 2001). The XFL's end-of-season championship game drew a Nielsen rating of just 2.1, almost half the rating expected by McMahon and Ebersol (Forrest, 2002). It was no surprise, then, that shortly after the game Ebersol and McMahon decided to cut their losses and disband the league.

After only one season and only three months of existence, the XFL was a financial and public failure for both the WWF and NBC. The WWF's stock, once trading at almost $35 per share, fell well below half that upon announcement of the league's closure (Forrest, 2002). Further, the WWF and NBC were widely ridiculed in the press after the league's demise. As one reporter put it, the league failed because it was made up of "everything a sports league should not be, drawn up on a marketing man's story board with no respect whatsoever for the fan, the game or the integrity of sport" (Todd, 2000, p. F6). Beyond scathing critiques levied by those in the media, however, questions about the league's downfall remained unanswered. Had the new league failed to reach the target, the young male demographic? Had McMahon and Ebersol overestimated their formulaic approach to producing mediated sport? Perhaps most significantly, is the NFL's stronghold over the football-consuming populace so tight that even the injection of WWF-style sensationalized hyper-marketing is not enough to render a viable football alternative?

Cursory observation suggests that the XFL did indeed isolate its core wrestling audience, males aged 18–34 (Fendrich, 2001c). Perhaps it lacked the carefully scripted dramatic and aesthetic elements of wrestling, or maybe, despite the innovations, the XFL too closely resembled an athletically inferior version of the NFL. Perhaps more significant, however, is the contention that the XFL's failure was in larger part owing to its inability to compete with an evolved NFL *spectacle,* already deeply entrenched in the American popular sporting imaginary. At the same time, the cultural cache of the WWF brand paradoxically served to further undermine the XFL. Thus, not only did the XFL as a popular cultural commodity fail to present the quality of football demanded by a sport savvy American consuming populace, it fell short of the extreme "attitude" consumers have come to expect from the WWF. The NFL represents the dominant model of contemporary corporate football; hence, it would be difficult for the XFL to penetrate, or deviate from, the pre-established archetype. Ironically, the WWF itself had set the standards for corporatized rebellion against the sporting mainstream: the core wrestling audience that the XFL coveted came with expectations of carefully manufactured sensationalized entertainment. Thus, in contrast to those who have pointed to the XFL's *over*emphasis on entertainment as reason for its failure (cf. Anderson, 2001), it is, arguably, more accurate to say that the XFL didn't go *far enough* in accentuating production values over sporting content. If the WWF represented the dominant model, then ironically the XFL may have fallen victim to the heightened audience expectations already set in place by its primary investor.

In conclusion, the league did not represent a *failed experiment* with regard to either its "sportainment" sensibility or hyper-commercialized structure. The XFL was not fundamentally different from other professional leagues in North America, or, indeed, globally. This is nowhere more evident than in comparisons with the NFL. While the XFL was supposedly the anti-NFL, the two leagues demonstrated more similarities than differences. As Wade (2001, D4) proclaimed during the first week of the XFL: "Yes, look. And see what [NFL Commissioner] Paul Tagliabue doesn't want you to see. After just one weekend, it's clear the XFL and NFL are more alike than different." While professional football has always possessed something that wrestling has generally lacked—the popular perception of sporting authenticity— in recent years wrestling's over-the-top production and marketing values have become the envy of professional football executives. Forrest (2002) argues that it was the perceived need to enhance and recreate its telecasts that led to the ABC network's hiring of comedian Dennis Miller, and more recently colorful ex-coach John Madden, for its pivotal *Monday Night Football* broadcasts (strategies which could not prevent the demise, in the face of steadily falling ratings, of primetime network *Monday Night Football* coverage as announced by its shift to the ESPN cable outlet from the 2006 season onwards). Across the game's expansive television landscape which ranges from coverage on CBS, NBC, Fox, and ESPN networks, to the NFL channel, and NFL Sunday Ticket packages on DirecTV (the generative sum of which, beginning in 2006, will approach $3.74 billion per year), the league has become ever more consciously designed, promoted, and delivered as ratings-driven entertainment. Thus, we have seen an increased emphasis on a visceral, violent, voyeurism (referee-viewpoint cameras, on-player microphones); the lionizing of hyper-masculine protagonists (Warren Sapp, Brett Favre, Ray Lewis); the involvement of highly objectified female figures in studio and sideline settings (Melissa Stark, Lisa Guerrero, Michelle Tafoya on ABC, Bonnie Bernstein on CBS); the fostering of celebrityhood both on and off the field (Dennis Miller, John Madden); the highlighting of particular player performances (in shows like Fox's *Under the Helmet,* and *Monday Night Football*'s puerile "You've Been Sacked" half-time segment). With this combination of features, the NFL could almost top the XFL.

As the latter examples suggest, the XFL was hardly unique in its blurring of popular cultural realms. Further, critiques of the XFL's explicit, profit-driven production values—which often forsook the on-field action—seem hypocritical given the state of the NFL and contemporary sport in general. While league executives were certainly more overt in their identification of the XFL's sportainment ethos— McMahon himself was quoted as saying "I don't care how [the fans] are entertained" (Morgan, 2001, p. D1)—to denounce the XFL as programming as opposed to sport (Anderson, 2001, p. D1) seems naïve if one pays closer scrutiny to any recent NFL broadcast. As journalist Juan Rodriguez so succinctly put it in his sardonic reply to coverage of the XFL in the popular press:

Take Bob Ryan of the Boston Globe. . . . He leveled the league for being "all about hits and leaving people crumpled on the ground." What does this make the NFL and its ace color man, John Madden, whose trademark word is "Boom!"? (Rodriguez, 2001, p. G1).

While, like professional wrestling, the XFL lacked the perception of authenticity, its production values have been paralleled within professional football, if not readily appropriated and deployed by pro-football executives. The XFL's business plan may have been to combine the "cultural standards of professional wrestling" with the "basest qualities of the NFL" (Bisher, 2001, p. 3D), but it would appear that the NFL itself had already been heading down the same path with a long-established if not always loyal audience already in tow. Certainly the NFL has been more covert in its conflation of sport and entertainment — an implicit rather than explicit blurring of sport, culture, and economics — the XFL nonetheless lies somewhere on the same continuum: although the XFL may be a more highly evolved form, the NFL must also be considered a form of sportainment.

Rather than being an ingenious (if ingenuous) marker of the future of football, the XFL was merely symptomatic of broader trends within the media-sport nexus and popular culture more generally. In the XFL, converging corporate and cultural interests manifest themselves in an institutional conglomeration whose façade only loosely resembled sport in its traditional guise. That the NFL now so closely resembles the XFL suggests modern sport has indeed reached a point of "total exhaustion of viable systematic alternatives" (Fukuyama, 1989, p. 3) to the sport-media-entertainment complex which so explicitly showed itself in the now departed football league. While it may not have lasted long on the cultural landscape, the XFL was a potent indication that we should not overlook the economic, technological, and political forces that come together to structure our experiences of contemporary sport culture. Viewers may have turned away from the XFL because it, too explicitly and unashamedly, blurred the lines between melodrama and sport, but the veneer of sporting authenticity that envelops leagues such as the NFL may be crumbling. Perhaps sport, to paraphrase Postman (1985), is in danger of amusing itself and us to death? That's sportainment!

4

GENDERED OLYMPIC VIRTUALITY

According to Hogan (2003), the *interpretive program* component of recent Olympic Games opening ceremonies constitute an evocative stage for the ethnic and gender inflected performance of the *home* nation. These ceremonies are directed to internal and external audiences alike, and for contrasting purposes, including the advancement of specific political propaganda, corporate investment, or tourism marketing objectives. Given the global visibility of such national stagings (Hogan, 2003), it was perhaps surprising that the interpretive program for the 2002 Salt Lake City Winter Olympic Games should have been so white and masculinist in its orientation. For instance:

> A key theme running throughout the interpretive program was humanity's relationship to and ultimate victory over nature. This was exemplified particularly in the "Fire Within" segments around which the interpretive program was structured. In the first of these segments, the "Child of Light," a young White boy struggled to make his way through a raging winter storm. A White man representing the fire within helped guide the boy to safety. The segment was a parable of humanity's (and America's) search for strength and meaning and the triumph of human will in the face of adversity. In this sense, the story was timeless and universal. Nonetheless, the fact that White males personified both humanity/America (the child) and its will and drive (the fire within) reveals the extent to which White male perspectives and experiences are still dominant in discourses of American identity. (Hogan, 2003, pp. 115–116)

Foregoing the opportunity to represent the US in more ethnic and gender in-clusive terms, and in the context of the political and cultural tumult resulting from the events of September 11, 2001 (Falcous & Silk, 2005; Silk & Falcous, 2005), Salt Lake City's performance positioned a familiar sense of white "na-tional manhood" (Nelson, 1998) at the heart of the nation's (and indeed of humanity's) origins.

At a time when the Olympic movement regularly congratulates itself for its move toward greater gender equality, usually expressed in terms of the growing numbers of female participants, the Olympic Games act as a context and mecha-nism for normalizing particular gender discourses and relations. The opening cer-emonies are only the initial, yet one of the most visible, vehicles through which the Olympic movement could, if it were so inclined, choose to depict gender and gen-der differences in a more progressive light (hence, the disappointment of the Salt Lake City debacle). Regardless of the organization's proclivity—or indeed antipa-thy—toward a more emancipatory gender politics, the representation of the Games by the commercially oriented popular media habitually advances a more traditionally gendered Olympic reality.

As numerous researchers have shown, the various strands of Olympic Games media coverage routinely resonate with, and indeed advance, the essentialist and hierarchically ordered notions of differential gender identities, practices, and expe-riences, which reside all too comfortably within the popular imaginary (Billings, Eastman, & Newton, 1998; Borcila, 2000; Chisholm, 1999; Duncan, 1990; Higgs, Weiller, & Martin, 2003; Jones, Murrel, & Jackson, 1999; Urquhart, & Crossman, 1999). In seeking to make a contribution to this established body of work, this chapter concentrates on the NBC's coverage of the 1996 Summer Olympic Games in Atlanta. Specifically, it examines how and why NBC consciously advanced tradi-tionally feminine codes within, and through, the content and structure of its primetime televisual discourse. This involves appropriating elements of French cultural commentator Jean Baudrillard's provocative contemporary cultural theor-izing as a suggestive framework for examining the nature and influence of the mass-mediated sport spectacles that dominate, and define, the representational politics of American sporting culture.

In 1991, Baudrillard wrote a series of articles in the French radical newspaper *Libération* focused on the Gulf War being "[p]romotional, speculative, virtual" (1995, p. 30). Published in English and collected in 1995 under the title *The Gulf War Did Not Happen* (Baudrillard, 1995), these writings created a welter of criti-cism even for an author thoroughly familiar with stirring intellectual controversy (see Norris, 1992; Rojek and Turner, 1993; Woods, 1992). Yet, Baudrillard's pri-mary thesis was hardly controversial. His main thrust was not to deny that over 100,000 people lost their lives in this conflict, but rather that the "reality of the media Gulf War" (Patton, 1995, p. 16) deviated from the actual experience of events as they unfolded. It was in this sense that Baudrillard asserted that the Gulf War did not take place for, on the level through which the conflict was consumed by its global television viewership, it was "a masquerade of information: branded faces delivered over to the prostitution of the image" (Baudrillard, 1995, p. 40). Hence, in texts intended to problematize what Kellner (1992) described as the "Persian Gulf TV War," Baudrillard (1995) sought to intervene into the uncritical appropriation of the simulated televisual discourse that framed the conflict within the global popular imaginary.

Within his Gulf War analysis Baudrillard adopted an interpretive method that fused the destabilizing influence of Brechtian paradox with the unsettling "fatal strategy" of taking radical notions to their [il]logical extremes (Baudrillard, 1993a, p. 180). Such epistemological and ontological radicalism has proved distressing to mainstream academicians, many of whose careers, and thereby lives, have clung to the hope of developing theoretical understandings that will definitively represent and explain the complexities of social reality. Baudrillard, in contrast, has shunned the scholarly responsibility, and indeed legitimation, proffered by such lofty goals, and instead focused on producing texts that are less attempts at representing and more concerned with transfiguring, in the sense of radically transforming, the perception and experience of mediated reality (Patton, 1995). So, although Baudrillard's writings are intentionally exaggerated, contradictory, and often bewildering, this does not diminish their potential to offer insightful readings of societies increasingly dominated by mass mediated imagery. As a consequence, this chapter illustrates how Baudrillard's extreme strategy for interpreting the Gulf War's "instant history TV" (Patton, 1995, p. 6), provides a productive schema for analyzing the mass mediated spectacles that dominate American sporting culture. Taking its leads from Baudrillard's work, explicitly his interrogation of the mediated Gulf War narrative, this preliminary discussion problematizes the images emanating from another media event (Dayan and Katz, 1992), namely, that fashioned by NBC's coverage of the 1996 Summer Olympic Games in Atlanta.

The content and structure of NBC's 79 hours of primetime coverage (of 171.5 hours total) demonstrated that, as with the Gulf War, so with the 1996 Summer Olympics, there is no guarantee as to the nature of the "event that it could be or that it would signify" (Baudrillard, 1995, p. 29). Rather, the American viewing public was confronted with NBC's promotional, speculative, and virtual representation of Atlanta reality: an Olympic simulation manufactured to serve definite purposes. In the lead up to the Atlanta Games Dick Ebersol predicted people will get the "results from CNN or the Internet . . . but they'll get the stories from NBC" (Impoco, 1996, p. 36). This Olympic production strategy was certainly not new; it merely represented the latest, and perhaps most sophisticated, attempt to transform televised sport in such a way that it could better compete with other forms of mass entertainment (see Barnett, 1990; Blake, 1996; Rader, 1984; Whannel, 1992). This discussion focuses on unraveling the motives behind, manifestations, and consequences of, NBC's decision to review, massage, and repackage (Zipay, 1996) Olympic reality for a female audience. Of course, television coverage of sport has long been produced according to a philosophy that positions the male viewer as the intended "subject of consumption" (Goss, 1995). For this reason, mainstream American televised sport came to be imbued with an aura of essentialized masculinity. The importance of

NBC's 1996 Atlanta Olympics lies in that it was perhaps the first primetime *global* sport spectacle to consciously fashion its production to attract a larger female viewership. However, rather than blithely celebrating the Atlanta Games as "the Gender Equity Olympics" (McCallum & O'Brien, 1996, p. 17), this discussion problematizes NBC's *discovery* of the female audience, and thereby imitates Baudrillard's project by challenging the popular perception and experience of mediated Olympic reality.

According to Baudrillard, within the contemporaneous age of instantaneous and global communication, the order of appearance and representation—and therefore the constitution and construction of social reality—has become defined through an ever-proliferating economy of televisual simulations. Contemporary culture can thus be characterized as being hyperreal, because, in Chen's neo-Baudrillardian terms, "What is real is no longer our direct contact with the world, but what we are given on the TV screen: TV *is* the world" (1987, p. 71). Preempting the hackneyed and superficial criticisms of Baudrillard's hyperontology, it should be noted that Chen's proclamation is in no way asserting that material existence has been rendered obsolete within the era of all engulfing televisual simulations. Rather, the triumph of the televisual image—resulting from innovations and expansions in the realm of communications technology—has had a profound effect on the way people engage, understand, and experience their material existence (Rail, 1991). Such was the case during the Gulf War, when the American viewer's engagement, understanding, and experience of the conflict were mediated through a combination of the Pentagon's conspiratorial editorializing and the American media's populist programming. Although the Gulf War hyper-narrative, beamed via satellite into American homes, bore little or no resemblance to the experience of those on the battlefield, the images of the war nonetheless had real effects and became "enmeshed in the ensuing material and social reality" (Patton, 1995, p. 11).

Once turned into media information, the Gulf War became a virtual conflict fashioned from and thereby symptomatic of the contradictory sensibilities of a postmodern America dominated by the televisual (Baudrillard, 1988; Kellner, 1995). Even though American media culture is dominated by images of "expertly choreographed brutality" (Gerbner, 1995, p. 547), the American viewing public was spared graphic representations of the mass slaughter inflicted by American forces. Because of a fear of "adversely affecting public sentiment" (Patton, 1995, p. 13), the American public was provided with "No images of the field of battle, but images of masks, of blind or defeated faces, images of falsification . . . which rendered the [Iraqi] other powerless without destroying its flesh" (Baudrillard, 1995, p. 40). According to the representational logic of this "'clean' war" (Baudrillard, 1995, p. 40), the televisual absence of charred and mutilated remains of Iraqi soldiers and civilians allowed the fragile American psyche to rest easily with the self-evident superiority, yet reassuring humanity, of its forces. In this way, a made-for-TV Gulf War simulacrum was fabricated into "less the representation of real war than a spectacle which serves a variety of political and strategic purposes on all sides" (Patton, 1995, p. 10).

The scripted hyperreality of the Gulf War spectacle was mirrored by that of NBC's coverage of the Atlanta Games, which fashioned a virtual Olympics comparably designed to seduce the American masses, and thereby to serve a variety of primarily economic—but nonetheless political—purposes. During the latter half of 1995, NBC signed two contracts with the International Olympic Committee (IOC), amounting to $3.6 billion, securing the broadcast rights to the Summer Olympic Games in 2000, 2004, and 2008, and to the Winter Olympic Games in 2002 and 2006 (*The Economist,* 1996). For the foreseeable future, NBC had bought the rights to America's Olympic coverage. In doing so, Dick Ebersol, president of NBC Sport and more pertinently executive producer of NBC's coverage of the Atlanta Games, had purchased the right to creatively suture the network's trademark peacock logo to the accumulated and emotive symbolism of the Olympic rings. As Richard Pound, then IOC vice president, brazenly admitted, "If you owe them [the bank] $10,000, you're a customer. If you owe them $10,000 billion you're a partner" (Thurow, 1996, p. 14).

With the "thoroughly modern marriage" (Knisley, 1996, p. S5) forged between NBC and the IOC, in an American context the Olympic Games are as much about the advancement of NBC stock as about covering the event (Peterson, 1996). This was particularly true since NBC had *guaranteed* its corporate advertisers a 17 Nielsen rating for the Atlanta coverage (equating to roughly 16.3 million TV households). Should Olympic broadcasts fall below that mark, the network would provide advertisers with free air time, an unwelcome eventuality that would eat into the anticipated return on NBC's $465 million investment (Farhi, 1996). Clearly, NBC was substantially more than a channel of transmission for the Olympic event, and the Atlanta Games were destined to become an NBC-directed deceptive televisual subterfuge: a pre-fabricated Olympic spectacle and "highly artificial construct, designed for maximum sentiment and ratings" (Remnick, 1996, p. 27).

NBC's stratagem for molding their Olympic spectacle illustrated Baudrillard's concept of the postmodern condition as a cybernetic visual culture directing a simulated order of appearance: "Whenever we switched on the tube, we saw what Ebersol wanted us to see, when he wanted us to see it. . . . Whether we like it, we watched. But we weren't watching the Olympics; we were watching Ebersol's vision of the Olympics" (Knisley, 1996, p. S5). Ebersol even brazenly acknowledged his role and influence at the helm of NBC's Olympic culture industry: "I get to arrange how all these things are perceived in the world" (quoted in Goodbody, 1996, p. 21). Ebersol's perceptions, and thereby NBC's contrived manipulation of the Olympic spectacle, were significantly informed by more than 10,000 interviews carried out by network researchers with the aim of "trying to pinpoint what viewers like and don't like" (Impoco, 1996, p. 36). The results of these interviews provided the basis for what NBC's director of research, Nicholas Schiavone, identified as the five principles, corresponding to the five Olympic rings, that provided the foundational philosophy for NBC's Olympic television coverage:

Ring I, Story: Viewers want a narrative momentum, a story that builds. Stories make connections with reality, among facts, and between the subject and the viewer. This is what the viewer takes away from the telecast.

Ring II, Reality: Perhaps the major hook for Olympic viewers is the unscripted drama of the Olympics, the idea that anything can happen, both of an athletic nature and a human nature. People look for real stories and reliability, things that apply to them. They are looking for real life and real emotion presented credibly.

Ring III, Possibility: This ring covers the feeling of self-realization. The audience experiences the rise of individuals from ordinary athletes and their humble beginnings to the company of the world's elite. This identification reinforces belief in their own ability to achieve. This embodiment of possibility gives the viewer a reason he or she can "make it through."

Ring IV, Idealism: The Olympics are still viewed by a vast majority in the contexts of purity and honor. They appeal to what is best in us. This area summarizes the viewers' need to integrate the intellectual and the emotional.

Ring V, Patriotism: Love of country is not just limited to an American viewer's love of the United States. National honor and Olympic tradition seem to go hand in hand. The viewer recognizes the love of his or her own country, but at the same time respects the international athlete's love of their nation as well. (Schiavone, quoted in Remnick, 1996, p. 27)

NBC's formulaic Olympic production was a prime example of mediated texts as imploded, reformulated, and bastardized interpretations of the real. For, as Baudrillard (1980, p. 141) noted, any information that "reflects or diffuses an event is already a degraded form of the event." Given the influence of interviewees' responses in shaping programming philosophy, what was presented as NBC coverage of the 1996 Summer Olympics was, in a Baudrillardian sense, the generation of a model of a real situation (Atlanta Games coverage) through reference to models that had already been reproduced (televisual simulations of previous Olympic Games). According to NBC's new Olympic reality logic, the "real is not only what can be reproduced, but that which is already reproduced. The hyperreal" (Baudrillard, 1983, pp. 146–147). NBC was thus responsible for creating a hyperreal Olympics that were "more real than reality itself" (Baudrillard, 1980, p. 139).

Driven by the economics of the marketplace, Ebersol freely admitted "ratings are the yardstick by which it [NBC] will judge its Olympic Games coverage" (*The New York Times,* 1996, p. 26A). As a result he had to "keep in mind appealing to the widest audience" (quoted in Sandomir, 1996a, p. 14B). For Ebersol, ensuring a wide audience meant capturing and sustaining the interest of women viewers (Zipay, 1996). Women were of particular interest to network executives because, through its ongoing research into the Olympic television audience, NBC had *deduced* that "men will watch the games no matter what" (Gunther, 1996, p. 43). This research also identified that, unlike other sporting events, the Olympics appeal to women in roughly equal numbers as men (Impoco, 1996; Remnick, 1996). Consequently, the size of NBC's female viewership would determine the difference between commercial success and failure, between reaping the financial benefits of charging up to $700,000 per 30 seconds of advertising, and being forced to offer free advertising time as a way of alleviating corporate customer dissatisfaction with poor ratings. Hence, NBC's brief involved packaging the Olympics in such a way "that women will stay glued" (Gunther, 1996, p. 43).

Atlanta represented the third consecutive Summer Olympics broadcast by NBC. So, in effect, the network was re-engineering the Olympic commodity-sign based on its accumulated knowledge of the processes of popular cultural production and consumption. During the 1988 Seoul Olympics NBC relied on live transmissions and, it has been asserted, floundered in the ratings due to the network's decision to adhere to a journalistic style of coverage that involved "hiring print reporters to investigate stories, splitting screens to show more than one event, stressing live coverage, results, and controversies" (Gunther, 1996, p. 43). Reflecting upon the Seoul debacle, NBC's coordinating producer David Neal opined that the mistake was "treating the games like a two-week Super Bowl" (quoted in Impoco, 1996, p. 36). Such a testosterone-rich Olympic reality was thought to have alienated female viewers who, according to NBC's audience research findings, tended "to be more interested in stories than in scores" than their male counterparts (Impoco, 1996, p. 36).

In order to accommodate the perceived masculine *and* feminine sides of its viewership, for the 1992 Barcelona Olympics, NBC relied on two differing production designs which created two distinct Olympic realities (Sandomir, 1996a). First, in conjunction with Cablevision Systems and designed primarily for the male portion of the sports viewing public, NBC offered its "Olympic Triplecast," which incorporated three channels of comprehensive live coverage for the 15-day duration of the games, and charged between $29.95 a day and $125 for the entire event. Second, designed for the high ratings demanded of primetime network television, NBC produced a female-friendly Olympics that relied almost exclusively on taped programming in order to massage "what has already happened in Barcelona . . . into a storytelling package with natural commercial breaks" (Sandomir, 1992, p. 11). Despite high ratings for its primetime telecasts, NBC was hampered by the financial outlay required of the "unmitigated disaster" (Albert Kim quoted in Edwards, 1996) that the triplecast became, and ended up losing $98.6 million on the games (Gunther, 1996, p. 42). Nevertheless, Barcelona proved a useful learning experience for NBC Olympic producers and provided the blueprint for the gendered strategy that framed coverage of the Atlanta Games.

To some commentators, 1996 witnessed the *discovery* of women as an important, and hitherto largely neglected, market segment: "From the Summer Olympics to the political conventions to car ads on TV, the marketers who shape our tastes tuned in to the sensible, compassionate, nonideological women who run so much of the country" (Alter, 1996/1997, p. 32). Just as political pollsters identified the hypermythologized "soccer moms" who were to become the sought-after voters in the 1996 US presidential campaign (Davies, 1996; MacFarquhar, 1996; Safire, 1996), so NBC's research of the Olympic audience identified women as its key constituency of viewers. NBC thus predetermined that, despite the merit or otherwise of the forthcoming exploits of female Olympians, the Atlanta Games would be a celebration of Olympic womanhood. Within the battery of promotions that prepared the American audience for the upcoming spectacle, NBC openly declared that its focus would be on women's sports (Schulian, 1996). The network's power to direct the popular articulation of the Atlanta Olympics was subsequently evidenced in the popular media's faithful replication of this female Olympic theme. NBC's female orientation was intertextually augmented by myriad media sources. The US women's basketball team was featured on the cover of the *Sports Illustrated* (July 22, 1996) double issue Olympic preview, and the front cover of *The New York Times Magazine* introduced the Atlanta Games as the Olympics in which "Women Muscle In" (June 23 1996). Before the ceremonial flame had been lit, and despite the fact that male athletes continued to outnumber female athletes (63.5 percent to 36.5 percent [Becker, 1996]), a complex illusion of Olympic gender equality and emancipation was already artificially piloting the popular signification of the Atlanta Games.

NBC's representational strategy for the actual coverage of the Atlanta Games involved manufacturing a stereotypically *feminine* Olympic spectacle. In creating this primetime "Oprah Olympics" (Gunther, 1996, p. 42), NBC manufactured its own Olympic reality centered around events deemed appropriate to female viewers and infused with sentiment intended to resonate with the female psyche (Remnick, 1996). According to production executives, NBC's conscious manipulation of the content and structure of Olympic reality "was based on a scientific campaign to shape their broadcasts to a feminine sensibility" (Remnick, 1996, p. 26). NBC appears to have followed a wider industry trend, which involves presenting market research data as "scientific" without fully considering "the assumptions built into its research procedures." Moreover, such research designs fabricate "more reified and more concrete" constructs of the consumer "despite the rather flimsy practical and pragmatic origin of the information being processed" (Lury and Warde, 1997, p. 95). Thus, it could be argued, NBC was complicit in unscientifically simulating traditional feminine sensibilities within and through its broadcasts. NBC's crude interpretation of its Olympic audience research findings exteriorized interiority, or objectivized the subjective (Goss, 1995), by reducing the complexities of consumer motivations and predispositions to a binary and essentialist model of gender norms and differences. In accordance with this reductionist model, NBC's manufacturing of its Atlanta Olympic reality was based on an understanding of gender identities, practices, and experiences, as unitary, stable, and fixed entities, to be engaged by providing programming that resonates with the essential features of our gendered beings. Certain sports are viewed as being popular among women simply because they incorporate and celebrate traditionally feminine traits such as bodily beauty, grace, and expression. Conversely, some sports are deemed to be unpopular among women because their embodied masculine characteristics are viewed as an anathema to feminine sensibilities. In an Olympic context, this point was succinctly expressed by Ebersol: "If you put boxing in the middle of the greatest family entertainment in all of sports, you're going to drive people away. . . . Women and children won't stand for it" (quoted in Gunther, 1996, p. 43).

NBC sought to hail, or interpellate (Hall, 1996), female members of the television audience by proffering essentialized feminine subject positions within its primetime Olympic discourse. NBC's Atlanta Olympic coverage highlighted events that represented women in ways that the network deemed would be gender appropriate for a middle American audience. Predictably, NBC's primetime coverage focused on the overdetermined hyper-femininity (Feder, 1995) of gymnasts (Shannon Miller, Dominique Dawes, Dominique Moceanu, and Kerri Strug), swimmers (Janet Evans, Amanda Beard, and Amy Van Dyken), and divers (Mary Ellen Clark and Becky Ruehl). Of course, there is nothing inherently *feminine* about these sporting activities, or any other activity for that matter. However, all of them have long been culturally coded as signifying the vulnerable, aesthetic, and hetero-sexualized embodied femininity around which NBC chose to center its Olympic reality (Duncan, 1990; Ryan, 1995; Whitson, 1994).

Feminizing the content of the primetime Olympic schedule was aided by the economic leverage held by NBC over the IOC, which allowed for, among other measures: the expansion of the gymnastics competition from 7 to 9 nights of primetime coverage; the inclusion of a made-for-TV champions gala as an audience-grabbing finale to the gymnastics competition; the enlargement of the swimming program from 6 to 7 days; and, the incessant promotion of the diving program within the Olympic schedule. Presumably because they were deemed not to have exuded the appropriate feminine aura, the highly successful US women's basketball, soccer, and softball teams received nothing like the same primetime coverage. Meanwhile, even less telegenic "boxers, wrestlers and weightlifters—hairy, sweaty undesirables" were left to compete in the "daytime ratings wars" (Schulian, 1996, p. 112).

The structure of NBC's Atlanta Olympic production was similarly framed by an essentialist understanding of gender as a binary category, within which the rational sports-loving male was positioned against the emotion-driven sentiment-loving female (Carlson, 1996; Gunther, 1996; Remnick, 1996). In one sense, NBC was corroborated Baudrillard's assertion that contemporary popular culture has become a domain of the affective: "They [the masses] delight in the interplay of signs and stereotypes and in any content, as long as it results in a dramatic sequence" (Baudrillard, 1980, p. 143). Whereas Baudrillard (1988) views the triumph of affect as seducing the American population en masse, NBC clearly perceives it as a particularly feminine attribute:

> while men enjoy sports "from the outside in"—that is, they want the event itself and then, possibly, some connection with the people involved—women come to sports "from the inside out." Before they get interested in an event, they need to know the characters and sympathize with them. (Dick Ebersol, quoted and paraphrased in Remnick, 1996, p. 27)

NBC felt it would "lose this special [female] audience" by treating "the Olympics as a normal, results-driven sporting event on TV" (Ebersol, quoted in Hruska, 1996, p. 9). Consequently, in an affective sense, NBC's strategy for hailing the female viewing subject revolved around producing sentiment-laden Olympic narratives designed to seduce the habitually empathetic female psyche.

The goal of fashioning the Atlanta Games into a feminine product designed to bring "a tear to the eye and bullion to the coffers" (Remnick, 1996, p. 26) necessitated NBC manipulating the structure of Olympic reality, akin to what occurred during the Gulf War. CNN's made-for -TV "Gulf War movie" (Patton, 1995, p. 13) was a "programmed and always delayed illusion of battle," a war "amplified by information . . . the systematic manipulation of data" and "artificial dramatisation" (Baudrillard, 1995, p. 58). The goal of this contrived media orchestration was to "control the production and meaning of information" in order to promulgate a "kind of affective patriotism" among the American viewers (Baudrillard, 1995, pp. 13, 50). In order to create the same type of affective link between the Olympic media spectacle and the desired female audience, NBC adopted a "highly elastic style narrative" (Remnick, 1996, p. 26) that artificially dramatized the event through the preprogrammed, and frequently delayed, manipulation and amplification of Olympic televisual discourse.

It has been noted that sport's unique quality over other forms of televised popular entertainment is the immediacy and uncertainty of sporting spectacles (*The Economist,* 1996, p. 17). Recognizing, yet subverting, the primacy of the *live sporting event,* NBC's Olympic televisual spectacle was consciously fashioned into a timeless and unreal space that, to the casual observer, *appeared* to be live even though up to 40 percent of it was not (Hruska, 1996). According to Dick Ebersol "In our minds, we'll be live at all times" (quoted in Sandomir, 1996a, p. 14B), and certainly the network's announcers expressed nothing that indicated to the contrary (Impoco, 1996; Levin, 1996a; *The New York Times,* 1996). In actuality NBC's nightly broadcasts were considerably more complex:

> Within NBC's broadcast of the Games, there are three types of production. The first is purely live, when something is shown in real time. . . . The second is called live-on-tape. . . . What viewers see is called live by the announcers but is shown several minutes or several hours later. . . . The third is taped coverage, which is usually easy to distinguish because there are breaks in continuity. A feature may be thrown in and special effects added. (Sandomir, 1996b, p. A1)

The motive behind the intermingling of purely live, live-on-tape, and taped coverage under NBC's deceptive rubric of being "plausibly live" (*The New York Times,* 1996, p. A26) was plain: "Its job was to build interest and drama in the unfolding panorama of the Olympic Games" (Crain, 1996, p. 15). The adoption of multiple programming formats allowed NBC's Olympic production team to artificially heighten and intensify the dramatic content of its broadcasts. This degree of creative flexibility simply does not exist in "purely live" production. The network utilized "pausibly live" programming to mold seamless and engaging narratives that invariably built to a suspenseful climax, but whose relation to unfolding real-time events was largely irrelevant. NBC simply chose to blur "reality in the name of a good story" (*The New York Times,* 1996, p. A26), with the rationale that if you "tell them stories . . . they will watch" (Impoco, 1996, p. 36).

The most conspicuous example of NBC's plausibly live strategy centered on the delaying, rearranging, and massaging (Sandomir, 1996b, p. A1) of Kerri Strug's final vault in the women's gymnastics team competition. The *historic* vault actually took place in the late afternoon, but it was not shown on NBC until almost midnight Eastern Time. Seizing on the emotive narrative of the injured athlete, NBC's primetime programming intensified the drama surrounding this heroic, triumphant, yet ultimately irrelevant vault. (The US had already won the gold medal prior to the vault.) The result was NBC's "highest, most emotional, most poignant moment" of the Olympic coverage, garnering a phenomenal 27.2 Nielsen rating (Sandomir, 1996b, p. A1). Despite the notoriety of this particular event, the repackaging of Strug's vault was indicative of NBC's production strategy throughout the Games:

> To NBC, the Olympics are episodes or segments in a prime-time show. It is all about stories, tales to be told, athletes to admire. Results are incidental. The events need not be presented on television in the linear fashion in which they unfold in real life. (Sandomir, 1996b, p. A1)

As well as creating a "zone of fictional time" (*The New York Times,* 1996, p. A26) an equally significant, and related, element of NBC's narrativizing of the Olympic schedule involved the strategic insertion of taped personal profiles as a means of creating emotional attachments between the television audience and certain athletes and their events (Levin, 1996a, p. 21). The influential Roone Arledge (see Rushin, 1994) developed "Up Close and Personal" profiling for ABC's groundbreaking coverage of the 1972 Munich Olympics. For the Atlanta Games, Ebersol (a longtime Arledge protégé) enthusiastically appropriated this technique, and commissioned 135 two- to three-minute emotionally charged segments featuring various athletes, personalities, countries, and events drawn from the televisual archives of Olympics past, present, *and* future. These syrupy examples of "formulaic hagiography" (Carlson, 1996, p. 48) focused on a broad array of athletes; from predictable features on high-profile American hopefuls such as Michael Johnson and Janet Evans, to stories on foreign notables such as the Belorussian gymnast Vitali Scherbo, the British triple jumper Jonathan Edwards, and the Canadian rower Silken Laumann, to more bizarre features such as that on the failed thoroughbred race horse, Nirvana II. These humanizing—sometimes anthropomorphizing—segments personalized "the competitors with feature stories that emphasize[d] family tragedies, childhood physical ailments and heartbreaking disappointments" (*The New York Times,* 1996, p. A26). By narrating contests through the stories of particular individuals, NBC framed the coverage of events in order to influence the way they were consumed. These "motivational infomercials" (Carlson, 1996, p. 48) acted as semiotic anchors for the audience by attaching an affective signifier to certain events and orchestrating viewers' emotional investment in the simulated narrative unfolding before their eyes. As in the Gulf War, the real-time Olympics were lost (Baudrillard, 1995) in the carefully scripted production of these "soap opera games" (Carlson, 1996, p. 48). NBC's fabrication of highly emotive narratives framed the Olympics into a "17-day marathon 'Melrose Place'" (Sandomir, 1996a, 14B) for women, who, according to the network, are "addicted to melodrama" (Zipay, 1996, A60). In this sense, NBC's *Olympic show* imitated the "army's television show" during the Gulf War, with entertainment the "leading character," and female support for the Games was the desired "discursive effect" (Poster, 1995, p. 160).

Mirroring the American media's strategic manipulation of the Gulf War, NBC's generation of a hyperreal Olympics produced a markedly different kind of event from that which actually occurred in Atlanta. The most striking difference was NBC's conscious decision to fashion the Games into a distinctly feminine televisual spectacle. This gendered Olympic strategy was seemingly vindicated by averaging a 21.6 Nielsen rating (translating to roughly 20.7 million TV households), an impressive 41 percent share of the television audience, which equated to a weighty 25 percent increase over the viewing figures for the Barcelona Games (Shapiro, 1996). In the coveted 18-to-34 female demographic segment, NBC's ratings improved 16 percent from the Barcelona figures, and a staggering 69 percent from Seoul (Levin, 1996a). These ratings far surpassed the guaranteed mark set for securing full payments for advertising air time. As a consequence, and even after sharing 10 percent of its profits with the IOC, NBC made a $70 million profit on its initial $465 million Olympic investment (Farhi, 1996; Levin, 1996b).

Given the economics of the television industry, Ebersol has already announced that, in regard to the network's Olympic production strategies, money talks, so "Get used to it. The ratings were so high that NBC will take the same tack into Sydney and beyond" (Knisley, 1996, p. S6). The complexities and contradictions of media consumption patterns have been rendered irrelevant by NBC's money hungry media machine, which directly and uncritically attributed the reasons for higher Olympic viewing figures to its innovative production strategies. No other explanation was even plausible. As a result, the widespread skepticism and resistance to the NBC Olympics expressed by many consumers was neutered, and became wholly submerged, under the symbolic weight of the network's increasingly reified, strategically concretized, and *evidently* satisfied "imaginary consumer" (Lury and Warde, 1996). Moreover, NBC's lucrative Olympic simulacra have become the hegemonic sport media production aesthetic, influencing the production of sport events by its rival networks (*USA Today*, 1996, p. 2C; Unger, 1996). Certainly, and despite disappointing ratings at the time-zone-challenged Sydney 2000 games, Ebersol continues to extol the importance of the Olympic Games as a commercial media spectacle:

> I don't care what people say about Olympic ratings—it's the last single event that puts the whole family together in front of the television set. Normally, in the case of Dad, his favorite team is on regional cable. Mom is watching a prime-time soap opera like "ER." The kids are down the hall watching MTV or playing video games. . . . The Olympics, at one time or another, grabs all of them.

Under Ebersol's domineering influence, coverage of the 2004 Athens Olympics was molded to the new dictates of an expanding television landscape (comprising 1,210 hours of broadcast coverage over General Electric's various cable and satellite outlets: CNBC; MSNBC; Telemundo, USA, Bravo and HDTV feed), while retaining its preoccupation with the production of primetime entertainment for the NBC network. As Ebersol himself acknowledged, "I live more than anything else to produce the Games" (quoted in Wise, 2004, p. C1).

In conclusion, and as evidenced by NBC's Olympic coverage, female athletes, and the very notion of female sport participation, are becoming more prominent in American popular culture practices and experiences. Conversely, the politically progressive potentialities of an increased female presence in the Olympic spectacle were neutered by the demeaning way in which NBC chose to represent women. In spite of, or perhaps even because of, being the focus of NBC's Olympic reality, female athletes and consumers were portrayed and engaged in ways that subtly devalued their existence. Fabricated "with Mrs. Six-pack and the kids in mind" (Gunther, 1996, p. 42), NBC's clean, face-lifted, and affectively engineered spectacle was modeled on stereotypical and demeaning models of women as both the *objects of production* (the fetishization of athletic hyperfemininity), and as the *subjects of consumption* (the affective interpellation of the hypersensitive female consumer). NBC's marketing, promotion, and mediation of Olympic reality served as a kind of electronic surveillance (Bogard, 1996; Goss, 1995; Lyon, 1994) that normalized hierarchically differentiated representations, embodiments, and experiences of gender, within and through the coded circuitry of its televisual discourse.

As it became absorbed into the depthless, timeless, and aestheticized reality of Baudrillard's third order of simulacra (see Baudrillard, 1983; 1993b; Featherstone, 1991), NBC's gendered Atlanta reality became a constituent part of the hyperreal media culture that surreptitiously directs and defines everyday American existence (Chen, 1987; Denzin, 1991; Kellner, 1995). As Knisley noted, "He [Dick Ebersol] manipulated us, and for better or worse, he manipulated the Games, the single biggest sporting event in the world" (1996, p. S5). If the aggressive inclusion of women in the promotional circus of the American sport media continues in such a regressive fashion, the result will be the further accentuation of the essentialized, stable, and hierarchically ordered gender categories which reside all too comfortably within the popular imaginary. In light of such eventualities, rather than celebrating Dick Ebersol "for adapting NBC's approach to today's world" (Knisley, 1996, p. S6), we would be well advised to heed Baudrillard's advice to "resist the probability of any image or information whatever . . . and to that end re-immerse the war [in this case, mediated sport spectacles] and all information in the virtuality from whence they come" (Baudrillard, 1995, p. 66).

5

CELEBRATING RACE

As cultural critic Todd Gitlin surmised, "To speak of a culture of celebrity nowadays is nearly to commit a redundancy" (1998, p. 81). However, merely acknowledging the existence of contemporary celebrity culture as a definer of the age, potentially obscures its broader significance and derivation. The contemporaneous preoccupation with "the personal, the intimate, and the individual" (Marshall, 1997, pp. xiii) is the product of definite social and historical forces and relations. The second half of the twentieth century witnessed the individualizing amalgam of: Western democracies' intensified emphasis upon personal rights and responsibilities; consumer capitalism's solipsistic regime of economic (re)production; and the celebratizing tendencies of the commercial television medium. The result is a culture within which an ever expanding, hierarchically ordered, economy of mass mediated public individuals can, and often do, engage and inform private experience through their position as contextually produced "embodiments of the social categories in which people are placed and through which they have to make sense of their lives" (Dyer, 1986, p. 18).

From the outpourings of the commercial media, whom Braudy (1997, p. 550) refers to as the "arbiters of celebrity," we are, at least superficially, privy to a wealth of information that encourages us to develop a sense of familiarity, intrigue, and, sometimes, obsession with celebrity figures. While the celebrity is usually a complete stranger—someone we are never likely to meet nor ever truly know—the virtual intimacy created between celebrity and audience often has very real effects on the manner in which individuals negotiate the experience of their everyday lives.

So, as well as being a consequential force within late capitalist Western liberal economies, celebrities are significant public entities responsible for structuring meaning, crystallizing ideologies, and offering contextually grounded maps for private individuals as they navigate contemporary conditions of existence (Marshall, 1997). The hyper-individualizing production regimes and aesthetics of the new "television culture" (Fiske, 1987) have resulted in the identification, nurturing, exposition, celebration, and castigation of public individuals. This is becoming a large part of the popular media universe: "everyone is involved in either producing or consuming celebrities. Through TV advertisements, restaurant openings, charity balls, trade shows, and sports events, our lives are celebrity saturated" (Rein, Kotler, & Stoller, 1997, p. x). Diverse arenas such as politics, religion, commerce, the judiciary, military, sport, and virtually all other forms of entertainment, have cultivated their own celebrity economies. As a result, social institutions, practices, and issues have become principally represented to, and understood within, the popular imaginary through the actions of celebrated individuals. This is particularly evident within the sporting realm, where the incestuous processes of commercialization and mass mediation have turned sport into a self-generating promotional circus. This sporting-media-industrial complex is driven and defined less by events, activities, and spectacles, than by the very presence of those most public individuals who actually play the game; celebrated individuals whose narrated sporting and extra-sporting exploits (either heroic or cowardly, triumphant or failing) further their hold upon the popular imaginary.

To all intents and purposes, the era of the modern sport celebrity began with William Randolph Hearst's establishing of the first newspaper sport section within *The New York Journal* in 1895. This popular initiative soon spawned imitations in numerous national settings and provided a mechanism and forum for the transformation of notable athletes into nationally celebrated figures. It was a process of familiarization which, given the public's voracious interest in their nascent sport stars, evolved as an effective means of increasing newspaper circulation. Hence, figures such as the English cricketer W. G. Grace, the Welsh Rugby Union player Gwyn E. Nicholls, and the American jockey Tod Sloan, all sprang to national prominence around this time, and could be considered among the first modern sport celebrities (see Dizikes, 2000; Rae, 1999; Williams, 1991). The next stage in the evolution of the sport celebrity can be traced to the mid-1920s and is exemplified by the popularizing of Harold "Red" Grange, the University of Illinois and Chicago Bears running back. Perhaps most significant in this process was the influence of the legendary sports journalist, Grantland Rice, and his newsreel reporting competitors, who mythologized Grange's pyrrhic exploits to the estimated 60 million Americans then visiting movie houses each week (Carroll, 1999; Harper, 1994; 1999). As Rader noted, Grange was one of a coterie of skillfully promoted sporting figures at this time (others included, Babe Ruth, Jack Dempsey, Bobby Jones, and Bill Tilden), raised to the status of popular "compensatory" heroes, through their imaged personas, which helped assuage public anxieties pertaining to the "passing of the traditional dream of success, the erosion of Victorian values and feelings of powerlessness" amidst the turmoil of the Depression (1983, p. 11).

The nature and influence of the sport celebrity was elevated to a considerably higher plane in the post-World War II era with the advent of a postmodern "civilization of the image" (Kearney, 1989), instantiated by the widespread adoption of televisual communications technology. Television's innate predilection for human intimacy, coupled with live sport's telegenic qualities (the drama of the uncertain outcome played out by a cast of definable characters), secured sport's place in the programming schedule during the early years of network television, and bred a new generation of television sport heroes such as Arnold Palmer, Mickey Mantle, and Joe Namath. In the intervening decades, the ever more collusive relationship between television and sport profoundly influenced the tenor of popular sport culture, such that sport is now "basically media-driven celebrity entertainment" (Pierce, 1995, p. 185). Sports are customarily structured, marketed, mediated, and experienced, as contests between identifiable individuals (or groups of individuals) with whom the audience is expected to possess (or develop) some kind of affective attachment. As Whannel identified, "Sport is presented largely in terms of stars and narratives: the media narrativises the events of sport, transforming them into stories with stars and characters; heroes and villains" (1998, p. 23). If, as Lusted claims, "Personalities are central to the institution of television" (1991, p. 251), then they are even more central to the institution and era of televised sport.

Given the centrality of noteworthy individuals to the constitution and experience of contemporary sport culture, it is little wonder that a thriving sport celebrity industry has come to the fore. Headed by such mega-agencies as IMG, Octagon, and SFX, the manufacturing of sport celebrities has become a highly rationalized, almost McDonaldized (Ritzer, 1998) process. The postmodern disposition toward the blurring of institutional boundaries has meant the spheres within which sport celebrities operate as cultural and economic agents have broadened beyond those of the playing field and the corporate endorsement. Indeed, the "sports superstar . . . has sufficient prominence . . . to spin off into the wider realm of popular entertainment" (Rowe, 1995, pp. 117–118) and is liable to appear in commercial settings ranging from ghosted autobiographies to television situation comedies, talk shows, mainstream movies, popular music recordings, animated video games, and websites. So, within today's multi-layered "promotional culture" (Wernick, 1991), the sport celebrity is effectively a multi-textual and multi-platform promotional entity.

Without question the sport celebrity possesses numerous qualities that distinguish it from the imaged embodiments of other cultural realms. On a positive note, as a celebrity domain there are certain tangible benefits derived from sport's historically configured social positioning and implicit structure. First, when positioned against other celebrity formations (within which inherited wealth and status frequently play an important role), sport is ostensibly meritocratic. Sport celebrity then becomes the assumed corollary of performative excellence:

The cultural illusion is fostered that, one day, the "ordinary but special" individual consumer may realize his or her unique qualities, and join the ever-changing pantheon of celebrities. Sport has a particularly potent role to play within this ideological formation. (Giulianotti, 1999, p. 118–119)

In true neo-liberal fashion, the ascent to sport celebrityhood is habitually reduced to individual qualities such as innate talent, dedication, and good fortune, thus positioning the sport star, within the popular imaginary, as a deserved benefactor of his or her devotion to succeed. Second, sport is an uniquely valued cultural practice: "Only sports has the nation, and sometimes the world, watching the same thing at the same time, and if you have a message, that's a potent messenger" (Singer, 1998, quoted in Rowe, 1999, p. 74). Although by no means guaranteed, sport figures are likely to possess a heightened presence and affection within popular consciousness, making the transition to potent celebrityhood that much easier. Third, in the cinematic and popular music industries, individual performers routinely adopt fictive identities within their primary performative realms (e.g., films and music videos). Conversely, in sport, there is a perception that spectators and viewers are confronted with *real* individuals participating in unpredictable contests. Hence, the seemingly visceral, dramatic immediacy of sport gives the sport celebrity an air of authenticity that sets it apart from celebrities from other, more explicitly manufactured and manipulated, cultural realms. More problematically, sport also incorporates a host of idiosyncratic instabilities that can affect the process of celebrity manufacture. For instance, in most cases, sport celebrities emerge and endure due to continued excellence within their respective fields of endeavor. This represents an added layer of instability for those managing sport celebrity, since carefully scripted and heavily invested imaged personas can potentially be compromised by declines in performative function or even individual failures on the field of play. In addition, off-the-field indiscretions can play a role in undermining the personal narrative associated with a particular sport celebrity (the most tragic example being O. J. Simpson [see Johnson & Roediger, 1997]).

Sport celebrities occupy complex and varied positions within today's cultural economy, encompassing functions and roles as diverse as athletic laborer, entertainer, marketable commodity, role model, and political figure, to name but a few. However, the contemporary sport celebrity is, almost without exception, overdetermined by his or her function as a commercial entity. As such, the sport celebrity represents an important point of entry into what Rowe (1999) described as the "unruly trinity" of commercial sport, the entertainment media, and late capitalist culture. As with any cultural product, there is no guarantee that sport celebrities will be consumed in the manner intended by those orchestrating the manufacturing process (workers within the marketing, advertising, public relations, and commercial media industries). Audiences are far from homogenous entities, and consumers habitually display contrasting expressions of celebrity appropriation according to the cultural, political, and economic contingencies of their social location

(Hall, 1980; Johnson, 1987). Given their contested nature, those within the celebrity industry seek to manufacture celebrity identities that acknowledge, and seek to engage, the perceived sensibilities of the audience in question. As such, sport celebrities are crafted as contextually sensitive points of cultural negotiation, between those controlling the dominant modes and mechanisms of cultural production, and their perceptions of the audience's practices of cultural reception. The celebrity is thus, at any given conjuncture, a potentially potent "representative subjectivity" (source of cultural identification) pertaining to the "collective configurations" (social class, gender, sexuality, race, ethnicity, age, nationality) through which individuals fashion their very existence (Marshall, 1997, pp. xi, xii). This is particularly true of the sport celebrities who provide the focus for the remainder of this chapter, for the commercially mediated identities of Michael Jordan and Tiger Woods emerged from, and indeed helped to constitute, particular moments in the evolution of the US racial formation.

Michael Jordan may have retired from the NBA, both as a player and latterly (if temporarily) as a team executive, however, he remains a "supremely instructive figure of our times" (Dyson, 1993, p. 71). As the most aggressively and successfully marketed professional athlete in American sport history, who also happens to be—lest we forget—an African American male, Jordan's persona offers insight into the cultural politics of the late capitalist American racial order. As such, he typifies the function of the (sport) celebrity acting as a "channeling" device for the "negotiation of cultural space and position for the entire culture" (Marshall, 1997, p. 49). In this case, Jordan's popular subjectivity both visualized and authorized particular understandings of, and responses toward, the enduring issues of race and racial difference. Within a society that continues to be cleaved by racial inequities, hostilities, and anxieties, Jordan emerged as the quintessential sporting embodiment of the American nation, a national icon with whom everyone could, seemingly, identify. The reasons for this apparent quirk of cultural appropriation and representation are complex (see Andrews, 2001). Hence, rather than tackle the question in toto, the aim of this discussion is to provide some insight into one important aspect of Jordan's emergence as "America's player" (Sakamoto, 1986, p. 10), namely, the role played by Nike, arguably the most important commercial and media force in Jordan's national deification, in fabricating Jordan as "the kind of [non-threatening] figure who goes down easily with most Americans" (race commentator Shelby Steele, quoted in Naughton, 1992, p. 137).

Although Jordan's stellar collegiate career at the University of North Carolina, the 1984 Los Angeles Olympics, and his outstanding rookie performances during the 1984–85 NBA season for the Chicago Bulls, garnered him considerable national publicity, his fledgling popular appeal was crystallized through the innovative promotional initiatives engaged by Nike. During the previous fiscal year, Nike had experienced an alarming decline in sales and sought to redress this by confronting its anonymous presence in both collegiate and professional basketball. In the spring and summer of 1984, the company surveyed the crop of potential draftees and set their sights on Jordan. According to Sonny Vaccaro, Nike's intermediary with the collegiate game, Jordan "was brilliant. He was charismatic. He was the best player Vaccaro had ever seen. He could fly through the air!" (Strasser & Becklund, 1991, p. 535). Vaccaro's enthusiasm for Jordan went as far as admitting "I'd pay him whatever it takes to get him" (quoted in Strasser & Becklund, 1991, p. 536). On Vaccaro's recommendation, Jordan was identified as the figure who could reassert Nike's position as the sport shoe industry's market leader. Such confidence in Jordan's playing and marketing potential was confirmed when the company signed him to a $2.5 million contract. Nike was ridiculed for taking such a financial risk on an untried player at a time when it was experiencing considerable economic troubles. In retrospect such concerns seem almost laughable, as the Air Jordan phenomenon grossed $130 million in its first year (Strasser & Becklund, 1991, p. 3). This financial boost reasserted Nike as the preeminent sports shoe manufacturer and elevated the company to the position of American corporate icon.

Given the exhilarating telegenicism of Jordan's play, Nike's advertising company at the time, the Los Angeles based Chiat/Day agency, chose to develop an innovative campaign for the equally innovative signature Air Jordan shoes. This involved saturating the electronic media with strategically coded images of Jordan wearing Air Jordan shoes. Hence, during early 1985 the first Air Jordan commercial was broadcast, a slot entitled "Jordan Flight" in which a slow motion Jordan executed a dunk on an urban playground to the sound of jet engines accelerating to take off. With this commercial, and especially his parting salvo "Who said a man was not meant to fly?" Jordan's identity was constituted in the minds of the American populace as Air Jordan, "the Nike guy who could fly" (Katz, 1994, p. 7). The locus of Nike's early Air Jordan initiative keyed on Jordan's physical prowess and thus corroborated assumptions pertaining to the naturalistic element of black corporeality. As Mercer has argued:

> Classical racism involved a logic of dehumanization, in which African peoples were defined as having bodies but not minds: in this way the superexploitation of the black body as a muscle-machine could be justified. Vestiges of this are active today . . . [in] that most commonplace of stereotypes, the black man as sports hero, mythologically endowed with a "naturally" muscular physique and an essential capacity for strength, grace and machinelike perfection. (1994, p. 138)

Jordan's repeatedly valorized physicality thus became an effective embodied corroborator of historically entrenched racist ideologies, the airborne Jordan representing a seemingly compelling material vindication of what popular racist discourse had long extolled.

The early stages of the Air Jordan promotional phenomenon were evidently dominated by the signification of Jordan's naturally athletic black body. However, although racial signifiers pertaining to black physicality have provided a backdrop for the promotional discourse that narrated his stellar career, to a large extent they have been subsumed by a more obtuse relationship to popular racialized codes. The prevailing racial politics of the American New Right were founded upon a paranoid defensiveness toward overt expressions of racial difference, and a concomitant dismissive attitude toward the existence of race-based discrimination. In accordance with these politics, Nike's subsequent Air Jordan campaigns inspired the multifarious segments of the American mass culture industry (who subsequently invested in Jordan) to nurture an intertextually informed identity, which explicitly invested in the affective epidemics that delineated Reaganite America at the time (see Grossberg, 1992). Thus, Jordan's carefully scripted televisual adventures on the corporate playground were designed to substantiate an All-American (a pervasive euphemism for white) hard-bodied identity (Jeffords, 1994), which would appeal to the racially sensitive American mass market. Jordan's phenotypical features could not be overlooked, but his imaged identity could be distanced from the racial signifiers that dominated popular representations of African American men. Jordan's corporate image makers recognized that if he was to become an American sporting icon, they could not afford to explicitly associate him with the threatening expressions of black American existence.

To facilitate this evolution from mall America's flavor of the month to enshrined All-American icon, Jordan's marketing directors realized he had to be packaged as a Reaganite racial replicant; a black version of a white cultural model who, by his very simulated existence, ensures the submergence and subversion of racial Otherness (Willis, 1991). As David Falk, Jordan's agent, surmised, the intention behind the Jordan project was to promote an "All-American image. . . . Not Norman Rockwell, but a modern American image. Norman Rockwell values, but a contemporary flair" (quoted in Castle, 1991, p. 30). This process was initiated by Nike's decision to move away from Air Jordan campaigns that only displayed Jordan's physical talents, to slots that furnished him with an identifiable, if superficial, personality. Thus, Nike's move from Chiat/Day to the more innovative Wieden and Kennedy agency saw the introduction of a series of groundbreaking advertising campaigns in which Jordan interacted with Mars Blackmon, Spike Lee's cinematic alter ego from the film "She's Gotta Have It." The apparent willingness of the basketball hero to spend time with his bicycle messenger fan and friend, demonstrated that, for all his success, fame, and fortune, Jordan was, reassuringly, just another "down-to-earth guy" (*The New York Times,* February 20, 1989, p. D7). In true Reaganite fashion, Jordan's self-evident wholesome humility, inner drive, and personal responsibility "allows us to believe what we wish to believe: that in this country, have-nots can still become haves; that the American Dream is still working" (Naughton, 1992, p. 7). In other words, through his comedic interludes with Mars Blackmon, Jordan was inextricably articulated as a living, breathing, and dunking vindication of the mythological American meritocracy. Through subsequent creative associations (see Andrews, 1998) with McDonald's, Coca-Cola (more latterly, Gatorade), Chevrolet, and Wheaties—significant All-American corporate icons—Jordan was similarly cast as a "spectacular talent, midsized, well-spoken, attractive, accessible, old-time values, wholesome, clean, natural, not too Goody Two-shoes, with a bit of devilry in him" (David Falk, quoted in Kirkpatrick, 1987, p. 93).

Unlike the stereotypical representations of deviant, promiscuous, and irresponsible black men that punctuated the ubiquitous populist racist discourse of the New Right, Jordan was identified as embodying personal drive, responsibility, integrity, and success. The flight metaphor that dominated the articulation of his imaged persona graphically encapsulated Jordan's decidedly individualistic and American demeanor: "striving for agency, self determination, differentiation from others and freedom from control" (Langman, 1991, p. 205). Here was the prototypical simulated Reaganite hard body (Jeffords, 1994), lauded by the popular media for being living proof of the existence of an "open class structure, racial tolerance, economic mobility, the sanctity of individualism, and the availability of the American Dream for black Americans" (Gray, 1989, p. 376). This ideology, and indeed the very image of Jordan, cruelly posited that anyone in America could realize the dream regardless of race, color, or creed, the only variable being the individual's desire to take advantage of the opportunities afforded by this great country. As Herman Gray identified, the repetitious celebration of this colorblind credo within the popular media does little more than reinforce the notion–propagated within more explicit channels of political communication–that the fault for the material and economic failure of the African American constituents of the urban underclass is "their own since they [apparently choose to] live in an isolated world where contemporary racism is no longer a significant factor in their lives" (1989, p. 384).

By creating an opposition between Jordan and *them* (the failing, and thereby threatening, African American throng), the concerted promotion of Jordan as the "embodiment of [Reaganite] American virtue" (Naughton, 1992, p. 154) had the desired effect of downplaying his racial Otherness in a way that mirrored the signification of his equally hard-bodied media contemporary, Heathcliff Huxtable (see Jhally & Lewis, 1992). According to novelist John Edgar Wideman, Jordan "escapes gravity" and "makes us rise above our obsession with race" because he leaps the great divide between races and classes by being a down-to-earth, middle-class, apolitical hero (1990, p. 140). This notion of Jordan as a figure who transcends race (and, indeed, sport) was certainly a common theme during the 1980s and early 1990s, voicing as it did the strategic evacuation of race so characteristic of the Reagan Revolution (Jeffords, 1994). As David Falk advanced, "He's the first modern crossover in team sports. We think he transcends race, transcends basketball" (quoted in Kirkpatrick, 1987, p. 93).

An extended article that astutely deconstructed "The Selling of Michael Jordan" (Patton, 1986), concentrated on the marketing of Jordan as an individual possessing "uncanny moves on the court and 'a charisma that transcends his sport,'" a personal attribute which turned him into "basketball's most lucrative property" (Patton, 1986, p. 48). Likewise Donald Dell, the chief executive of Pro-Serv (the sports agency with whom Jordan was associated in the early phase of his professional careeer), commented that Jordan was a rare commercial property because he "has a charisma that transcends his sport. He belongs in a category with Arnold Palmer or Arthur Ashe" (quoted in Patton, 1986, p. 50). Clearly, sport in this context (specifically Jordan's sport, basketball) is a euphemism for race. Jordan is the figure who has transcended the black identity of professional basketball and thus garnered a widespread and inclusive simulated appeal that resulted in his becoming America's favorite athlete, a status which no black man before him had achieved (Naughton, 1992, p. 137). In doing so, Jordan played a crucial role in making the NBA accessible to the white American populace who had previously been turned off and turned away by the game's overtly black demeanor (see Cady, 1979; Cobbs, 1980; Cole & Denny, 1995; and Cole & Andrews, 1996).

Michael Jordan's carefully engineered charismatic appeal (Dyer, 1991), which had such an impact on popularizing the NBA to corporate and middle America alike, is not an example of racial transcendence; rather, it is a case of complicitous racial avoidance, facilitated through the displacement of racial signifiers. Jordan's hyper-real image was charismatic inasmuch as it set him apart from the popular representations of *ordinary* black males, by endowing him with "supernatural, superhuman or at least superficially exceptional qualities" (Weber, quoted in Eisenstadt, 1968, p. 329). The most pertinent of Jordan's "exceptional qualities" related to his understated racial identity, as opposed to his superlative athletic displays. After all, there was nothing about demonstrations of African American physical excellence that the popular imaginary would have considered exceptional. Hence, Jordan's image was coveted by the media primarily because of its reassuring affinity with the affective investments associated with America's white-dominated national popular culture. Although the media could not escape the fact that Jordan is of African American descent, his identity has been shrewdly severed from any vestiges of African American culture. Some black superstars, the most prominent being Jordan, have been able to pander to the racial insecurities and paranoia of the white majority primarily because of their ability to shed their black identities in promotional contexts. In doing so, these black mediated icons have achieved a degree of popular approval which superficially would seem to argue against the presence of race-based discrimination within American society. As Marvin Bressler, noted, "It has always been possible in the history of race relations in this country to say that some of my best friends are X. Such people are very useful in demonstrating our own benevolence. We must be good people—we love Michael Jordan" (quoted in Swift, 1991b, p. 58). Nevertheless, the compulsion for African Americans to disavow their blackness in order to harness rather than alienate popular opinion, is indicative of the ingrained hegemonic racism within American society. American culture simply does not tolerate individuals who are, to put it plainly, too black.

Like the reactionary colorblind cultural politics that nurtured it, the notion of racial transcendence supposedly embodied by Jordan was a seriously flawed and contradictory concept. Racial discourse is never transcended; it is in a Derridean sense *always already there* (see Smith, 1994). Jordan is not an example of racial transcendence; rather he is an agent of racial displacement. Jordan's valorized, racially neutered, image displaces racial codes onto other black bodies, be they Mars Blackmon, Charles Barkley, or the anonymous urban black male habitually criminalized by the popular media. Nike's early promotional strategy systematically downplayed

Jordan's blackness by contrasting him with Mars Blackmon, Spike Lee's somewhat troubling caricature of the young, urban, African American male. The contrast fortified Jordan's wholesome, responsible, All-American, and hence non-threatening persona, and became the basis of his hyperreal identity, which was subsequently embellished by the multiplying circuits of promotional capital that enveloped him. Thus, despite allusions to racial invisibility, Jordan's image exemplifies what Reeves and Campbell identified as "a spectacle of surveillance that is actively engaged in representing authority, visualizing deviance, and publicizing common sense" (1994, p. 49) in a way that has profound implications for the representation, and indeed experience, of race and racial difference in contemporary America.

Tiger Woods is, in many ways, the direct heir to Jordan's mantle as the acceptable embodiment of race within the sport celebrity economy. Again, Nike has played an important role in the manufacturing of this commercially palatable icon of racial Otherness. Notably, Woods also provided an important point of contrast to more strident forms of commodified blackness (Boyd, 1997), with which the NBA became associated toward the end of Jordan's playing career, when his imaged identity began to assume a residual, as opposed to a dominant, cultural presence. As a *Business Week* columnist explained, Woods was a breath of fresh air for an American public "tired of trash-talking, spit-hurling, head-butting sports millionaires" (Stodghill, 1997, p. 32). Although race is not explicitly mentioned, Stodghill's reference is clearly to African American professional basketball players who are routinely depicted in the popular media as selfish, insufferable, and morally reprehensible. Woods's cultural significance was further embellished through repeated reference to his multicultural identity, which challenged America's rigid understanding of race and racial difference:

But times are changing. Interracial marriage and reproduction are on the upswing, and a new generation of post-1960s multiracial children is demanding recognition, not in the margins of society but as a mainstream of their own. . . . To get a glimpse of its future, look at Eldrick "Tiger" Woods, the golf prodigy. His mother, from Thailand, is half Thai, a quarter Chinese, and a quarter white. His father is half black, a quarter Chinese and a quarter American Indian. (Page, 1996, pp. 284–285)

In the wake of his decision to turn professional in August 1996, Woods's assumed multicultural appeal, coupled with his boundless playing potential, prompted a heightened sense of commercial anticipation from within the ranks of the golf industry. According to the PGA Tour commissioner, Tim Finchem:

I just think that there are three major elements to Tiger Woods. One is . . . the level of his competitive skills he has demonstrated time and time again. Secondly, he is from a multi-racial ethnic background which makes him unique. And, third is, he has exhibited the poise, and the integrity, and the image, of the kind of players who have performed well on the PGA Tour. And that is the package, and it's a very marketable package. (ABC's *Nightline*, September 2, 1996)

Finchem's "very marketable package" was taken up by the expectant titans of the American sport industry. Mark McCormack's International Management Group (IMG) had so aggressively courted the 15-year-old Woods that they offered his father, Earl Woods, a paid position as "talent scout" for the American Junior Golf Association, whose tournaments his son was then dominating. Upon turning professional, Woods officially signed with IMG. He also signed a 5-year $40 million sponsorship deal with Nike, which expected that Woods's racial difference and prodigious talent would "revolutionize" the public's relation to golf. Nike anticipated that Woods, as a multi-market endorser, would resuscitate its stagnant golf division and, in so doing, significantly bolster the company's overall profits. The success of America's latest revolution, orchestrated around Woods's body and style, would be measured in terms of the diversification and expansion of the market for golf-related products and services both in the US and abroad.

In August 1996, two days after Tiger turned professional and on the eve of the Greater Milwaukee Open, Woods held his first press conference as a PGA Tour player. At the microphone, a seemingly sheepish Woods intoned, "I guess, hello world." The familiar global address simultaneously insinuated the decline of national boundaries and trumpeted the significance of Nike's latest worldly American citizen. The faux spontaneity of this carefully scripted sound-byte was made evident when, the next day, Nike launched a print and television advertising campaign featuring Woods, entitled "Hello World." Despite Nike's claims that they had merely made a swift and creative response to a national moment in the making, the commercial was, rather an example of the sort of strategic marketing that placed Nike at the vanguard of contemporary promotional culture (Wernick, 1991).

The "Hello World" television campaign introduced Woods, as he was ostensibly introducing himself, to "the world at large" (Allen, 1996, p. 11C), by interspersing and overlaying the following text between and upon images of his early golfing exploits and recent successes at US Amateur championships:

Hello world.
I shot in the 70s when I was 8.
I shot in the 60s when I was 12.
I won the US Junior Amateur when I was 15.
Hello world.
I played in the Nissan Open when I was 16.
Hello world.
I won the US Amateur when I was 18.
I played in the Masters when I was 19.
I am the only man to win three consecutive US Amateur titles.
Hello world.
There are still courses in the US I am not allowed to play because of the color of my skin.
Hello world.
I've heard I am not ready for you.
Are you ready for me?

Wood's recitation was accompanied by an emotive musical score, whose pseudo-African tones and timbre added to the dramatic—and familiarly exotic—content of the visual narrative.

As Nike's "Hello World" advertisement reinforced a familiar aesthetic, it seemingly presented a challenge to America by disrupting and violating America's unwritten racist ("no national critique, particularly in terms of racism or sexism") code. By highlighting Woods' energy, skill, and earned successes and then deliberately confronting America with a "racial dilemma," America's ideals of colorblindness and proper citizenship were—at least apparently—being challenged. Moreover, while previous annotations to the burgeoning Woods phenomenon exploited his difference in ways that maintained a non-threatening ambiguity concerning his *precise* racial identity, the "Hello World" campaign flouted such American racial propriety by "determining" his African American-ness. According to Henry Yu, the "Hello World" campaign was evidence of Nike's attempt to "African Americanize" Woods: "To Nike *(at least at this juncture),* he was African American" (Yu, 1996, p. 4M, italics added).

Although the "Hello World" campaign identified and named racism, it did so through the familiar and acceptable terms of social criticism. Capitalizing on narratives already in place—and particularly narratives that America loves to consume through sport—Woods's entry into professional golf was cast as an event of national magnitude. Consumer identification was invited and secured by cloaking Woods in overt patriotism: He was vaunted as an emblem of racial progress, a righter of wrongs like foundational figures Jackie Robinson and Arthur Ashe. Indeed, the extraordinary proliferation of allusions to Robinson surrounding Woods underscore the sort of pleasures promised to American consumers: The "Hello World" campaign announced itself as America's quintessential tantalizing tale of racial progress, one that combined race, sport, masculinity, national healing, and proper citizenship. Thus, through Woods and Nike, consumers hailed as compassionate and informed citizens, were invited to recollect mediated national-ethical moments of the past and to participate in a national-familial-ethical moment of the present.

In this way, Woods became the latest version of a commercialized, raced masculinity implicated in political backlash while certifying national transformation, progress, and equality (see Andrews, 1996; Cole, 1996). One commentator pointedly captured the conservative "some of my best friends . . ." orientation of Woods' enthusiastic appropriation by the hearts and minds of the American establishment:

> the core constituency of golf, those "members only" who have managed to make the country club, after the church, the most segregated institution in America, think Tiger will get people off their backs. How can you call golf racist now, you liberal jogger, just look who we invited to tee? (Lipsyte, 1996, p. 11)

Woods, like Colin Powell, Michael Jordan, and Oprah Winfrey, was thus used by the populist defenders of core American values and ideologies (those cultural producers operating within the ratings-driven media and poll-driven centrist politics), as self-evident proof of the existence of a colorblind meritocracy. In a time of increasing racial polarization along social and economic lines (c.f. Kelley, 1997; Wilson, 1997), Tiger Woods emerged as a popular icon from whom the American populace could derive a sense of intimacy, pride, and reassurance.

To the extent that Woods was perceived to be an activist, it was clearly a nationally sanctioned activism linked to media, family, and consumption. In this case, a familiar dramatic and heroic narrative—in and through which consumers could participate—was fabricated against the backdrop of an exceptional experience. In a national context ostensibly already devoid of racism, Woods and Nike had identified a local and temporary situation of racial discrimination in the private and protected elite space of golf. Under the guise of public debate and intervention, America's self-congratulatory mood was affirmed. Thus, rather than encouraging critical thought about contemporary national politics and the complexity of racism, the "Hello World" campaign relied on, and reproduced, a mediated patriotism. Ironically, racial discrimination, formulated as a holdover from another time, was used to reauthorize the nation's view of itself as beyond race.

During the fall of 1996, the media coverage of Tiger Woods reached extraordinary proportions following his victories at the 1996 Las Vegas Invitational and 1996 Walt Disney World/Oldsmobile Classic tournaments. As much as they were interested in his exploits on the golf course, the popular media were obsessively concerned with documenting, and thereby advancing, the "Tigermania" seemingly sweeping the nation. Paradoxically, Tigermania was represented through the dramatically increased viewing and attendance figures for tournaments and blanket media coverage incited by the popular media (Potter, 1997; Stevens & Winheld, 1996; Williams, 1996). Nike, in a moment symptomatic of this expansion of Woods's celebrity-citizenship, debuted their second Tiger Woods commercial. Nike's Tiger Woods Mk II was revealed to an expectant primetime American viewing public during coverage of IMG's made-for-TV "Skins Game," which ran on the ABC network over Thanksgiving Day weekend in 1996. In this commercial, Nike further took advantage of Woods' accruing cultural capital as the unequivocal embodiment of America's future multicultural citizenry. Capitulating to dominant cultural norms and values in a more banal and therefore even more powerful way, Nike contributed to the fabrication of Woods as the latest version of the *new* face of America. In a sixty-second commercial entitled "I am Tiger Woods," Woods' racial image was re-engineered through a mixture of black and white and color images with still, slow, and full motion footage, accompanied by a musical soundtrack incorporating an understated mix of drum beats and chorus harmonies. Visually the commercial centered on a cast of racially diverse and geographically dispersed children (on golf courses and in distinctly urban settings), who collectively embodied Nike's vision of Tiger Woods's essential heterogeneity. Moreover, they signified, by inference, the future American populace. The result was a somewhat pious celebration of that which Tiger Woods had come to represent. Borrowing the "I am . . ." strategy previously adopted in both Stanley Kubrick's *Spartacus* (1960), and more recently Spike Lee's *Malcolm X* (1992), each carefully chosen child representative proclaimed, with varying degrees of solemnity, "I am Tiger Woods." The golfing Woods is periodically glimpsed as young males and females possessing characteristics stereotypically associated with African Americans, Asian Americans, or European Americans offer invocations of "I am Tiger Woods." The commercial ends with slow-motion footage of Woods hitting a drive down the center of a tree-lined fairway. As he reaches the apex of his follow-through, "I am Tiger Woods" in white text appears in the bottom center of the frame, followed by Nike's global-local sign, the obligatory swoosh.

Less than three months earlier, the "Hello World" campaign had enabled, despite its swift removal, the possibility of reading Woods as an outspoken racial insurgent. Now, Woods was clearly re-presented and re-articulated into a multicultural figure who, like his young imitators, was framed as the pre-political and post-historical embodied manifestation of contemporary racial politics. Moreover, a significant change is claimed for the golf world: not only have we witnessed an immediate change in personnel, but golf's future will include a significantly different cast of characters. Indeed, through what Yu (1996) depicts as a shift away from Nike's African Americanized representation, Woods, Yu argues, was conclusively cast as "a multicultural godsend to the sport of golf" (1996, p. 4M). Under the sign of Woods' multiculturalism, and in America's (golfing) future, everyone will be included.

While African American basketball players are regularly charged with violating national core values, Woods has therefore become revered for his cultural heritage and cultural literacy. Yet, aware that earlier promotional incarnations of Tiger Woods persona had created media and popular interest but not the desired level of commodity consumption, Nike has subsequently sought to appeal to the "classic" golfer (middle class and white), whose high levels of disposable income sustained the golf economy. So, Nike's Tiger Woods strategizing sought to evoke a brand image that was "more Armani than Gap" (Meyers, 1998, p. 2B). This involved the use of more conservative designs and materials for the Tiger Woods apparel collection and, more crucially, it signaled a distinct change in the way Woods was represented within Nike advertising campaigns. This shift is exemplified in the deeply reverential "I am lucky" Nike advertising campaign that followed the "I am Tiger Woods" commercial:

> Hogan [Ben Hogan] knows, Snead [Sam Snead] knows, Jack [Jack Nicklaus] knows. I am lucky. Everything I have I owe to golf, and for that I am lucky.

This appeal to Woods's position among the litany of golfing greats was indicative of the "revamping" of the "Woods brand" (Meyers, 1998, p. 1B), in that it highlighted and mobilized another dimension of contemporary cultural dynamics and larger political concerns in America. Its rhetoric, a conservative appeal to tradition, draws a connection between Woods and those who came before him, thus furnishing Woods with a reassuring sporting and national cultural lineage. Unlike popular reactions to rank and file NBA players, Woods was thus codified as a multicultural agent who restores virtue to, as he is designated an extension of, America's sporting tradition.

Woods's iconic national sporting pedigree was subsequently underscored by his superlative displays during the 1999 and 2000 PGA seasons. In 1999 Woods won eleven events, including the US PGA Championship, his second major title, to finish at the top of golf's world rankings and the PGA money list. Even these stellar achievements were surpassed in the 2000 season when Woods won the US Open, the British Open, and the US PGA Championship (three of golf's four major championships), and a total of nine PGA tour events. In the wake of his domination of golf, Woods—by now everybody's favorite multicultural American—has been rendered a cultural phenomenon, distinguished by his ability to stimulate popular interest, as measured by either the number of spectators at events or television audience ratings figures, rather than incite critical reflection. The forces of corporate capitalism have effectively neutered this potentially progressive cultural figure, such that, presently:

> Most of us don't need him to be a savior or a hero or a role model. We simply want the spectacle: Tiger gliding down the fairway, Tiger hitting rainmaker drives, Tiger pummeling his opponents and then putting his arm around them, Tiger hugging his mom. If he turns and winks back at us every once in a while, that will be enough. (Ratnesar, 2000, p. 66)

The popular spectacle that Tiger Woods has become was evidently enough for Nike which, in September 2000, signed him to a new 5-year endorsement contract worth $100 million. Nike paid this exorbitant sum in order to augment its brand identity through a continued association with the ambiguously exotic, yet suitably benign, multicultural face of America's future citizenry that is Tiger Woods. In a complementary yet different vein to Jordan, Woods became the personification of publicly authorized embodiments of (multi)racial difference: an intimate instantiation of a (multi)racialized public common sense (Reeves and Campbell, 1994). Woods thereby became a normative reference point against which the less accommodated constituencies within the contemporary American racial formation (specifically that of the African American man) were made ever more visible. Hence, both Jordan and Woods could be considered important embodiments of the contested racial categories "in which people are placed and through which they have to make sense of their lives" (Dyer, 1986, p. 18).

6

SUBURBAN SOCCER FIELDS

According to Markovits and Hellerman, the popularity of recreational soccer in the United States has not translated into mass audiences for televised soccer, hence they conclude there is "Still no soccer in the United States, at least on any meaningful scale" (1995, p. 255). One wonders what compelled the authors to make such an assertion. Even in purely economic terms, soccer is a meaningful entity within contemporary America: Nike/IMG's $500 million investment in the US Soccer Federation over the next decade and the estimated $245 million in soccer equipment sales during 1998 both attest to that fact (see Sporting Goods Manufacturers Association, 1998; Sunderland, 1998). In Nike representative Sandy Bodecker's terms, "The biggest trend I see in the [apparel] market is that soccer is transitioning from a sort of sub category to a core sport at a much broader level than it had been before" (quoted in Soccer Industry Council of America, 1997). Moreover, soccer's most profound incursion into American existence can be discerned from its central location within the lives of millions of suburban American families. No longer a "mini-passion of suburban America" (Post, 1994, p. 61), youth soccer participation has emerged as a defining practice within this economic, political, and cultural core of American life. Indeed, such has been youth soccer's material and symbolic penetration of the suburban landscape, that the game presently enunciates the dominant rhythms and regimes of suburban existence every bit as naturally—or organically—as the single family home, ballet classes, sport utility vehicles, lawn sprinkler systems, the Gap, and Williams Sonoma.

Rather than evolving from a specific research study or location, this chapter draws from a multitude of ethnographic experiences gathered from over ten years of observing suburban soccer cultures in a number of metropolitan areas across the Mid-South and Mid-West regions of the US. Adopting the cultural studies method of "articulation," this experiential data is used as a resource for the "practice of drawing lines, of mapping connections" (Grossberg, 1997a, pp. 260–261) between broad societal forces and the practices of everyday life, from which it is possible to begin to interpret the suburban American soccer phenomenon. In the tradition of cultural studies within which "context is everything and everything is context" (Grossberg, 1997b, p. 7), the aim of this discussion is to contextualize—in a way that renders it meaningful—the suburban soccer practice. Following a genealogy of soccer in the US, this discussion forges an understanding of this peculiarly American soccer scenario, by making connections (or articulations) between soccer and the broader social forces that coalesced to form post-war suburban spaces, populations, and experiences. This evolves into an explication of how soccer has been appropriated as part of the innately competitive, socially differentiating, and highly stylized lifestyles through which individuals attempt to exude conspicuous membership of the valorized suburban middle class.

According to Hank Steinbrecher, executive director and general secretary of the US Soccer Federation:

> What has happened is that soccer was viewed by the general populous [sic] as ethnic, urban and very blue collar. What we find, however, is that while there is still a base of ethnic and urban supporters, the reality is that soccer today is mom and dad, two kids, two lawn chairs, Saturday afternoon with the family dog, watching the kids play, $40,000 income, mini van. (quoted in Pesky, 1993b, p. 31)

Despite the current dominance of American football, baseball, basketball, and to a lesser extent ice hockey, in intercollegiate and professional manifestations, it should not be overlooked that soccer has had a presence on the American continent for over three centuries. As Sugden noted, "In terms of longevity and international competition soccer is the elder statesman of American sport" (1994, p. 219). Although originally cast as a pastime for young males attending East Coast preparatory schools and universities (Dunning & Sheard, 1979; Holliman, 1931; Lucas & Smith, 1978; Reisman & Denny, 1951), for much of its history within the US, soccer has been primarily identified as being an activity associated with successive waves of immigrant populations (Jose, 1994; Mormino, 1982; Riess, 1991; Sugden, 1994). Soccer—like aspects of diet, religion, customs, and folklore—played a more obvious function in assuaging new immigrants' feelings of cultural dislocation, than either baseball, basketball, or football. Played by primarily "hyphenated Americans" of whatever origin (European, Central, or South American) (Anon, 1993, p. 100), soccer thus became identified as a multi-accentual ethnic, and hence definitively non-American, urban pastime.

Despite soccer's enduring marginality, since the end of the Second World War there have been numerous efforts to set up professional soccer leagues, each attempting to take advantage of the increased discretionary income of middle America. Thus, at various times and within varyingly expansive ambitions, the International Soccer League (ISL), the National Professional Soccer League (NPSL), the North American Soccer League (NASL), and the United Soccer Association (USA), all competed for customers (Gardner, 1996). The overcrowded nature of the soccer marketplace, coupled with the undersized soccer market, provided a poor prognosis for these leagues and, as a consequence, only one of them (the NASL) made a significant, if fleeting, impact on American sporting culture. Founded in 1968, the NASL rose to prominence through the signing and innovative marketing of a number of foreign soccer mercenaries. The popularity and economic viability of the league peaked in the mid-1970s, from whence steadily declining spectator attendance coupled with a flawed economic and managerial plan, sent the league into a terminal decline. In 1985 the NASL—up to that point the most concerted effort at popularizing soccer to a mass American audience— folded (Toch, 1994).

Although an ephemeral aspect of the American professional sporting scene, the NASL did have a "significant American legacy" (Gardner, 1996, p. 225) in terms of its impact upon youth soccer participation. From the early 1970s, NASL teams such as the Tampa Bay Rowdies, the Seattle Sounders, and the Chicago Sting, implemented grassroots youth soccer programs designed to stimulate interest in the NASL product among the nation's expanding suburban hordes. By the 1980s, "All that NASL missionary work, all those clinics" (Hersh, 1990, p. C1), in conjunction with Title IX of the 1972 Education Amendments Act (a piece of legislation designed to address issues of gender equity within publicly funded education), heightened soccer's visibility and increased opportunities for organized involvement in the game. As a consequence, between 1981 and 1991 participation in high school soccer increased 83.78 percent, from 190,495 to 350,102, while the number of private and community-based teams expanded, as did the quantity of soccer programs offered at the collegiate level (Pesky, 1993a; Schrof, 1995).

The expansion of youth soccer programs continued into the 1990s. By 1997, soccer was firmly established as the second ranked sporting activity for 6–11-year-olds (8,646,000 participants), sandwiched between basketball (11,014,000) and baseball (4,400,000). Soccer was also the third ranked sporting activity for 12–17-year-olds (4,981,000 participants), behind basketball (12,409,000) and volleyball (7,493,000) (Soccer Industry Council of America, 1998). Steinbrecher (1996) even identified a soccer-involved sub-population of some 45 million "Soccer Americans," comprising of 18 million direct participants (70% of whom were under age 18), and 27 million "involved family members." Moreover, with registered soccer players approaching 20 million, and roughly 50 million people described as "soccer literate," there is compelling evidence that the evolution of soccer in the post-war era has been "America's silent sporting revolution" (Anon, 1996, p. 27).

Beyond youth participation, soccer has also moved to establish itself on the professional sporting landscape. Seeking to harness America's silent soccer revolutionaries and spawned as part of the political process that brought the 1994

World Cup to the US, Major League Soccer (MLS) debuted in 1996, and represents the latest attempt to establish a truly national and economically viable professional soccer league. The "quirky demographics" (Anon, 1996, p. 27) of MLS's stated core constituencies of consumers are the numerous ethnic minority populations (primarily those of South and Central American descent), many of whom inhabit America's impoverished inner urban and economically transitionary suburban locales (Delgado, 1997; Hayes-Bautista & Rodriguez, 1994) , and the legions of "Soccer Americans" of predominantly European descent residing in the affluent suburban subdivisions on the peripheries of the America's Metropolitan Statistical Areas (MSAs) (Markovits & Hellerman, 2001). Clearly, soccer's appeal in America transcends a number of demographic boundaries, equally as evident is the differential manner in which the game resonates within divergent socio-cultural settings:

> Rather than expressing a common affinity toward the game, America's starkly contrasting soccer cultures express the structural inequalities that continue to blight the American social formation. While in many impoverished urban Hispanic American communities, soccer is often fervently upheld as a symbol of hope, pride, and identity, within the predominantly European American spaces of suburban affluence, the game has been conclusively appropriated into everyday regimes of privilege. (Zwick & Andrews, 1999)

The marketing strategy of the MLS is at least partly based on an intuitive understanding of the multi-accentual relationship between soccer participation/interest, place of habitation, socio-economic status, and ethnicity. The suburban rendition of this correlation has been concretely confirmed in one examination of soccer within metropolitan areas (Andrews, Pitter, Zwick, & Ambrose, 1997). In this study, registered youth soccer players in Memphis were found to be disproportionately represented in areas whose geographic location and per capita income designated them as spaces of American suburban affluence. These elite suburbs accounted for 89.89 percent of metropolitan youth soccer players, yet only 37.01 percent of the metropolitan under-18 population. Within Memphis's conglomeration of affluent suburban neighborhoods, there existed a distinct ethnic homogeneity, with European Americans comprising 84.90 percent of the total population. Given these sporting, socio-economic, and ethnic spatial distributions, it was no surprise that the ethnographic phase of this study concluded that soccer in suburban Memphis was an almost exclusively European American practice: "Of the hundreds of players observed during the course of the interviewing process, only 2 were black" (Andrews, et al., 1997, p. 274).

While it would be imprudent to extrapolate the Memphis suburban soccer scenario to the rest of the US, there is considerable anecdotal evidence corroborating the widespread existence of similar patterns of youth soccer distribution and constitution within other metropolitan locales (Anon, 1993; Coughlin, 1997; Gardner, 1996; Harpe, 1995; Russakof, 1998; Sugden, 1994; Walker, 1997; Winner, 1998). Notwithstanding its multi-ethnic manifestations, today soccer in the US can be considered "a white, middle-class, suburban sport, just the opposite of the game's demographics in most of the world" (Hersh, 1990, p. C1). Following Grossberg's understanding of cultural dialectics, a popular practice like suburban soccer can only be understood as being "always constituted with and constitutive of a larger context of relationships" (Grossberg, 1997a, p. 257). For that reason, the rest of the chapter will identify the social, historical, political, economic, and cultural arrangements responsible for shaping the contemporary suburban context out of which this peculiarly American soccer phenomenon emerged.

Although this discussion is focused on soccer's relation to the suburban American experience at the end of the twentieth century, it should not be overlooked that contemporary manifestations of suburban existence represent the latest (and by no means the last) phase in the ongoing reformation of metropolitan spaces and populations around the central logic of commodity consumption (Binford, 1985; Fishman, 1987; Jackson, 1985). Within the post-war context, the nature of "decentralisation of population from the cities" (Savage & Warde, 1993, p. 76) to suburban peripheries was markedly different from previous enactments, particularly in terms of scale and scope. Between 1950 and 1970 the suburban American nation grew from 41 million (27 percent of total US population) to 76 million (37 percent of total US population). Indeed, by 1970, and for the first time in the nation's history, suburban dwellers outnumbered both their urban and rural counterparts (Holleb, 1975). Continuing this trend, the 1990s has witnessed the ascension of American suburban dwellers to the absolute majority of the national population (Kleinberg, 1995; Lemann, 1998; Thomas, 1998). The spatial relocation of millions of predominantly young, yet hugely expectant, Americans during this era represented an unparalleled movement from urban cores to suburban peripheries, of a sizeable—if relatively homogenous—proportion of the nation's populace. This mass in-migration from city to suburb spawned a statistically, economically, politically, and culturally imposing home-owning suburban middle class, located both spatially and symbolically between city and country, that subsequently delineated suburban American spaces and populations (in Zukin's terms, the suburban American landscape [1991]) within the post-war national popular imaginary (Silverstone, 1997).

It should be noted, however, that despite their cultural, economic, and political presence, American suburbs are by no means homogenous bastions of upper middle class affluence, for "within contemporary America, the adjective suburban could legitimately encompass anything from zones of underclass poverty, to sectors of middle/upper class affluence, and a multitude of variations in-between" (Zwick & Andrews, 1999, p. 211). This became particularly relevant among America's maturing post-war suburbs, where populations began to differentiate themselves based on the variable acquisition and mobilization of economic capital. Subsequent phases of outward residential development spatialized and materialized this socio-economic suburban fragmentation through the construction of ever more spacious and opulent homes, and the occupation of older housing stock by less affluent, often ethnic minority, inhabitants. By the 1980s the post-war American suburb approximated an ever extending patchwork quilt, patterned by variously sized consumption communities (ranging from collections of houses to vast subdivisions) whose common lifestyle practices exhibit contrasting degrees of affluence. Nevertheless, despite its inherent variability and fluidity, the vision of the American suburb that pervades the popular imaginary continues to be that of the European American post-war bourgeois utopia: those metropolitan peripheries and populations dominated by an aesthetic and consumer-oriented possessive individualism, that underlies a more self-righteously advanced adherence to notions of achievement, morality, and privilege.

The process of post-World War II suburbanization was inextricably tied to the need to reactivate America's burgeoning mass consumer culture, which—having sprouted in the early decades of the century—was temporarily derailed by the Great Depression, and diverted by the forces of military Keynesianism. With apologies for oversimplying the complexities of Keynes' economic theory, the stimulation of widespread home ownership (through the suburban relocation of large swaths of America's post-war population) was an important mechanism for successfully regulating the balance between the productive and consumptive forces of the Fordist economy:

> [O]pening the suburbs to massive residential development spatially defined a new market culture. Suburbia's socio-spatial patterns typically anchored in place the market arrangements of the postwar period. Moreover, mass suburbanization offered a macroeconomic solution to prewar problems of underconsumption. (Zukin, 1991, p. 140)

Certainly, the calculated post-war activation of American home ownership addressed a number of inter-meshing social and economic problems. First, it alleviated the chronic housing shortage created by, among other things: Depression and wartime economies; millions of returning GIs; and the rapidly expanding post-war populace. Second, it regenerated the American building industry, a key economic impetus and indicator, that had lain relatively dormant during the Depression and war years. Third, it greatly stimulated the post-war economy by providing privatized settings (homes) for the actualization of a revitalized consumerist aesthetic and culture:

> [S]uburbanization necessitated a more expensive way of life than people had known in modest urban apartments; television told people what they needed to buy; and in the empty leisure left by equally empty work, buying itself became a way of life. (Ehrenreich, 1989, p. 35)

Without wishing to understate the importance of the first two factors, this discussion reflects on the third, since the relationship between home ownership policies and post-war mass consumer culture was crucial in molding today's suburban landscapes of consumption.

The American government's championing of home ownership as a catalyst for economic growth was initiated in 1934 with the passing of the National Housing

Act. This legislation established the Federal Housing Administration (FHA) as an agency for prompting the growth of moderately priced private housing. The subsequent 1944 Serviceman's Readjustment Act (part of the GI Bill) and the 1949 Housing Act, made house mortgages—thereby, home ownership—even more accessible to the general public, and large scale residential building ever more profitable for private investors. Consequently, single-family housing starts escalated from 114,000 in 1944 to a record high 1,692,000 in 1950 (Jackson, 1985). Huge tracts of America's metropolitan peripheries were rapidly transformed into the types of mass residential suburban communities (epitomized by the prototypical Levittown, on Long Island, New York) so famously dissected by William H. Whyte (1956), and Herbert J. Gans (1967). The multiplier effect of mass home ownership led to increases in mass consumption, stimulated by the purchase of the consumer durables required to furnish and maintain the dream home. This postwar repositioning of the suburban home as a "temple to consumer society" (Fine & Leopold, 1993, p. 68) escalated the demand for consumer goods, which assured relatively high levels of mass employment, and subsequently created a stable and affluent workforce ready and able to partake of the new consumerist ethos. Thus, as Lears noted, the term "'consumer culture' had unprecedented validity as a description of the sprawling suburban society developing in the wake of war-built prosperity" (1994, p. 247).

In at least two senses, the first post-war suburban Americans were a homogenous group. First, due to overtly segregationist public and private housing initiatives, suburbanites were almost exclusively of European American descent (Jackson, 1985; Wright, 1983). Second, they were of sufficient financial means to be able to partake in this internal migration (Zukin, 1991). Nevertheless, the mask of whiteness and relative prosperity belied the inherent diversity of these new suburbanites. Many of those relocating from America's inner urban cores had lived in close proximity to others from the same ethnic grouping. The preponderance of urban neighborhoods dominated by Italian Americans, Polish Americans, or Slovak Americans, had ensured cultural and ethnic distinctions were preserved, and in some senses enhanced. Wrenched from culturally and ethnically distinct social milieus, many postwar suburbanites found themselves ensconced in homogenizing suburban spaces, within which differences were relegated to the "ghostly images of family albums" (Silverstone, 1997, p. 7). Within this "present-tense culture" (Hitchens, 1998, p. 37), commodity consumption became the primary lingua franca through which an unfolding suburban identity and existence was realized to self and others.

Although many of the structural foundations were being put in place (i.e., mass employment, mass home ownership, and mass transport), it would be remiss to assume there existed a seamless transition between America's military and suburban-based consumer economies. Late 1940s America was wracked by an internal contradiction between the values of a fledgling economic system that demanded accelerating rates of commodity consumption, and the purchasing reticence expressed by a financially shell-shocked populace not far removed from economic depression and wartime insecurity. Thus, many Americans in the immediate post-war era understandably adhered to those residues of the Protestant work ethic prefigured on an ascetic discipline of "thrift, hard work and sobriety" (Featherstone, 1982, p. 19). For America's consumer economy to become a viable proposition, the American population (and most importantly, those millions embarking on the post-war suburban adventure) needed to be educated with regard to the morality of, and authorized pleasures derived from, unbounded commodity acquisition. In other words, the notion of the freely consuming subject had to be substantiated and legitimated in the minds of the American public.

As with many cultural changes within modern America, the post-war shift from a "puritan orientation" to a "hedonistic ethos of spending and credit" (Slater, 1997, p. 28) was engineered by the advertising industry which, at this time, entered a new realm of creativity and influence with the rampant spread of network television. During the 1950s, television soared from a position of relative exclusivity to being a popular institution at the core of American life. In 1950 only 9 percent of American households owned a television, this figure escalated to 86 percent in 1959, when the average American watched more than five hours of programming per day (Stark, 1997). As an advertiser-supported mass medium, virtually from its inception, American network television was a selling machine that infiltrated the American psyche by concocting commercial narratives that assuaged the guilt felt by many post-war Americans with regard to unfettered spending. Exemplifying the stratagem of nurturing consumer self-confidence, a well known contemporary commercial byline exclaimed: "You deserve the right to drive a Cadillac." In concert with stimulating the ethos of consumption in general, network television championed utopian visions of suburban existence centered on commodity acquisition (Ewen, 1976; Lasch, 1979). Thus, through mainstreaming narratives such as the television situation comedies *Leave It to Beaver* and *My Three Sons,* the populist American Dream discourse (historically associated with the popular practices and ideologies of the American middle class) was thus relocated to the new consumer middle class living in America's new suburbs (Clarke, 1991).

During the 1950s, membership of the new suburban class was exhibited through the consumption of particular domestic commodities, the acquisition of which set suburban individuals apart from the urban throng. By being "defined and asserted through difference," the post-war suburban landscape became a material expression and mechanism of class-based power, prestige, and privilege (Bourdieu, 1984, p. 172). In an era not far removed from the deprivations of the Great Depression, the commodified suburbanization of post-war American culture—or what Schlesinger described as America's new-found "godly materialism" (1963, p. 84)—resulted in the fearless frontiersman being usurped by the unbounded suburban consumer within the national popular imaginary. In other words, the democratic mythos of the freedom-seeking American citizen was replaced by that of the commodity-seeking American citizen-consumer (Slater, 1997). The advancement of unreserved suburban materialism as the new American way of life fuelled an epidemic of peer-referenced spending:

By the fifties, the Smiths had to have the Joneses' fully automatic washing machine, vacuum cleaner, and, most of all, the shiny new Chevrolet parked in the driveway. The story of this period was that people looked to their own neighborhoods for their spending cues, and the neighbors grew more and more alike in what they had. Like compared with like and strove to become even more alike. (Schor, 1998, p. 8)

The normalizing rhythms of commodity-based suburbanism prompted many social commentators to decry the unimaginative, bland, and monotone culture it created: "In their very inoffensiveness and desire to fit in, suburban Americans seemed to critics to embody our own national version of the 'self-policing state'—the society that had sailed into a calm, dead-level ocean of conformity" (Lears, 1994, p. 252). Such criticisms, however perceptive, failed to recognize the stultifying suburban homogeneity of the early-mid 1950s as merely a phase in the relentless commodification of American existence.

Toward the end of the 1950s, maturing economies of scale within America's Fordist economy reduced production costs for mass consumer goods, and allowed previously restricted commodities such as automobiles, refrigerators, and televisions, to be accessible to a broader spectrum of the population. Since affluence and the social status accrued from it are primarily relational constructs, the appropriation of the working class into America's consumer culture created anxiety among a suburban American populace now challenged to differentiate their lives from lower status groupings. Rejecting the conformist consumption that framed the immediate post-war suburban experience, many suburbanites thus sought to (re)affirm an elevated social standing by engaging in escalating cycles of competitive consumption (Schor, 1998). In simplistic terms, the doctrine of "Keeping up with the Joneses" was rejected in favor of an obsessive desire to stay one step ahead of the Joneses. Rather than being allayed, middle class insecurities were heightened by the advancement of a culture of unremitting competitive upscaling. Through "fear of falling" (Ehrenreich, 1989) down the American class ladder, suburban consumers were compelled to continually aspire to bigger and better things, and were thus consigned to what Lasch (1979, p. 72) characterized as feelings of perpetual dissatisfaction and status anxiety: the "new forms of discontent peculiar to the modern age." Out of this fundamentally competitive cultural context, the American suburban soccer phenomenon was to emerge.

During the mid-1980s, the aggressively individualizing neo-liberal economics of the Reaganite moment encouraged an epidemic of consumer spending which further blurred traditional socio-economic boundaries (Clarke, 1991; Grossberg, 1992). America's maturing commodity democracy meant the process of suburban differentiation could no longer effectively be realized through the acquisition of commercial goods, regardless of their economic worth (Fine & Leopold, 1993). As a result, the suburban middle class turned to a more sophisticated mechanism for securing social distinction, broadly characterized by a turn to the aesthetic (Clarke, 1991; Duncan & Duncan, 1997; Ehrenreich, 1989; Schor, 1998).

As novelist Stephen King noted sardonically, "My generation . . . traded God for Martha Stewart. She's this priestess of etiquette who says that when you shovel snow from your drive, you oughta leave an inch or two at the sides, because it looks so nice" (quoted in Conrad, 1998, p. 1). Conjoining financial (economic capital) and educational resources (cultural capital), the suburban middle class presently derives its superior sense of self (social capital) from the assemblage of "goods, clothes, practices, experiences, appearance and bodily dispositions they design together into a lifestyle" (Featherstone, 1991, p. 86). This focus on the aesthetic rendered suburban existence an effect of consumer taste, not necessarily linked to the possession of the economic capital necessary for its realization. Prompted by the overt individualism and cultural moralizing of the Reagan revolution, lifestyles thus became viewed as an effect of individual choice and sophistication, rather than being necessarily overdetermined by "the choice of destiny," which for those less fortunate is "produced by conditions of existence which rule out all alternatives as mere daydreams and leave no choice but the taste for the necessary." Being steeped in spurious notions of freedom and individuality, the notion of suburban lifestyles as "tastes of luxury" conveniently obscured the privileged social and economic conditions of which they are a product (Bourdieu, 1984, p. 178).

By exuding a persuasive sense of consumer sovereignty (Slater, 1997) the practice of competitive lifestyling also concealed the collective regulation that continues to frame suburban existence. Assembling a particular lifestyle is evidently an active process, but one simultaneously enabled and constrained by the distinguishing influence of the class habitus. As an "internalized form of class condition and of the conditionings it entails," the habitus acts below the level of consciousness, and in concert with the possession of various forms of power (capitals), to shape subjective experiences (practices) within objective structures (fields). Suburban lifestyle projects are less a search for true individualism and more a stylized expression of class-based cultural associations. As Bourdieu noted, taste is an "acquired disposition to 'differentiate' and 'appreciate'. . . to establish and mark differences by a process of distinction" (Bourdieu, 1984, p. 101). In this sense, the habitus is a learned, yet wholly internalized, system of dispositions, preferences, and tastes, which informs an individual's capacity to act in the social world in a way that embodies their class position (Lury, 1996). Hence, suburban lifestyle assemblages can be viewed as aesthetically oriented "classified and classifying practices" that betray collective belonging even as they appear to celebrate consumer individuality (Bourdieu, 1984, p. 171).

The late twentieth century American suburb represented a complex social space, comprising multiple interrelated fields and sub-fields (housing, decor, diet, employment, education, dress, leisure, sport) in which individual agents competed for the various types of capital (economic, cultural, intellectual, physical), with which they seek to constitute their lifestyle practices in accordance with the regulatory codes of suburban taste cultures. Within such settings, acts of consumption (sometimes discrete, but often not) constitute the lifestyle projects through which suburban subjects become actualized to selves and others. The ontological well-being of the suburban populace is always in the process of being realized (if never actually achieved), through the implicit challenging of fellow consumer adversaries in the competitive marketplace. For this reason, the ritualized public forums of suburban display—excessive malls, extravagant country clubs, and indeed, exclusionary soccer fields—have become civic promenades for the performance of an individual's carefully managed commodity-based lifestyle.

Over the past two decades, youth soccer has become entrenched in the suburban context to the extent that it contributes to the very constitution of this competitive "universe of practices and consumptions" (Bourdieu, 1990, p. 159). According to Joe Povey, editor of *Soccer Jr.* magazine:

> Parents say they want their kids to have the absolute best opportunity—whether it's a camp, a private school or an elite soccer team . . . The emphasis shifts from fitting children into a community as peers of others to giving them an edge or an advantage. To explain why would be a sociological question. It's just something our generation has been guilty of. (Quoted in Russakof, 1998, p. A1)

Soccer's socio-spatial distribution is at least partly attributable to its position as "an elective luxury," only afforded by parental possession of considerable economic capital (Bourdieu, 1984, p. 178). As an illustration, participation in competitive youth soccer has been estimated to cost between $3,500 and $4,000 per year, a figure that includes the direct (annual membership fees, uniforms, cleats, and soccer balls for practice sessions) and indirect (entrance fees, travel, accommodation, meals, and entertainment expenses incurred during regular trips to weekend tournaments) costs of participation (Zwick & Andrews, 1999). The economics of competitive soccer instantiate a degree of social exclusivity, from which the game derives a "distinctive rarity" (Bourdieu, 1978, p. 835). This at least partly explains the bifurcation existing within many youth soccer communities, between low status, relatively inexpensive and relaxed recreation teams, and their high status antithesis, the costly and competitive travel teams with which suburban soccer is synonymous. Predictably, the competitive ethos of suburban culture has normalized the travel team as the de rigueur form of soccer involvement. Access to the considerable amount of spare time (identified by Bourdieu [1978, p. 834] as a transformed form of economic capital) demanded by soccer involvement is also a telling determinant in the class distribution of suburban soccer participants. Quite simply, the lives of affluent youthful suburbanites incorporate an "absence of necessity," meaning there exists no financial compulsion to enroll in the part-time workforce in order to augment their own, or their families', economic capital (Bourdieu, 1986). Evidently, only those from sufficiently affluent backgrounds are afforded the luxury of participation in soccer games and practices five days a week during the season, as required by many coaching regimes (Zwick & Andrews, 1999).

Although steeped in the economics of suburban privilege, youth soccer represents an important cultural field upon which the aesthetic logics of the suburban habitus are practiced and displayed (Bourdieu, 1993). This observation would be of little surprise to any card-carrying historical materialist, for as Marx famously noted, "even the most abstract categories . . . are by the very definiteness of the abstraction a product of historical conditions as well, and are fully applicable only to and under those conditions" (Marx, 1977b, p. 355). Thus, as "a unitary set of distinctive preferences which express the same intention in the specific logic of the symbolic sub-spaces, furniture, clothing, language or body hexis" (Bourdieu, 1984, p. 173), the differentiating taste culture of the suburban middle class has been faithfully transposed to the soccer field.

Having been raised within a climate of competitive aestheticism, the children of the suburban middle class are fully attuned to the nuances of converting economic capital to cultural capital, through the ever-evolving process of consumer stylization of the self (Lury, 1996). The search for distinction through the aestheticization of existence is an important part of the soccer experience, especially for older children. The increasingly convoluted taste cultures of middle class youth are apparent within the soccer setting: there is even evidence to suggest that "soccer style" has informed wider aesthetic trends (Grish, 1998; Perez, 1997). Thus, merely responding to the fleeting ascendancy of particular fashion statements (Adidas, Nike, Umbro, Puma, or alternative "other"; single colored or multi-colored; round-necked or v-necked; cotton or nylon; "grunge," "retro," or "urban") requires considerable financial investment on the part of parents. Clearly youth soccer cultures represent an adolescent arena for the playing out of the suburban middle class habitus. In order to ensure a sense of cultural belonging, it is vital that individuals are attuned to ever-changing codes of aesthetic propriety: "Wearing a passé t-shirt, sporting an unsuitable haircut, or having a bad hair day, would be immediately criticised for being an indication of lack of care of the 'self'" (Zwick & Andrews, 1999, p.220). Moreover, given the visible nature of soccer involvement, parents are equally aware of its importance as a forum for the aesthetic projecting of the self. This is evident in the near parodic uniformity of cosmetic appearance, dress, and choice of luxury vehicle exhibited by parents at games, practices, and meetings, vividly illustrating the normative regulation underpinning consumer individuality. Thus, although manifest in very different cultural products and expressions, both players and parents use the soccer field as a context for the expression of the middle class habitus, through which they exude membership of the suburban elite.

Suburban youth soccer is also a particularly interesting site of lifestyle differentiation, since it can be viewed as a sub-field within the larger field of child-rearing (among the most outwardly visible, and hence obsessively nurtured, sites of suburban lifestyle consummation):

> The one place where keeping-up behavior is paramount and conscious is where the kids are concerned. Whatever doubts the average American parents may have about the importance of the Joneses' new kitchen, there's little doubt that they are worried about whether their children are maintaining the pace with the Joneses' offspring (Schor, 1998, p. 85).

As embodied signifiers of parental lifestyle, and thereby class position, every aspect of a middle class child's life have been exposed to the suburban regime of competitive lifestyle consumption. The constitution of a child's education, apparel, footwear, toys, body, teeth, and even soccer cleats are points of social distinction and comparison that compel parents to conform to ever-escalating norms of stylized existence. This phenomenon is readily apparent within the realm of children's leisure practices, hence what Schor (1998) pointed out as the escalating standard for children's birthday parties, manifest in the predilection for outsourcing the "entire event to Chuck E. Cheese, the Discovery Zone, the Mining Company, or some other business that stages a memorable event for the kids" (Gilmore, 1998, p. 97).

Suburban soccer culture evidences the extent to which the more mundane aspects of children's leisure time have been engulfed by the normalizing competitive lifestyle ethos: this "generation of parents . . . keeps starting children off younger and younger, pushing them harder and harder, not just in soccer but in music, competitive-admissions preschools, ballet, foreign languages" (Russakof, 1998, p. A1). Apparently no longer allowed to engage in unstructured or unsupervised play, many young suburbanites are pressed by their parents into grueling after-school schedules of commercially organized "extended education," despite the financial, logistical, and emotional problems frequently posed to children and parents alike (Ehrenreich, 1989, p. 82). Exhibiting the kernel of the suburban habitus, the motivation for such prompting appears to be the conspicuous manufacturing of healthy, cooperative, goal-oriented, and competitive children. Suburban parents routinely regale soccer as an appropriate activity that encourages the "right" type of corporeal aesthetic for boys and girls alike. It is cast as a healthy alternative to the abnormalizing and aggressive masculinity of American football (Hornung, 1994; Wagg, 1995); it instills a teamwork ethic and achievement orientation that can be transferred to other realms of existence; it provides a competitive environment within which their offspring are challenged to excel; and, it represents yet another structured activity designed to create and monitor productive youth bodies. These sentiments betray the extent to which suburban soccer has become a "wholly owned subsidiary of competitive adults" (Russakof, 1998, p. A1), in that parents use it to assuage anxieties about their own lives. Moreover, for many suburban parents, not providing one's offspring with the requisite experiences derived from competitive soccer represents suburban failure tantamount to child neglect.

Fully and enthusiastically incorporated as part of the suburban aesthetic, youth soccer participation has become the sporting version of "Tuscan extra virgin olive oil," a manifest expression of suburbanite lifestyle sophistication (Sugden, 1994, p. 247). This observation has been noted and nurtured by the denizens of Madison Avenue, the hub of America's advertising culture, who—within a multitude of advertising campaigns for products as diverse as Lender's bagels, Dutch Boy paints, Cellular One mobile phones, and McDonald's fast food—have used soccer referents to substantiate their objects of production (archetypes of the utopian suburban lifestyle) and interpellate their preferred subjects of consumption (consumers identifying with, or aspiring to, the utopian suburban lifestyle). This ubiquitous representational strategy is ably illustrated within a television commercial for the Buick Regal automobile:

> [An affluent suburban subdivision]. Some families get more done in a day than others do in a week.
>
> [The family is introduced, smiling in front of their spacious single family dwelling. They jump into the car, hasten to a soccer game, and return rapidly] They're the first to do anything, including to say. . .
>
> [One of the daughters greets the audience] "Hey, how's it going?" Now there's a car that does as much as your supercharged family.
>
> [The family embarks on another journey]. Introducing the new supercharged Regal GS. No other sports sedan squeezes so much supercharged "fun," power, and standard safety features into your daily routine.
>
> [Having returned home, the family sets out for a children's party. The son is wearing a banana costume]. Regal GS by Buick.
>
> [Their bassett hound howls. The car returns to pick up the dog]. "Hey, life's a blur."
>
> [The dog is put in the back of the car, and once again the family is on its way]. The all new Regal GS, the official car of the supercharged family.

Within this commercial—as in its broader cultural appropriation—suburban soccer is used as a benchmark constituent of the supercharged suburban aesthetic. As such, the game acts as a principal "source, as well as an indicator of social differentiation" for the innately competitive suburban middle class (Schor, 1998, p. 30). However, as with many other suburban practices, participation in youth soccer is commonly viewed as a lifestyle choice, thereby effectively obscuring the very real economic barriers that preclude many from involvement. In so doing, the uncomfortable notion of socio-economic class is erased, and the suburban middle class allowed to bolster its overactive sense of self-righteous achievement and privilege. Thus, and somewhat refining Zukin (1991), although a central feature of the suburban topography, youth soccer represents an effective sublimation of the very real social class relations (and, indeed, gender and race relations only implied herein), through which a suburban landscape of the powerful (white, middle class) is both structured and experienced.

7

ROT BENEATH THE SPORTING GLITTER

Since 1990, in an era of shrinking fiscal and legislative support for urban welfare initiatives, city and state governments throughout the US have spent more than $10
billion to subsidize the construction of facilities for major league sports teams (Kaplan, 2003). There are, of course, well-rehearsed political and economic imperatives
driving such public policy initiatives; however, this chapter focuses on the cultural
derivations and implications associated with the sporting-based, built spectacularization of the contemporary US city. The aim is to contribute to the growing literature
that critically examines the role of professional sport teams, elite sporting events, and
sport venues in creating and projecting a city identity (see Belanger, 2000; Schimmel,
Ingham & Howell, 1993; Silk, 2002, 2004; Silk & Amis, 2005; Smith, 2001; Smith &
Ingham, 2003; Whitson & Macintosh, 1993, 1996; Waitt, 1999). Through recourse to
the instructive example of Baltimore, Maryland, this project elucidates the manner in
which cities have utilized professional sports venues and facilities as central components of broader urban redevelopment initiatives and assesses the consequences of
such strategic policy decisions for city inhabitants. More specifically, this discussion
focuses on Oriole Park at Camden Yards (OPCY), constructed in downtown Baltimore during the late 1980s and early 1990s. More than just a trendsetter for sports facility design (Bale, 1994; van Rooij, 2000), OPCY is an integral part of Baltimore's
evolving plan to transform its urban core into a vibrant entertainment and recreation
zone. As such, OPCY represents an important point of entry into debates on the spatial reorganization of contemporary American cities around a domineering logic of
consumer- and service-oriented capital accumulation.

Baltimore certainly provides an interesting view of the forces driving the late capitalist reconstitution of the urban condition. As David Harvey noted, it is a city "emblematic of the processes that have moulded cities under US capitalism, offering a laboratory sample of contemporary urbanism" (2001a, p. 7). Characteristic of this new urbanism, changes in the global flows of production, commodities, and information radically reconfigured the spatial arrangements underpinning the logic of accumulation. This resulted in the emergence of new roles, regimes, and relations for cities within developed economies (Sassen, 1991; 2001). In the second half of the twentieth century, the mass manufacturing economy evacuated its traditional urban home in the northeastern and midwestern cities of the US, and concomitantly urban tax bases, populations, and public expenditure steeply declined (Goodwin, 1993). In order to inoculate against what threatened to be a terminal malaise, many cities expedited a shift from a managerial to an entrepreneurial style of governance. Less interested in enhancing public welfare than attracting private capital, the post-industrial city thus emerged with the overriding aim of luring "highly mobile and flexible production, financial, and consumption flows into its space" (Harvey, 2001b, p. 359).

In today's ever more entrepreneurial climate, cities compete against each other to attract capital investment from corporate, governmental, and retail sectors. Although much of the attendant inter-urban competition revolves around the advancement of subsidization and infrastructure incentives (Harvey, 2001b), the focus herein is the manner in which cities have reconstituted the function and structure of the urban environment. Shorn of their traditional industrial manufacturing economies, many North American cities have become preoccupied with the shift to commercial initiatives that engage—and seek to reconstitute—the urban environment as a multifaceted space of consumption and capital accumulation (Lowes, 2002; Sassen & Roost, 1999; Zukin, 1991). Thus, the post-industrial city has emerged as a "spectacular urban space" (Harvey, 2001b, p. 92), replete with obligatory components and expressions of contemporary urban viability: shopping (festival marketplaces and malls); dining (theme restaurants and cafes); entertainment (theaters, sports facilities, museums, live music, casinos); and visitor infrastructure (hotels, convention centers) (Gottdiener, 2001; Hannigan, 1998; Ritzer, 1999). Both individually and in combination, each of the aforementioned resources are designed to attract corporate and consumer interest and investment and thereby secure a competitive advantage for cities within the "place-wars" that organize the spatial distribution of contemporary capital (Robins, 1997). In order to address the negative preexisting perceptions of the urban environment (Judd, 1999)—and thereby assuage the concerns of potential consumers and investors alike—urban redevelopment and regeneration projects have tended to concentrate on relatively small areas "cordoned off and designed to cosset the affluent visitor, while simultaneously warding off the threatening native" (Fainstein & Gladstone, 1999, p. 26). So, as "islands of affluence . . . sharply differentiated and segregated from the surrounding urban landscape" these "tourist bubbles" (Judd, 1999, p. 53) project a reassuringly dislocated experience and perception of safety, fun, and vitality for downtown areas (Eisinger, 2000).

Certainly, major sporting events, franchises, new stadia and other sport-related experiences have become among the most effective vehicles for the advancement of internally and externally identifiable places (Bale, 1994; Chalkey & Essex, 1999; Rowe & McGuirk, 1999; Stevenson, 1997; Whitson & Macintosh, 1993, 1996; Wilcox & Andrews, 2003). As Waitt proposed in relation to the Sydney Olympic Games, "imaging a city through the organization of spectacular urban space by, for example, hosting the Olympic Games, is an important mechanism for attracting capital and people in a period of intense inter-urban competition and urban entrepreneurialism" (1999, p. 1062). So, while the 1980s featured the proliferation of festival malls, the 1990s featured sport stadia as anchors of urban regeneration and differentiation (Austrian & Rosentraub, 2002; Hannigan, 1998; Turner & Rosentraub, 2002). Like Debord's (1995) "veil of appearance," through their very physical form, spectacular built structures—monuments of sporting consumerism (Coors Field in Denver, Safeco Field in Seattle, and Conseco Fieldhouse arena in Indianapolis, among others)—frequently obscure the complexities and contradictions of urban life and the experiential realities of a deeper social malaise. Following Belanger (2000), this discussion problematizes the position and influence of one celebrated sport stadium complex, as part of a broader strategic "spectacularization of urban space." This is realized through an examination of Baltimore as an exemplar of the processes and effects of consumption-based urban entrepreneurial strategies. More specifically, this discussion focuses on the manner in which the material and symbolic presence of OPCY acts as both a compelling marker of urban regeneration, and, as such, an effective mask for continuing structural decline within Baltimore's urban core.

In many respects, Baltimore has long been a microcosm of broader patterns of social, economic, and urban development. During the 19th century, the Baltimore and Ohio Railroad was a key connection between the East and Midwest and, as a marker of Baltimore's importance, Camden Station was the world's largest train station when it opened in 1857. During the first half of the 20th century, Baltimore was a major manufacturing center. During the 1930s and 1940s, it ranked seventh among US urban centers in industrial production, with steel, shipbuilding and repair, and the Port of Baltimore serving as the city's major employers. By 1950, Baltimore had grown to 950,000 people (Harvey, 2000), but, owing to accelerating rates of US deindustrialization, soon went into a period of population stagnation followed by significant decline starting in the late 1960s. Although reversing the city's decline has been among the central issues for Baltimore's civic leadership, conditions in Baltimore continue to deteriorate. The city's population has dropped by almost 33 percent since 1950, and the manufacturing sector has virtually disappeared as two thirds of the city's manufacturing jobs have been lost since 1960 (Harvey, 2000; Morton Hoffman & Company, 1964; US Census Bureau Data, 2001).

As high-paying jobs and well-paid workers left Baltimore, causing the city's tax base to erode, the quality of life for its remaining residents has declined as poverty and its related social ills have increased substantially. In 1999, Baltimore ranked first among large cities in the US for murder, violent and property crime, and drug-related emergency room visits (Linder & Associates, 1999). An esti-mated 23 percent of the city's residents lived in poverty as Baltimore's per capita income level fell to 57 percent of Maryland's average (Johns Hopkins Institute for Policy Studies, 2000). Public health suffered as city residents had life expectancies 14 years under national averages, and in 1999 Baltimore's rate of teen pregnancy was the highest of the 50 largest US cities (Harvey, 2000; Johns Hopkins Insti-tute for Policy Studies, 2000). Overall, Baltimore has become trapped in a spiral of deterioration as its declining tax base and social services have accelerated the flight of corporations and residents from the city. This has left a higher concentra-tion of lower-income residents who are in greater need of services, such as educa-tion, health care, housing, and public safety, from a government with less ability to provide them (Schimmel, Ingham, and Howell, 1993). Faced with the corol-lary of deeply entrenched socio-structural problems and attendant inequalities (urban deindustrialization, depopulation, tax base diminution, and elevated pov-erty and crime rates), Baltimore's policy makers in government and the private sector have focused on the development of the service, leisure, and entertainment sectors within the downtown core. The assumption was that increased economic activity would create sufficient tax revenues to allow the city to address its other problems (Hula, 1990; Levine, 1999).

While many American cities have met the challenges of the postindustrial econ-omy through entrepreneurial strategies harnessing the force of private investment capital, Baltimore's downtown redevelopment has been widely lauded as a model for such urban regeneration schemas (see Harvey, 1992/2001b; Hula, 1990; Levine, 1999). Redevelopment of Baltimore's central business district started in the 1950s with the $180 million Charles Center office and retail complex, which was de-signed for white-collar professional corporations in the legal, finance, insurance, and real estate industries (Harvey, 1992/2001c; Hula, 1990; Wagner, 1996). Busi-ness leaders then turned their focus to the Inner Harbor, which was the "cradle" of the city's development and had long been a center for Baltimore's industrial, ware-housing and wholesaling activities, but had fallen into disuse and decay by 1960 and was characterized as an area of urban blight (Morton Hoffman and Company, 1964; see also Wagner, 1996). In a market analysis prepared for business leaders, Morton Hoffman and Company (1964) recommended redeveloping the 250-acre area as a mixed-use commercial, residential and recreational area featuring up to 900,000 square feet of office space, 3,000 housing units, waterfront public parks, an expanded marina, a "boatel" featuring 300 hotel rooms, a science center, aquar-ium, eating and drinking places, a maritime museum with "historic vessels," and a community college.

The potential of the Inner Harbor began to be realized after the election of William D. Schaefer as mayor in 1971. Schaefer's campaign and administration fo-cused on the redevelopment of downtown and the Inner Harbor (Hula, 1990), and within a short time, the Inner Harbor began to be transformed into a con-sumption space. The *U.S.S. Constellation,* an early 19th century US Navy ship, was berthed there (1972); the Baltimore City Fair, attended by 2 million people, was relocated from the Charles Center to the Inner Harbor (1973); and the Maryland Science Center (1974) and the 27-story World Trade Center (1977) were completed (Hula, 1990; Wagner, 1996). The next round of development, despite opposition from citizens who wanted to preserve the waterfront for public use, was manifest in the Inner Harbor's flagship projects: the Harborplace festival mall, the National Aquarium, the Hyatt Regency Hotel, and the Baltimore Convention Center—none of which was part of the original redevelopment plan (Harvey, 2001c; Hula, 1990; Wagner, 1996).

Such was the impact of the Inner Harbor development that Baltimore was widely praised in the (inter)national media as having undergone a stunning "urban renaissance": the London *Sunday Times* claiming in 1987 that "the decay of old Baltimore slowed, halted, then turned back" (in Harvey, 2001c, p. 139). Seeking to perpetuate this perception of urban development, the Strategic Management Committee (1991) published *The Renaissance Continues: A 20 Year Strategy for Downtown Baltimore*. This vision of Baltimore in 2010 projected the downtown area as "a place for people," a place of "opportunity," "uncommonly livable," "easy to get to," and "especially attractive" (p. 5) for visitors and residents, who could choose from a diverse array of leisure options offered around Baltimore's Inner Harbor. Despite such praise and self-aggrandizing, the city's redevelopment efforts have garnered criticism for some important perceived failings. As a motor for capital accumulation, the varied development projects have required considerable public subsidization such that they have been identified as economic failures and debilitating drains on local government coffers (see Harvey, 2001c; Levine, 1999). Moreover, the perceived success of the Inner Harbor prompted other cities to revitalize their waterfronts through the development of entertainment and recreation facilities similar to Harborplace (Judd, 1999; Levine, 1999). With the serial repetition of this successful form of built environment, and as consumers "grow bored easily" with duplicative consumption spaces, Baltimore had to create "increasingly spectacular displays and a continual escalation of efforts to lure consumers" (Ritzer, 1999, p. xi). Thus, the seemingly perpetual need to revitalize the Inner Harbor development—in order to keep it competitive with the urban initiatives it inspired—has required an ever-larger commitment of public funds into the project.

In order to differentiate Baltimore from other cities and keep consumption environments fresh and attractive to potential consumers of the spaces and its associated services, Baltimore unveiled plans in the late 1980s for the construction of a baseball stadium at Camden Yards. Located on the western border of the Inner Harbor area and at the end of the I-395 access ramp into downtown, Camden Station and its 1016-foot-long warehouse (the longest building on the East Coast) were highly visible to visitors to Baltimore, and "deeply rooted in the history of Baltimore and its development as a center of trade and commerce" (Maryland Stadium Authority, 1987, p. 7). Despite their spatial and cultural centrality, the Camden Station and warehouse were abandoned in the early 1970s as industrial production in the city waned. Although there were many similar decaying industrial sites throughout Baltimore, the highly visible position of the station and warehouse was noticeably inconsistent with the nearby revitalized waterfront. The area's future was a topic of concern for city leaders and the subject of several redevelopment plans, including one that would convert the warehouse into an industrial museum and another that would convert it into residential space (Richmond, 1993).

As the future of Camden Yards was being considered, the city's continued relationship with major league sports was in doubt. MLB's Orioles had arrived in Baltimore in 1954 and, along with the NFL's Colts, helped substantiate the city's "major league" status (Johnson, 1986). The two teams shared Memorial Stadium, which was located in an urban residential neighborhood three miles north of the Inner Harbor, built during the 1920s and renovated during the 1950s. However, by the mid-1980s, according to a State of Maryland report by the Special Advisory Commission on Professional Sports and the Economy (1985), Memorial Stadium had "serious deficiencies when compared with stadiums in other major-league metropolitan areas" (p. 59). In particular, the Commission identified the stadium as possessing inadequate parking, poor highway access, many obstructed view seats and few premium seats, a shortage of concession stands and restrooms, a long climb to the upper deck, and inadequate press facilities and locker rooms. Both the Colts and the Orioles had recognized the deficiencies of Memorial Stadium long before the state report, and both teams had begun seeking new facilities in the early 1970s. In 1972, the Maryland Sports Complex Authority (MSCA) recommended Camden Yards as the site for a 70,000 seat, $114 million domed stadium. However, the inability of the teams, the MSCA, and the Maryland General Assembly to agree on financing led to the abandonment of this plan (Miller, 1990).

The request by the Orioles for a new stadium was only considered with greater urgency after the departure of the Colts for Indianapolis in 1984, as civic leaders were concerned that Orioles owner Edward Bennett Williams would move the team to Washington, DC (Johnson, 1986). In 1985, the State of Maryland formed a special advisory commission to analyze the role of professional sports on the state economy and to recommend a course of action, which led to the establishment of the Maryland Stadium Authority (MSA) the next year. Simultaneously, consultants were identifying and investigating sites for a new stadium. One report ranked Camden Yards as the top among 22 sites in Baltimore City (Hellmuth, Obata & Kassabaum, 1985), but in another study Camden Yards ranked third behind suburban sites in Lansdowne (at the intersection of I-95 and the Baltimore Beltway) and Anne Arundel County, because Camden Yards did not compare favorably with regard to traffic, land use, local compatibility, cost, and economic impact (HNTB & Touche Ross and Co, 1986). As the consultants were generating their reports, Mayor Schaefer, who was running for governor in 1986, actively promoted Camden Yards for its proximity to the Inner Harbor. Shortly following Schaefer's election as Governor, the MSA selected Camden Yards after the Lansdowne site was discovered to require expensive infrastructure upgrades, and renovation of Memorial Stadium was ruled out (Miller, 1990).

The construction of the publicly financed $210 million OPCY offered solutions to many of Baltimore's problems. First, it ensured that Baltimore retained its status as a "major league" city, as the Orioles signed a 30-year lease to stay there. Second, the presence of a major league edifice would—unlike the decaying buildings previously sited there—enhance rather than detract from the city's reimaging efforts, while extending the Inner Harbor retail and commercial zone all the way to I-395. Finally, in its cutting-edge, retro architectural design, OPCY provided Baltimore an imageable landmark that caught the attention of baseball fans and players, professional sports owners, the general public and architectural critics. Writing in *The New York Times,* Paul Goldberger (1989, p. H39) claimed that OPCY "is a building capable of wiping out in a single gesture 50 years of wretched stadium design, and of restoring the joyous possibility that a ball park might actually enhance the experience of watching the game of baseball." When OPCY opened, *GQ Magazine* wrote "every baseball fan should kneel down this moment and thank God for Baltimore" (quoted in Maryland Stadium Authority, 1992, p. 5).

The early designs of OPCY, however, provided no indication that it would be dramatically different from the late modern facilities preceding it (Ritzer & Stillman, 2001). In architectural renditions prepared for the Baltimore Corporate Stadium Task Force in 1985, the stadium architecture firm Hellmuth, Obata, and Kassabaum (HOK), who were to gain widespread acclaim for the eventual design of the stadium, initially presented a multi-use, primarily concrete vision of Camden Yards stadium, which placed it amid parking lots and excluded the warehouse (Hellmuth, Obata & Kassabaum, 1987). However, in concert with the Orioles, the MSA (1987) developed guidelines for architects that requested stadium designs creating "intimacy, character and an 'old fashioned park'" (p. 10). Moreover, the stadium had to be integrated into and be consistent with the existing renewal projects and neighborhoods that surrounded Camden Yards. Overall, the MSA (1987) stated that its goal was "to have a modern stadium, yet retain the warmth and intimacy of an old-fashioned ball park" (p. 10).

In one fell swoop, the era of postmodern stadium development was born (Ritzer & Stillman, 2001), as HOK set about randomly cannibalizing the past (Jameson, 1991, p. 18) to create a baseball environment replete with a faux historical authenticity that was, in effect, prefigured on the use of "nostalgia as an antidote to modernity" (Bale, 1994, p. 170). Of course, such "new-old" structures (Bale, 1994, p. 170), of which OPCY was to become emblematic, incorporate technologically advanced engineering and internal systems, while simultaneously fostering a "look and feel like what fans think the old-time fields must have looked and felt like" (Epstein, 1996, p. A13). In Ritzer and Stillman's (2001) terms, the aestheticized nostalgia of such environments provides a superficial, yet seductive, covering to what is a highly rationalized "McDonaldized" commercial enterprise.

Through its advancement of what became dubbed a "high-tech nostalgia" (Epstein, 1996, p. A13), HOK's revised design for OPCY met the MSA's requirements and goals. A pivotal aspect of the new rendering was the incorporation of the monolithic Camden Yards Warehouse as a distinctive feature of the design. In doing so, HOK used a symptomatic postmodern architectural practice: the construction of an essentially new building within the shell of an old built form. With this architectural façadism, there exists little or no "relationship between the façade and the rest of the building in terms of style, proportion and structure" (Richards, 1994, p. 11). As such, there is a fundamental disconnect between the external appearance of the building and its underlying structure. The viewer is deceived regarding the building's function, by its historically imbued decorative skin (Richards, 1994).

This is certainly true of the Camden Yard's Warehouse, whose historical patina belies the contemporaneously apportioned and appointed commercial spaces (many of which are used by the Baltimore Orioles organization) found beneath its red brick surface. Interestingly, OPCY also utilizes the backdrop of the Baltimore cityscape to further the historical façade perpetrated through the imaginative reuse of the Warehouse. No part of OPCY is taller than the Warehouse, allowing the ballpark to seamlessly integrate into its urban surroundings. According to Goldberger (1989, p. H39), "that is the goal at Baltimore: not a strained and self-conscious eccentricity, but just enough of a sense of the city to make it clear at every moment, from every seat, that you are under the sky of Baltimore." This integration is achieved in several ways. First, the city's skyline and the distinctive Bromo-Seltzer clock tower are clearly visible beyond the left field wall. Second, Eutaw Street has been incorporated into the stadium as a pedestrian concourse. Third, rather than using structural concrete, as in the majority of late modern stadia (Ritzer & Stillman, 2001), the exterior design of the stadium uses bricks of a color similar to the warehouse and surrounding community.

The brick façade is emblematic of the depthless aesthetic so closely associated with postmodern cultural forms, perhaps most graphically exemplified in the various structural and symbolic design elements used to engage the collective memory, and to assuage collective anxiety about the present (Featherstone, 1991; Healey, 1997; Jameson, 1991). John Bale has referred to this "postmodern stadium" as an architectural repository of history (1994, p. 170), and certainly OPCY deploys a variety of historical signifiers to assert its spatial provenance (however inauthentic). It is in this sense that OPCY most vividly, and indeed randomly, cannibalizes the past, as storied baseball signifiers are torn from their spatial and temporal moorings, and un-self-consciously juxtaposed, in a pastiche of postmodern baseball historicism (Jameson, 1991). HOK mined some evocative elements of the classic early modern ballparks (Ritzer & Stillman, 2001), drawing features from Wrigley Field in Chicago (the ivy-covered batter's eye), Fenway Park in Boston (accentuated right field wall), Forbes Field in Pittsburgh (upper deck sun shade), and the Polo Grounds in New York (wrought-iron row ends), into the hybridized pseudo-historical space that is OPCY.

Although OPCY's postmodern façade spatially historicizes the relationship between Baltimore and baseball, its internal structure is designed to facilitate and enhance the Orioles' profitability. In Ritzer and Stillman's (2001) terms, OPCY is a late modern stadium in terms of comfort, access, and revenue-generating capabilities. It was designed with 72 luxury suites, a club level with 5,000 seats, and wide concourses allowing for ease of movement and an increased number of points of sale for food and merchandise. While Eutaw Street is reminiscent of Yawkey Way outside of Fenway Park with its vendors and shops, unlike Yawkey Way, Eutaw Street is contained within OPCY, giving the Orioles organization direct access to revenues generated there. Fan comfort is further enhanced through its accessibility to I-95 (the highway connecting Baltimore to the rest of the East coast), which allows suburbanites to attend games without traveling through city neighborhoods. Not surprisingly perhaps given its populist "high-tech nostalgia" (Epstein, 1996, p. A13), in terms of attracting spectators, OPCY has been one of the most successful MLB stadiums. Since its opening in 1992, more than 3 million fans attended Orioles games in each of OPCY's first full nine seasons, not including the strike-shortened 1994 season (Baltimore Orioles, 2002).

However, similar to the Charles Center and Inner Harbor components of Baltimore's urban regeneration, the socio-political impact of OPCY has been much greater than its economic impact (in this case, the ability to attract paying spectators in sizeable numbers). OPCY represents a compelling manifestation of urban development, one regularly used as a means of redefining the image of the city to residents and external audiences alike. Thus, OPCY provides a "veil of appearance" (Debord, 1995) abstracted from its surroundings and conditions of existence, and subsequently mobilized through place-based marketing as the sanitized and sanctioned image of Baltimore. Following the argument of Belanger (2000), OPCY thus represents a self-portrait of, and indeed justification for, the urban entrepreneurialism currently operating in the city of Baltimore. However, while responsible for the commercial reengineering of the city—like OPCY itself—such strategizing functionally and institutionally excludes certain segments of the population who reside, precariously, in the shadows of such development initiatives.

The project is promoted as a public-private partnership, but the public has assumed the risk of the $210 million stadium and the private sector has reaped the rewards. According to Hamilton and Kahn (1997), OPCY is subsidized annually by $14 million of public money in excess of the taxes collected from economic activity and employment related to the Orioles and ballpark. These subsidies have been reflected in the escalating value of the team. When Williams purchased the Orioles in 1979, the team's value was $13 million, but following Maryland's commitment to building OPCY, financier Eli Jacobs paid $70 million for the team in 1988 (Quirk & Fort, 1992). The value escalated further after OPCY opened. After the failure of Jacobs's other investments, the team was sold for $173 million through bankruptcy proceedings in 1993 (Hamilton & Kahn, 1997).

While the subsidy has helped to further enrich team owners, the burden of the stadium's financing was borne mostly by people from lower socio-economic groupings. Following the recommendations of the Special Advisory Commission report (1985), OPCY was financed by the State of Maryland through revenues dedicated to the MSA from sports-themed lottery scratch-off games. According to Nibert (2000), lotteries represent a form of regressive taxation as studies have shown that people from lower income households are the most likely to play lottery games (see also Eitzen, 1996). OPCY, therefore, represents a transfer of wealth from lower income residents to the wealthy owners of the Orioles and the team's high-salaried players. The arrangement has further decreased the welfare of lower income residents as revenue, which was initially authorized in the 1970s to raise funding for education, has also been diverted to OPCY (Maryland State Lottery, 2002). Moreover, as OPCY is smaller and tickets are more expensive than at Memorial Stadium, lower income residents have had less opportunity to attend games. In fact, during the Orioles' first season in OPCY, there was a 93 percent decrease in the number of seats available for less than $8 (Orioles, 1991, 1992).

In addition to the negative economic results of OPCY, the stadium's impact on Baltimore's image may be diminishing. As suggested by Harvey (1989) regarding the serial replication of successful styles, although OPCY's nostalgic design was unique when it opened in 1992, the stadium's success has rendered it commonplace. Similar to Harborplace's initial success and the subsequent proliferation of festival marketplaces, OPCY's design is no longer unique, as it has become the template for baseball stadium design throughout the US. Each of the 14 major league stadiums that have opened since 1993, or are under construction, and many minor league facilities, have incorporated nostalgic elements into their physical environments. According to van Rooij, "there are now so many of these nostalgic stadia in the United States that the retro stadium, originally intended as a specific building for a specific location, has already been reduced to a cliché" (2000, p. 131).

As one response to the shift to the post-industrial economy, city governments have utilized a range of entrepreneurial strategies to increase tax collections in order to provide services and other benefits to urban residents. Throughout the US, city governments have responded to the challenges of deindustrialization, shrinking tax bases and reduced federal government spending, by subsidizing construction of sports facilities, shopping malls, hotels, and convention centers, to enhance the attractiveness of their downtown areas for corporations, tourists and suburban visitors. Successful urban regeneration projects have been replicated by other cities, leading to a virtual standardization of urban commercial development zones: Each possesses a festival marketplace with similar shops, themed restaurants, the obligatory "new-old" sports facility (Bale, 1994, p. 170), and a convention center with an attached luxury hotel managed by an international chain. Because of the relentless competition of cultural capitalism, these signature retail and commercial spaces require constant reinvestment as urban governments attempt to ensure that they do not have lesser amenities than comparable cities. Moreover, the result of consumption-based, visitor-oriented redevelopment may be to create little more than a veneer of change and vitality within the city. Beneath the façade of an improved civic image, the underlying realities of urban life frequently remain unaltered.

Specifically referring to Baltimore, Harvey describes the "rot beneath the glitter" (2001c, p. 140) as conditions for urban residents have deteriorated despite the city's much heralded revitalization campaign focused on the Inner Harbor (including OPCY):

The Inner Harbor functions as a sophisticated mask. It invites us to participate in a spectacle. . . . Like any mask, it can beguile and distract in engaging ways, but at some point we want to know what lies behind it. If the mask cracks or is violently torn off, the terrible face of Baltimore's impoverishment may appear. (Harvey, 2001c, pp. 143–144)

So, while façadism has architecturally been employed for specific redevelopment projects (such as OPCY) in an effort to express the postmodern urban aesthetic, it can also be understood as a metaphor that reveals the more general strategies employed by entrepreneurial cities. While the vibrant retail and commercial zones are the public face of the city, touted as representative of its overall redevelopment, they are, in many cases, and certainly in Baltimore's, islands of prosperity and affluence in a sea of urban decay and disinvestment (Judd, 1999).

It may be spurious to conclude direct causation between two multifaceted social phenomena (Baltimore's enduring crisis and the presence of the OPCY complex). Still, there is some explanatory worth in comparing some broad-based indicators of the urban experience in pre- and post-OPCY Baltimore. Between 1990 and 2000, the long-term depopulation of Baltimore continued, with a decline of 11.5 percent from 736,014 to 651,154. During the same period, Baltimore household income rose 25.1 percent, from $24,045 to $30,078, which amounts to 63 percent of the national average. Most disturbingly perhaps, over the decade while the number of people living in poverty dropped by more than 5 percent nationwide, in Baltimore the poverty rate rose by some 4.6 percent (US Census Bureau Data, 2001). The quality of services received by Baltimore residents reflects this earnings gap as students in Baltimore's public schools are 2 years behind the national average in reading, and 83 percent of the schools in Maryland eligible to be taken over by the state (based on poor overall performance) are located within the Baltimore city school district (Harvey, 2000). Despite the presence of "some of the finest medical and public health institutions in the world" (Harvey, 2000, p. 136), health services for city residents are inconsistent and difficult to access. Drug use and crime remain significant problems as well. The Office of National Drug Control Policy (2002, p. 6) described Baltimore as having "one of the most serious heroin abuse problems in the country" in 1999. Baltimore also ranked first per capita for drug-related emergency room visits (Linder & Associates, 2002). Crime risk in 2002 was 4.83 times higher than the national average, with Baltimore ranked 1235 out of 1240 and rated among the top five most dangerous metropolitan areas in America (CNN Money.com).

These disturbing social realities and deep-rooted structural inequalities belie the successful public image presented by urban redevelopment strategies. In this way, just as the façade of the building is separated from its underlying structure, Baltimore's aesthetic rejuvenation is a veneer masking the city's deep-rooted structural problems. Within this context, the metaphor of façadism also can be seen as an implicit critique of urban redevelopment policies, which focus on projecting civic image over improving citizen welfare. Rather than focusing on the problems of urban life and improving the welfare of residents, city governments have developed retail and commercial zones and amenities designed to attract the discretionary income of various constituencies of visitors, while simultaneously dissuading use of, or disconnecting lower-income residents from, these areas (Eisinger, 2000; Fainstein & Gladstone, 1999). Beneath the rhetorical veneer of improving the welfare of low-income urban residents through increased income derived from increased tax revenue (something rarely realized as this requires operational subsidies and ever-increasing public investments in infrastructure and amenities [Eisinger, 2000]), the true beneficiaries of using diminishing government resources to spectacularize the city (Harvey, 2001b; Ritzer, 1999) have been the upper and middle classes. Few benefits would seem to have trickled down to the urban poor. As a consequence of many urban regeneration schemes, "there are sections of the populations—the unemployed, the underemployed, women, the racialized or otherwise discriminated against—who are institutionally excluded from the high table of the global feast" (Brah, 2002, p. 37).

While championed under the mantra of state-sponsored capitalism that relied on federal and state bonds, grants, and subsidies (the Harborplace festival mall, for example, enjoys a $1-per-year lease on city property even after the city demolished the existing waterfront structures, rebuilt the bulkhead along the harbor, and agreed to provide ongoing maintenance), Baltimore's urban renewal, for all its glittering facade, is emblematic of the potential pitfalls of state capitalism (Smith & Siegel, 2001). Although public investment in the Inner Harbor was justified on the basis of economic growth and job creation, which in turn would improve the welfare of urban residents, the true beneficiaries of the redevelopment have been the entertainment-consuming visitors and the developers who have received substantial revenue-generating opportunities while the financial risks were assumed by local taxpayers. The publicly financed construction of OPCY helped to increase the value of the Orioles by $160 million within 14 years and provided an enhanced space in which baseball fans in the Baltimore region could enjoy the consumption of major league sports. Conversely, the redevelopment of the area has drained economic resources and attendant services from the adjacent downtown neighborhoods (Smith & Siegel, 2001). The urban residents who rely on Baltimore's government for public services have been excluded, both by price and physical design, from enjoying the benefits of the Inner Harbor and OPCY, while bearing much of the financial costs (either directly or indirectly).

Baltimore's spectacular space of sporting consumption is thus juxtaposed with the lived reality of life outside the "tourist bubble" (Judd, 1999), providing a paradigmatic exemplar of what John Mollenkopf and Manuel Castells termed a "dual city" (1991). Within this context, the success of the downtown renaissance, the Inner Harbor, and OPCY act as a "sophisticated mask" (Harvey, 2001c, p. 143) obscuring the underlying realities and socio-structural polarizations of the urban experience (Bianchini & Schwengel, 1991; Harvey, 1989; Whitson & Macintosh, 1996). In Baltimore, and through such simulated environments as OPCY, visitors experience the fantasy of a revitalized city while cosseted securely within the tourist bubble; yet the city's reality just outside the entertainment zone has not changed. Despite the improvements within the Inner Harbor, Baltimore's education system continues to crumble and urban residents increasingly are concerned about their safety. Although the industrial blight in Camden Yards has been replaced, urban residents have not had increased access to health care and their life expectancy has continued to decline. Despite the gentrification of some urban neighborhoods, the middle class has not returned to the city, which "has left Baltimore the home of the comfortable and the prison of the choice-less" (Johns Hopkins Institute for Policy Studies, 2000, p. 48). However, rather than facing these underlying socio-structural problems, contemporary cities like Baltimore seem to have a propensity for misguided reliance on the façade of (sporting) redevelopment in response to the profound challenges posed by the post-industrial condition.

8

GOING GLOBAL,
IMAGING THE LOCAL

Globalization is "a process (or set of processes) which embodies a transformation in the spatial organization of social relations and transaction—assessed in terms of their extensity, intensity, velocity and impact—generating transcontinental or interregional flows and networks of activity, interaction and the exercise of power" (Held, McGrew, Goldblatt, & Perraton, 1999, p. 16). While most contemporary commentators (Hirst and Thompson [1999] apart) would doubtless concur with this assertion as to the existence of globalizing economic, political, cultural, and technological processes, there is widespread disagreement as to their effects. This is particularly true when considering the ramifications of globalization for the future of the nation state. While many learned commentators decry the demise of the nation at the hands of rampant globalization, some display a steadfast belief in the enduring relevance of the nation as a source of identity and differentiation. This fracture is equally evident among those working in the global marketplace, particularly within the marketing and advertising nodes of transnational corporations (e.g., Sony, Volkswagen, and Disney), whose corporate footprints transcend the boundaries of nation states and who operate "simultaneously in different countries around the world, on a global scale" (Morley & Robins, 1995, p. 223). Located as it is in the "pivotal position between production and consumption, the advertising industry plays a key role in constituting the geographic boundaries of markets and in the internationalization of consumer culture" (Leslie, 1995). Consequently, it is the strategizing of the promotional arm of transnational corporate entities that provides the present focus. Certainly, the penetration of local cultures by the economics and imagery of global capitalism represents the latest and most sophisticated attempt by transnational corporations to command the widest possible market base and thereby accrue the benefits of colossal economies of scale. Rather than attempting to neuter cultural difference through a strategic global uniformity, many corporations have acknowledged that securing a profitable global presence necessitates negotiating in the language of the local. This chapter outlines some of the ways that sport—as a compelling cultural shorthand—has been appropriated by, and mobilized within, the advertising campaigns of transnational corporations as a means of contributing to the constitution and experiencing of national cultures.

Within the contemporary advertising industry it is possible to discern both indifferent and enthusiastic engagements with the concepts of nation and national identity. In terms of the former, and perhaps prompted by the hegemonic "borderless world" (Ohmae, 1990) rhetoric of the global marketplace, many advertising agency account directors eschew the utility of national cultures in providing the basis for profitable consumer segmentation and targeting. Instead, they focus on developing what are deemed to be more cost effective "global" campaigns, that circumvent national borders by creating more expansive global consumer tribes linked by lifestyle values or preferences rather than spatial location (Leslie, 1995). Numerous corporations possessing the technological wherewithal (networks facilitating the instantaneous global flow of capital and information), political approval (major Western democracies' perception of market globalization as an unavoidable force of nature), and economic structure (deregulationist initiatives that have lowered trade and tariff barriers) have sought to rationalize their products and promotional strategies into single globally focused directives. In seeking to transcend national boundaries, these corporations look to benefit from the massive economies of scale derived from the establishment of a truly global market. By way of illustration, this notion of post-national geographies of consumption (Leslie, 1995) clearly underpins the work of 180, the innovative Amsterdam agency founded by defectors from Wieden and Kennedy (the agency responsible for most of Nike's advertising).

The corporate mission of 180 speaks to universal traits, experiences, and emotions, in a manner designed to have appeal beyond the specificities of national cultural boundaries. With this objective in mind, 180's creative director Larry Frey outlined:

> When we execute things we work very hard to make sure it doesn't look like it's from one specific place and we are really picky about directors. We like international looks that make it difficult to pin down where this director makes their home. We use this checks and balances system on the music we select, on the editing techniques we use, on casting and on all of the directors we choose . . . We ask, is this thing too American, too German, too Spanish. We identify what are the styles that tend to emerge out of those countries and make a conscious effort to avoid them. (Hunter, 2000)

180's placeless universality is perhaps most graphically exemplified within their recent global "Adidas makes you do better" campaign for the sports footwear and apparel giant. In four separate television commercials, English soccer player David Beckham (clearing the streets of litter), Trinidadian sprinter Ato Boldon (returning a stolen television), Russian tennis starlet Anna Kournikova (challenging cheaters at a video arcade game), and New Zealand rugby player Jonah Lomu (rescuing a suffocating fish), all utilize their sporting or physical skills for the good of humanity. By focusing on such seemingly universal moralistic and heroic traits, the campaign transcends the nationality of the athlete and the national cultural context within which the advertisement is consumed. As Frey opined, "I think the Adidas spots we've done prove we can create and cross borders effectively" (Hunter, 2000).

In contrast to the aforementioned cultural globalism, the global-local element within the culture industries actively affirms the continued relevance of national cultures. According to this line of thinking, the "old structures and boundaries of national states and communities" (Robins, 1997, p. 12) have not been dissolved. Rather, we are ensconced in a historical moment wherein the symbolic analysts (Reich, 1991) of the global advertising industry play an ever more significant role in the process whereby the nation becomes imagined, understood, and experienced. Although the advancement of capitalism has always been about the overcoming of spatial constraints as a means of improving the flow of goods from producer to consumer (Hall, 1991; Morley & Robins, 1995), the intrinsically rationalizing logic of market capitalism initially came unstuck when faced by the "warm appeal of national affiliations and attachments" (Robins, 1997, p. 20). So, rather than attempting to neuter cultural difference through a strategic global uniformity, many corporations have realized that securing a profitable global presence requires negotiating with the local, "and by negotiate I mean it had to incorporate and partly reflect the differences it was trying to overcome" (Hall, 1991, p. 32). It is in this sense that Robins acknowledged "globalization is, in fact, about the creation of a new *global-local* nexus" (1997, p. 28). It is about the ability of transnational corporations to seamlessly operate within the language of the local, simultaneously, in multiple locations (Dirlik, 1996). As Dirlik proposed, "the radical slogan of an earlier day, 'Think globally, act locally,' has been assimilated by transnational corporations with far greater success than in any radical strategy" (1996, p. 34). Yet the locals produced in this context are little more than transnational corporations' commercially inspired inflections of local cultures. As such they are liable—though certainly not preordained—to be superficial caricatures of national cultural differences.

Dirlik continues, "The recognition of the local in marketing strategy, however, does not mean any serious recognition of the autonomy of the local, but is intended to recognize the features of the local so as to incorporate localities into the imperatives of the global" (1996, p. 34). According to the logic of global capitalism, transnational corporations that seek to be "part of that culture too" (NBC vice president J. B. Holston III, quoted in Morley & Robins, 1995, p. 117) effectively are involved in the production of localized spaces, identities, and experiences that facilitate the "continuity of flow" (Harvey, 1985, p. 145) between global production and local consumption. Hence, it is possible to refer to transnational capitalism's role in the delocalization (Castells, 1983), detraditionalization (Luke, 1996), or decentralization

(Robins, 1997) of national cultural production. In this sense, the material has been superseded by the cultural, and the physical by the symbolic, as new televisual, satellite, digital, and Internet-based technologies play an ever more central role in the mapping of national cartographies. As the key mechanism in the reconstruction of national spaces, cultures, and identities, new communications technologies are deeply involved in the "ongoing construction and reconstruction of social spaces and social relations" (Morley, 1992, p. 272). In cultural terms, the global mass media can thus be argued to have created new electronic spaces (Robins, 1990, 1997), whose presence has prompted the argument that the *space of flows* has superseded the *spaces of places* (Castells, 1996; Luke, 1996, 1999).

So, while in political and economic terms it could be argued that we are careering headlong into a "'post-national' world" (Smith, 1991, p. 143), in a cultural sense we are witnessing not a "withering," but rather a "changing" of the nation under the logic of transnational corporate capitalism (Hannerz, 1996, p. 89). Evidently Bensimon Byrne D'Arcy, the Toronto advertising agency responsible for the popular Molson Canadian "I am Canadian" advertisement, were working under similar assumptions when considering the relevance of national cultures within the contemporary global marketplace:

> Hey, I'm not a lumberjack or a fur trader.
> And I don't live in an igloo, or eat blubber, or own a dog sled.
> And I don't know Jimmy, Sally, or Susie from Canada, although I am certain they are really, really nice.
> I have a Prime Minister, not a President.
> I speak English and French, not American.
> And I pronounce it about, not a boot.
> I can proudly sew my country's flag on my backpack.
> I believe in peacekeeping, not policing; diversity not assimilation; and that the beaver is a truly proud and noble animal; a toque is a hat; a Chesterfield is a couch; and it is pronounced zed, not zee, zed!
> Canada is the second largest land mass, the first nation of hockey, and the best part of North America!
> My name is Joe, and I am Canadian!
> Thank you.

The undoubtedly humorous "I am Canadian" spot succinctly captures the type of—somewhat defensive—cultural nationalism that has evolved in a time of increasing extensity and velocity of global economic, political, cultural, and technological flows (Appadurai, 1990; Held, et al., 1999). While Canadian identity has long defined itself against the domineering cultural and economic influence of its neighbor to the south, the experience of similar engagements between global and local cultures is becoming ever more prevalent, as is the resistant (re)assertion of national and regional cultural traditions and identities in the face of such encounters. Indeed, according to Glen Hunt, Bensimon Byrne D'Arcy's creative director, "With globalization and the Internet, there are no more borders that help to define our territory.

. . . As we become less and less definable in our groups we look for something to hold onto and identify ourselves" (quoted in Fetto, 2000, p. 49). That "something to hold onto" is the reimagined and thereby reconstituted nation, which is a potent source of cultural identification and differentiation, as globalizing forces compromise its viability as an institution of political and economic organization.

While it is difficult to assess the precise impact that transnational corporate capitalism is having upon the nature and efficacy of national cultures, it is easier to point to the processes through which such changes are occurring. Given their preoccupation with knowledge-intensive, dynamic, and flexible "think work" (Allen, 1992), the marketing and advertising armatures of the new culture industries have become the core vehicles of surplus value production, and therefore capital accumulation, within late capitalist economies. In order to realize the goal of creating global-local markets for their products, transnational corporations increasingly concentrate on the promotional nodes of their respective commodity chains, thereby manipulating "the image which crosses and re-crosses linguistic frontiers much more rapidly and more easily, and which speaks across languages in a much more immediate way" (Hall, 1991, p. 27).

Following Tomlinson (1999), rather than viewing the power of transnational capitalism as distributing a "capitalist monoculture," the global strategies of postindustrial leviathans involve a greater degree of engagement with the local than is credited by many commentators. In some intellectual quarters, the resilience of the nation is widely acknowledged, but this recognition has tended to be expressed in terms of the localized consumption of global cultural products. Arguments are thus made pertaining to the necessarily varied processes of translation, adaptation, and indigenization of various cultural texts as they are appropriated within particular national locales (Appadurai, 1990; Morley, 1992; Robins, 1991; Tomlinson, 1999). The efficacy of the local is equally evident, though perhaps less researched, within the realm of global cultural production. Most significantly, it is the denizens of Madison Avenue, spiritual home to the marketing and advertising armatures of the new culture industries, who clearly recognize (and have sought to capitalize upon for their transnational corporate clientele) the mainstream populace's residual attachment to the nation. In order to recover a corporation's escalating production costs by exploiting the maximum possible market base, this new class of cultural intermediaries (Du Gay et al., 1997) must create global images and campaigns that resonate with local experience and sensibilities. As such, they understand the importance of "achieving a real equidistance, or equipresence, of perspective in relation to the whole world of their audiences and consumers" (Morley & Robins, 1995, p. 113). Far from transcending or eradicating difference, today's global advertisers recognize the central and prefigurative importance of the local, and routinely incorporate difference and particularity in their strategies (Dirlik, 1996; Morley & Robins, 1995). What we appear to be witnessing is the capitalization upon, and redefinition of, national "belonging-ness" by the promotional and marketing agents of transnational corporations intent on inserting their products into diffuse and diverse markets.

According to Bell and Campbell, sport has become one of the "world's biggest obsessions" (1999, p. 22). Clearly, advertisers and promotional innovators have operated under the assumption that, and indeed capitalized upon, the stylized excitement and glamour that characterizes most contemporary consumer-oriented sporting forms. As Daniel Beauvois of ISL, a leading sport marketing agency, has indicated, "Sport is probably the only thing that fascinates everyone in the world. . . . Many people now feel more concerned by sport than almost anything else in their lives" (quoted in Bell & Campbell, 1999, p. 22). While clearly an exaggeration—what else would one expect from an employee of one of the world's largest and most influential sport marketing agencies?—this remark suggests the way in which the corporate world has come to view sport, and its marketing potential, as a means of engaging and mobilizing consumers around the globe. It is argued then, that sport is mobilized as a major cultural signifier of nation that can engage national sensibilities, identities, and experiences. As such, sport is used as a cultural shorthand delineating particular national sentiments. That is, within the logic of transnational corporate capitalism, sport is a globally present cultural form but one that is heavily accented by local dialects. It is this notion of sport as a globally present, but locally resonant, cultural practice that advertisers seek to mobilize in their promotional strategies and campaigns.

Certainly, the Coca-Cola corporation represents a graphic example of a global corporate entity seeking to mobilize locally resonant sporting practices and personalities as a means of engaging local markets, thereby confirming its truly transnational reach and influence. In earlier phases of Coca-Cola's globalization, the corporation routinely adopted standardized advertising campaigns regardless of the national context within which consumption was being encouraged. This frequently meant the indiscriminate running of advertising campaigns originally produced for the "home" (American) market. Whether intentional or otherwise, this inevitably led to charges of a cultural imperialism: perhaps better expressed as an America flavored "Coca-Colonization," a bringing of "America to the world through Coca-Cola" (Leslie, 1995). Coca-Cola ultimately acknowledged the pitfalls of such blanket strategizing and modified its global marketing strategy, initially by producing nationally ambiguous and thereby globally inclusive advertising campaigns exemplified by the "I'd like to buy the world a Coke" television commercial that first aired in 1971 (Prendergrast, 1998). Latterly, in an attempt to further distance its brand image from its storied American roots, certain Coca-Cola campaigns focused more narrowly on specific regional and national cultures, many of which used sport as the vehicle of local inflection. In terms of the former strategy, the "Eat Football, Sleep Football, Drink Coca-Cola" campaign is most relevant to this discussion. In separate pan-North American (American Football), pan-European (Association Football), and pan-Australasian (Australian Rules Football) television advertisements, Coca-Cola was unself-consciously conjugated with regional sporting cultures through commercial narratives that featured the passion, intensity, and excitement of the various football codes and, by inference, that of drinking Coca-Cola.

Coca-Cola's subsequent incursion into the realm of national cultures is most poetically illustrated in the 1996 "Red" commercial developed by Wieden and Kennedy, Portland, as a means of furthering Coca-Cola's presence on the Indian subcontinent. The very real poverty experienced by much of India's vast populace would suggest little consumer interest in a carbonated soft drink that to many would represent an unattainable luxury. Nevertheless, the sheer volume of the Indian population (approximately 1 billion) means that—although small in percentage terms of the total populace—the potential market for Coca-Cola, India's middle and upper classes, is sizeable enough to encourage global corporations to enter the Indian market. This was the rationale behind the "Red" commercial, a 60-second depiction of the vibrancy and complexity of Indian culture keyed on the byline "Passion has a color." The color in this, Coca-Cola instance, obviously being red: the red of chili peppers drying in fields; of a Rajasthani man's turban; of the *bindis* adorning women's foreheads; of the *dupata* drying on river banks; of the cricket balls that regularly punctuate the visual narrative; and, of course, the red of the Coca-Cola brand symbolism, subtly and seamlessly inserted into this panoramic sweep of Indian culture. Using hypnotic Sufi-inspired devotional music along with all these images, the commercial brazenly synthesizes India's passion for cricket (red ball) with a desired passion for Coca-Cola (red logo). Through this association with the cricket thematic, Coca-Cola sought to thrust itself into the mainstream of Indian culture by providing itself with a seemingly natural place within local culture and experience.

McDonald's is another common signifier of transnational capitalist expansion, as well as being among the most targeted recipient (along with Nike) of anti-capitalist protest. Having long nurtured its explicitly American demeanor, in recent times, McDonald's appears more concerned with melding its brand identity into the superficial vagaries of local culture. In Britain, perhaps unsurprisingly, McDonald's has regularly drawn upon British football (soccer) heroes in order to cement its place in the British national imaginary. In one television advertisement, Alan Shearer, then England's football captain, embarks on a nostalgic journey through his native Newcastle, visiting his old school, his youth football club, and then, of course, a McDonald's restaurant. Significantly, the advertisement draws upon the best-known cultural signifiers of Newcastle: Shearer himself,; Newcastle United, the football club for which he plays; and, the evocative Tyne Bridges. Hence, McDonald's invokes the cultural specificities of an English locale as it embeds itself ever deeper in the experience of everyday British life. A more recent promotional offering operates more explicitly at the national level. As an element in the commercial production process, McDonald's revised and revisited the now-fabled 1966 FIFA World Cup Final between England and West Germany. The advertisement depicts Geoff Hurst, mythologized in English history for his three goals in the 1966 World Cup final, scoring his third goal in the game, a goal made immortal in English consciousness by the accompanying commentary from Kenneth Wolstenholme, "There's some people on the pitch, they think it's all over, it is now!" Rather than the ball entering the net for Hurst's third goal, the ad revises history by showing a streaker running on to the pitch, causing Hurst to miss the shot. The ad concludes with Hurst consuming the new product in McDonald's range, the McDonald's Triple Burger with "twisty fries," the narrative defining the revised footage as "a triple with a twist." The Shearer and Hurst campaigns, however parodically, attempt to insert the global McDonald's brand into the imaged recollections of the national psyche. Specifically, the advertisements used selected imagery, both concrete signifiers and sporting celebrities, to nurture the distinctly local national demeanor of the global brand.

The advertising and promotional operatives within transnational corporations, that actively endorse the implausibility of a global culture that extinguishes national difference, have also constructed initiatives that seek to engage a multitude of markets at the same time. Specifically, these campaigns rationalize the escalating costs of reaching the maximum market base by producing single, multivocal, multinationally oriented texts. These texts appeal to a number of different local markets and thus simultaneously exhibit both the global reach and the local resonance of the brand. Despite the globalizing cosmopolitan logic underpinning such campaigns, the producers of these initiatives are aware that the particularities of place and culture can never be entirely transcended. Rather, they recognize that "globalization is like putting together a jigsaw puzzle: it is a matter of inserting a multiplicity of localities into the overall picture of a new global system" (Morley & Robins, 1995, p. 116). For instance, through its transnational advertising agency, Wieden and Kennedy, who have offices in Portland, New York, London, Amsterdam and Tokyo, Nike has produced a series of global multivocal promotional campaigns that select various "authentic" national traditions in the form of sporting heroes and combine them to exhibit both the global ubiquity and the local pertinence of the brand. This trend is most evident within Nike's expansion into the nationally charged global football marketplace: An initiative prompted by Nike's recognition that if it were to become a truly global sport corporation, it would need to secure a global presence within what is unquestionably the global game (Giulianotti, 1999).

Initially, Nike's multivocal football campaigns selected specific physical locales and corroborated them with images of complementary national football heroes, as they sought to engage the national sensibilities and affiliations of multiple and dislocated consumers. Nike's first incursion into global football was realized in their 1994 "Wall" campaign, created within Wieden and Kennedy's main office in Portland. In this spot Nike selected a series of football heroes, hijacked from the cultural memory of particular localities, and positioned them as representatives of their respective nations. Significantly, the advertisement depicted these celebrities within their own localities, and it was a football that orbited a time-space compressed "Nikeworld." The advertisement highlighted various football celebrities, moored, quite literally, in the bricks and mortar of their own locales, while kicking a ball around a compressed globe. The ad depicts Eric Cantona, a former French international and Manchester United player on a billboard next to the Eiffel Tower in Paris. Cantona, sporting a Manchester United shirt (perhaps to engage the

French and the global Manchester United marketplace at one and the same time), beats a nondescript opponent also moored onto the billboard and kicks the ball over the English Channel, past the Houses of Parliament and into a billboard in London's Leicester Square. Here, Ian Wright, then of Arsenal and England controls the ball and fires it past Tower Bridge. The ball continues its flight around the world, passing between various national symbols and heroes, such as a Rio de Janeiro beach and the Brazilian player Romario, finally ending up in Mexico City where the ball is saved by the Mexican goalkeeper, Jorge Campos.

As Nike's global football strategizing has evolved, however, explicit representations of place would appear to have been discarded in preference to a sole focus on football heroes as signifiers of national cultural difference. In 1996, Wieden and Kennedy's Amsterdam office produced the direct successor of the "Wall" campaign, with an advertisement, titled "Good versus Evil," which highlighted football stars from a whole range of countries demonstrating how the game can unite the planet against the forces of evil. "Good versus Evil" did not define the other (opponents) as place-bound; rather the selected heroes were pitted against opponents that were both temporally and spatially ambiguous. Set in a Roman amphitheater, the ad depicted the selected celebrities (good) playing, and ultimately beating, a team lead by a representation of the devil and his underlings (evil). Herein, Nike complicated local affiliation, for some players wore their national team uniforms, and others sported their club uniforms. Paolo Maldini and Ronaldo, for example, wore their Italian and Brazilian national team shirts, respectively. However, Ian Wright (Arsenal), Patrick Kluivert (Ajax), Luis Figo (Barcelona), and Eric Cantona (Manchester United) wore their club shirts, arguably to appeal not only to a multitude of markets but also an attempt to capitalize on the market within which the player was best known. Cantona, resplendent in Manchester United livery, proved the central figure in the advertisement, by destroying "evil" with his deadly penalty kick. At the time, Cantona was better known for his exploits with Manchester United than with the French national team. Evidently, Nike sought to capitalize on the global appeal of Manchester United (and likewise in the case of Figo, Kluivert, and Wright, with Barcelona, Ajax, and Arsenal, respectively) as symbols that would better engage multiple markets than national team uniforms. And yet, given Italy's and especially Brazil's globally acknowledged and celebrated football heritage, Maldini and Ronaldo wearing national team uniforms could be seen as an attempt by Nike to constitute a global (as well as national) market for these globally admired national football dynasties.

The direct successor to Nike's "Good versus Evil" campaign once again emanated from Wieden and Kennedy in Amsterdam and was timed to coincide with the 1998 World Cup. Nike "Beach" rendered a new assemblage of burgeoning football celebrities (Ronaldo, Ariel Ortega, Christian Vieri, Nankwo Kanu, Ibrahim Ba, Roberto Carlos, Luis Enrique, and Hernan Crespo). These players were located in a distinctly ambiguous space, a remarkably indistinct beach idyll that could have been located anywhere from the Brazilian beach to the French Riviera or Australia's Gold Coast. The transnational thematic has been transposed subsequently to Nike's latest band of football celebrities (now christened the Nike "Geoforce") in the 2000 television commercial "The Mission." Within this highly stylized commercial, the Nike Geoforce set out to reclaim the new "GeoMerlin" soccer ball stolen from Nike by "Uri," a fictional character who seeks to impose a defensive approach to the game. The GeoMerlin soccer ball is seen as a threat to Uri's dour football, a game dominated by standardized and mechanized robots that replace human players and, thus, eliminate irrational and risk-taking individuals from the game. The "Mission" advertisements, and its accompanying promotional mechanisms, depict how Nike's Geoforce use their inventive football skills to storm the defensive fortress, destroy the robotic leader of Uri's operation, blow up Uri's headquarters and his soccer-playing robots, and return the prototype ball to Nike. The Geoforce was made up of Edgar Davids (the Netherlands), Oliver Bierhoff (Germany), Francesco Totti (Italy), Jose Guardiola (Spain), Luis Figo (Portugal), Lilian Thuram (France), Andy Cole (England), Dwight Yorke (Trinidad and Tobago), and Hidetoshi Nakata (Japan), all wearing the latest range of Nike "Mercurial" apparel. According to Nike (www.nikefootball.com), these "agents" have been selected for this particular mission because of their demonstrated courage, aggression, determination, "deadliness," and their natural athletic ability. In selecting these "agents" and their concomitant skills, Nike is involved in the transnational reconstitution of the cultural experiences of football, yet at the same time, Nike retains elements of particular localities through the selection of sporting heroes whose distinctly different skills evoke distinctly different national (football) cultures (Giulianotti, 1999). For example, the German, Bierhoff, is defined as a natural leader who is creative, intelligent, and determined, while the Japanese Nakata is composed, consistent, and instinctive. As such, Nike incorporates within its transnational campaign the very local differences that global capitalism has attempted to overcome (Hall, 1991). However, rather than romanticize or celebrate the sophistication of such campaigns, it is important to say that these campaigns point to the ways in which transnational corporations are providing commercially inspired representations of locality. In this case, Nike has done little more than select celebrities who represent a depthless caricature of national cultural differences, sensibilities, and experiences; modern nation-statehood effectively is replaced by late capitalist corporate-nationhood.

Like Nike, Adidas has produced transnational campaigns that are multivocal in nature by selecting particular national heroes and events with which audiences in different localities can affiliate. The futuristic "Soccer Reinvented" campaign featured "Team Adidas," made up of, among others, the Italian Alessandro Del Piero, the Argentinean Fernando Redondo, the Dutchman Edwin van der Sar, the Englishman Paul Gascoigne, and the American John Harkes. The advertisement depicts two teams of identical clones, each kitted out in bland Adidas uniforms. The only difference is that one team dons Adidas "Predator" cleats and provides player names on the back of their uniforms. Not surprisingly, the "predator" team plays the more inventive, exhilarating, and ultimately successful football. Like Nike's "Good versus Evil," the game is played in a "non-place" (Augé, 1995), a vacuous, neo-stadium resembling an immense bank vault devoid of signs, symbols, or color. The only spectators in the stadium are depthless simulations (Baudrillard, 1983), for the "fans" in this campaign are surface representations spatially constrained in television screens adorning a small area of the vast stadium. The advertisement thus eliminates physical place and replaces it with a spatial ambiguity, a "placenessness" that removes any relational or historical attachment the consumer may have to a particular sport stadium (Bale, 1998, p. 268). By removing all referents to place, but selecting national football heroes, Nike and Adidas are able to promote their brands transnationally, effectively engaging and invoking national sensibilities and experiences within a multitude of markets at the same time.

Clearly, the cultural innovators responsible for global marketing and promotional strategies are keenly attuned to the continued resonance of the nation within the logic of transnational corporate capitalism. In exposing the durability and resilience of the nation as a cultural entity, it is possible to refute the "end of the nation" rhetoric rooted in the global panic brought about by the instantiation of a globally homogenous commercial culture. In many ways, the nation has assumed a new importance, in that it has become a central and prefigurative element in global promotional initiatives. However, initial investigations suggest that these commercially inspired reflections are likely to be depthless caricatures of nation that delineate particular national contexts through drawing out, or selecting, stylized signifiers of (sporting) traditions, pastimes, and celebrities. Of interest here is the centrality of sporting forms and sporting celebrities in what Hannerz (1996, p. 89) describes as a "changing" of the nation under the logic of transnational corporate capitalism. Sporting spectacles and celebrities, or perhaps more accurately, commercially inspired representations of sport that emphasize entertainment, glamour, and at times violence, are increasingly incorporated into these transnational campaigns. This observation points to a troubling new global problem: that cultures, both sporting and national, are increasingly shaped by an external commercial locus of control. Clearly, we need to be attuned, and ready to respond, to the political and cultural economies propelling these "new dynamics of re-localization" (Morley & Robins, 1995, p. 115).

Conclusion

THE END OF SPORT HISTORY?

In 1989 Francis Fukuyama's article "The End of History" appeared in *The National Interest* and ignited a fierce debate over the nature of contemporary, and indeed future, socio-structural existence. According to Fukuyama, the solidifying global hegemony of Western liberalism, ushering the protracted conclusion to the Cold War, foretold the "total exhaustion of viable systematic alternatives," and hence predicted the "end of history as such: that is, the end point of mankind's ideological evolution and the universalization of Western liberal democracy as the final form of human government" (Fukuyama, 1989, p. 3). As with any such grand assertions, Fukuyama received a welter of criticism, specifically directed at the perceived totalistic Americo-centrism implicit in his argument. The "Third Way" centrism of subsequent Clinton, Blair, and Schröder administrations would also appear to mark a shift in the political landscape, thereby challenging Fukuyama's position. However, some commentators, particularly those from the intellectual left, tacitly endorsed the "end of history" thesis when chiding Clinton and Blair for being the torchbearers of the 1980s New Right project. In muted Fukuyama-esque tones, Stuart Hall observed that, rather than reinventing the Left, Blairism was disappointingly faithful to the tenets of Thatcherism, prompting Hall to parody New Labour as the "Great Moving Nowhere Show" (Hall, 1998). Far from being incontrovertible, Fukuyama's position nevertheless offers a suggestive starting point for interpreting the relationships between politics, economics, and culture at the beginning of the twenty-first century. Furthermore, these ideas are particularly germane to those interested in deciphering the corporate sport order that dominates contemporary sporting culture.

Prefigured on an economic system shorn of overt government intervention that regulates itself according to the "natural" rhythms of the marketplace (or so neo-liberal "invisible hand" apologists would have us believe), the complementarity between laissez-faire, free market economics, and ideologically individualist governments is self-evident (Hobsbawm, 1998). Despite numerous catastrophes resulting from the adoption of unfettered economic deregulation and privatization—most notably the human and ecological tragedies unfolding in the former Soviet Union and Indonesia—there persists a largely unquestioned acceptance of neo-liberalism as the economic modus operandi. Hence, Fukuyama's notion of a globalizing liberal democracy simultaneously proclaims the end of economic and political history, and "the market could be declared the final form of human history itself" (Jameson, 1998, p. 88).

During this time of global "free-market triumphalism" (Hobsbawm, 1998, p. 6), sporting culture has also been appropriated by oligopolistic transnational conglomerates. Indeed, the sport industry is a vivid example of Ernest Mandel's (1999) third multinational phase in the evolution of capitalism. This prognosis is substantiated by even the most cursory examination of the contemporary sporting universe: sport franchises and leagues commandeered by—or indeed turned into—transnational corporations seeking to add multiple revenue streams derived from the all-important entertainment economy; sport spectacles manipulated by commercial media outlets pursuing the audience demographic most desirable to their corporate advertisers; and, sport stars as embodied advertisements acting on behalf of their endorsement affiliations. From Los Angeles to London, Sydney to Sao Paolo, Tokyo to Turin, such is the uniformity of the corporatized sport economy that the assemblage of players (corporations, networks, athletes) may change, but the product (media-entertainment experiences) and purpose (profit maximization) are unerringly similar. While distinctions between the NFL Super Bowl and FIFA World Cup Final may have been palpable during the formative stages of the global sport economy (Real, 1989), today it is becoming increasingly difficult to differentiate between the constitution and experience of these and other major sport spectacles (e.g., the Tooheys New Super 12 Final, the Coca-Cola Football League Championship, or NASCAR's Pepsi 400). Hyper-commercial organization, formulaic production, and trite hagiography combine to create a ubiquitous late capitalist "structure of [sporting] feeling" (Williams, 1981) that goes beyond traditional sporting, and indeed national, boundaries. These "prolympic" (Donnelly, 1996b) sports are less contexts for the expression of national cultural difference, and more indicative of pervasive political, economic, and cultural processes shaping the global sport system.

Although sport is becoming ever more homogenized by the globalizing forces of the media-entertainment industrial complex, it is important to acknowledge the varying degrees to which particular sports have been engulfed by late capitalism. According to Fukuyama, histories are expressed in and through localized struggles over forms of governance. From this assertion, he makes the distinction between states "still in history" and those "at the end of history": essentially a separation between developing (historical) and developed (post-historical) political economies (Fukuyama, 1989). This mode of differentiation is applicable to the contemporary sporting arena, wherein certain sport forms are "still in history," while others are perceptibly "at the end of history." Until recently it would have been possible to cite a number of sports "still in history," as indicated by ongoing struggles for survival against the perceived threat of corporate capitalism (e.g., ultimate frisbee, rugby union, and mountaineering). However, these and other one-time harbingers of traditional (non-commercial) sporting values are in the midst of capitulating to the late capitalist marketplace. For example, organizations such as US Track and Field, English Test and County Cricket Board, and AMF Bowling Worldwide, have been involved in aggressive structural and cultural reformations motivated by the desire to become more appealing to the denizens of the sport-media-entertainment complex. These sporting bodies may be "still in history," in the process of evolving, but they aspire to the post-historical inertia that would signal membership in the new sporting establishment.

Sport practices positioned "at the end of history" are those that have already succumbed, willingly or otherwise, to the advances of transnational corporate capitalism. The National Basketball Association, the Australian Football League, and even the Olympic Games (until recently perceived as a sacrosanct bastion of anti-commercialism) are all examples of explicitly commercial entities focused on profit maximization–through the delivery of entertaining sport products–as their unashamed and overarching goals. The domineering cultural and economic presence of these hyper-commercial spectacles effectively nullifies the perceived viability of alternatives to the corporate sport model. So, competing elements within the contemporary sporting universe are either firmly entrenched in post-historical mode, are actively seeking its realization, or are rapidly disappearing from popular sporting consciousness. In a Fukuyamian sense, the end of sport history would seem to be upon us.

Although the hegemonic positioning of late capitalist corporate sport proclaims the end point of sport history, we are nevertheless presently bombarded by historical sporting referents within product design, advertising, television broadcasting, the celebrity economy, and the built environment. Close examination reveals that this apparent "historical" contradiction is anything but. The prevailing sporting historicism is propagated by the very conditions of contemporary existence responsible for the end of sporting evolution. In Jameson's terms, contemporary sporting culture can thus be characterized by a "return of history in the midst of the prognosis of the demise of historical telos" (Jameson, 1991, p. xii). So what is it about late capitalism that has spawned this "return" to (sport) history, and what is the nature of the (sport) history to which we are returning?

The demise of alternatives to free market neo-liberalism (socialism, communism, welfare capitalism) in the last third of the twentieth century, coupled with the stagnation of Fordist production and post-war advances in mass communication and manufacturing (particularly those related to television and computer technologies), advanced an era of flexible specialization and accumulation wherein economies of scale (mass output) have been replaced by economies of scope (varied output). Within this post-Fordist regime of economic production, consumers are bombarded with an ever-expanding array of new items across product lines. The goal is to fragment the traditional mass market into more compelling and lucrative consumer niches that would, in aggregate, increase market share (see Amin, 1994; Harvey, 1989). Evidently, the transition to post-Fordist production was contingent on the intensification of what Poster (1990) described as the "mode of information," particularly as it related to the rapid dissemination of knowledge of new products and changing product styles. Facilitating such transformations in the capitalist system, the new culture industries (media, advertising, marketing), and their core product (information), assumed primacy in the production process over more traditional modes of industrial manufacture, much of which has been relocated to the industrializing peripheries of the global economic system. Since carefully manufactured symbolic or sign values stimulate the flow of capital within the contemporary economy, the commodity has been usurped by the commodity-sign as the core of capitalist exchange. As a consequence, the unrelenting output of the new culture industries within the late capitalist economy has facilitated the ascension of symbolic value over the use and exchange values that dominated earlier stages in capitalist evolution. This has led to the postmodern imaged civilization characterized by cultural artifice, depthlessness, and discontinuity of culture (Jameson, 1991; Kearney, 1989).

The incessant production of commercially based images associated with the postmodern "implosive socius of signs" (Best & Kellner, 1991, p. 89) has created a "vast synthesis of fictions and realities into which traditional reference points collapse" (Featherstone, 1983, p. 6), including the modern meta-narratives of universal knowledge, progress, evolution, and thereby history. Confounding the ability to think of the present in traditionally historical terms—as part of an evolving age, epoch, or conjuncture—postmodern cultural logics of ontological flux and indeterminacy have been charged with contributing to a palpable weakening of modern linear and evolutionary historicism. With the endless cycle of product and stylistic innovation associated with post-Fordist regimes of flexible accumulation, the material and symbolic world is "changing constantly and arbitrarily," primarily in order to increase sales. Hence, the "value of the new and innovative is lost in this steady stream of variation that goes nowhere" (Gartman, 1998). The present thus becomes a random moment, which may or may not bear any relationship to the past, or indeed to the future. Ironically, with this crisis of the present, "producers of [postmodern] culture have nowhere to turn but to the past" in their attempts to design angst-assuaging representations of contemporary existence (Jameson, 1991, pp. 6, 17–18).

Postmodernism's turn to the past is most evident in the work of architects Michael Graves (Public Services Building, Portland), Charles Moore (Piazza d'Italia, New Orleans), and the later work of Philip Johnson (AT&T Building, New York), all of whom mined and amalgamated cultural referents from various historical periods into an eclectic contemporary aesthetic. As well as architecture, the "random cannibalization" (Jameson, 1991, p. 18) of the past as a means of constituting the present in times of ontological crisis, is discernible in film, television, art, advertising, and commercial design. It also exudes from retail outlets that satiate—and, indeed, help to stimulate—the nostalgic yearnings of many historically uncertain consumers:

> Restoration Hardware is unabashedly nostalgic. But wander around one of their stores and you begin to realize it's a strange kind of nostalgia that's being promoted. It's totally amorphous. The focus isn't on any particular time period, but rather on the past in general. The store sells a type of furniture wax inspired by a formula dating back to the 1700s, turn-of-the-century lamps, and schoolroom clocks from the 1950s. Also, the store is no stickler for authenticity. Furniture is designed to suit modern shoppers accustomed to modern conveniences. (Chaplin, 1999, p. 69)

History endures, but only in the form of historical simulations (Baudrillard, 1987), stylistic expressions of "pastness" that "have no understanding of history in depth, but instead are offered a contemporary creation, more costume drama and re-enactment than critical discourse" (Hewison, 1987, quoted in Harvey, 1989, p. 87). In this way, postmodern culture fosters a pseudo-authentic historical sensibility, as opposed to a genuine historically grounded understanding of the past, or, indeed, of the present. By rendering history a vast, yet random, archive of events, styles, and icons, that can be appropriated in any combination or sequence, commercial culture has fatally disrupted traditional chronology, leading to the compression of time (Harvey, 1989). As a consequence, we are ensconced in a culture of the present tense that has propagated a "historical amnesia" among the consuming populace (Jameson, 1998, p. 90). Surrounded by historical simulations, signs of "pastness" are widely revered, but precise provenances are little known and little cared about. A piece of "Mission style" furniture may be an obligatory feature in the suburban home of today's Americans—at least of those who aspire to the latest Sunday supplement chic—but there exists little widespread knowledge of, or interest in, the genealogy of the "Mission" aesthetic. What matters is that it is *the* latest approved lifestyle signifier. Differently put, history has become little more than a design element, a "superficial decoration" (Gartman, 1998, p. 125) used to differentiate products (and, by association, consumers) in the late capitalist marketplace.

Sport's expansive and comprehensive appropriation by the forces of late capitalism has meant today's corporatized sport environment is replete with such instances of this *random cannibalization* of the sporting past. The remainder of this conclusion outlines three illustrative vignettes pertaining to the superficial historicism through which products, celebrities, and spectacles are differentiated within the crowded sport marketplace. First, a Reebok "Ryan Giggs" television commercial, aired in the UK in the early 1990s exemplifies the commercial manufacture of history as pure simulation, and the attendant attenuation of conventional chronology. Within the 30-second spot, Ryan Giggs—a Manchester United and Wales forward and fledgling football idol of the moment—was provided with an instant Manchester United pedigree by being linked to a simulated expression of the club's heritage. The commercial opens with nostalgic images of youthful football supporters, circa 1950, bedecked in red and white scarves and enthusiastically waving football rattles. Setting the scene, the familiar voice of Bobby Charlton, a revered symbol of Manchester United's past triumphs and tragedies, encourages the audience to "Just imagine their [Manchester United's] greatest side." Charlton's call to historical reflection is subsequently curtailed by the unfolding televisual narrative, which selects Manchester United's transhistoric team of the ages for the audience.

Through computer-generated composition, accompanied by the voice of Kenneth Wolstenholme (a renowned English football commentator) and the strains of an emotive orchestral backdrop (ironically, an arrangement of the American Civil War song "Marching through Georgia"), Giggs is seamlessly inserted into a televisual pastiche of noted players drawn from various periods Manchester United's post-war history. Dismantling historical boundaries, the advertisement depicts Giggs as the orchestrator and finisher of a move that is designed to trigger the embodied memories of English football's collective consciousness (George Best's hip swerve, Steve Coppel's scuttling runs, and Bobby Charlton's passing). Having curled the ball with the outside of his left foot into the top right corner of the net (a move thrust into collective consciousness as a sign of "Giggsness"), Giggs is then flanked in celebration by the talismanic Best and Charlton, as Charlton himself proclaims "Their greatest ever side. Giggs would be in it, and he'd be wearing Reebok boots." Herein, Reebok erased historically bounded differences in playing personnel, style, team success, and even corporate sponsor, as it grafted Giggs—and by association Reebok—into the eternal present of Manchester United's lucrative heritage industry, which sets it apart from equally historical but less successfully marketed professional football clubs.

Preying on the *historical amnesia* instantiated through the outpourings of postmodern culture, the renaissance of Muhammad Ali's imaged identity in America in 1990s speaks to an even more cynical form of superficial historical revisionism. During the 1970s when Ali reached the nadir of his career in the US, he was controversial: outwardly Muslim, Pan-Africanist, anti-colonial, and against American imperialism. Yet according to Barry Frank, his agent with IMG, by the late 1990s Ali has become "universally loved" (Horovitz, 1999, p. 2A). Some may credit Ali's evolution from pariah to deity to an American civic consciousness that is more progressive and accepting of difference. More skeptical commentators attribute this metamorphosis to the workings of Ali's promotional entourage—including the nine IMG employees that comprise "Team Ali"—who shaped his mediated identity into one that positively engages the mainstream sensibilities of America's consuming populace.

Through carefully and consistently choreographed advertising campaigns for Apple, Wheaties, Morton's steakhouse, and Rockport shoes, and judiciously chosen public appearances (most notably as the igniter of the Olympic flame at the 1996 Atlanta Games), Ali corroborated his status as a cultural icon of historical proportions, while simultaneously erasing his threatening political stridency.

Vague allusions to his controversial and outspoken past, coupled with the public sympathy derived from his apparent physical decline due to the ravages of Parkinson's Disease, gave Ali an aura of authentic individuality: a prized commodity in the culturally and politically myopic 1990s. As a result, Ali became a culturally resonant exemplar of postmodern American individualism and was thereby symbolically severed from his role as torchbearer for a collective struggle against various forms of American oppression. Ali has thus become an example of what the novelist E. L. Doctorow described as the "disappearance of the American radical past" (quoted in Jameson, 1991, p. 24), a potentially progressive figure whose insurgent history has been creatively revised, and by that means neutered, in the name of commercial avarice.

Finally, returning to architecture, the aforementioned crucible of postmodern cultural innovation, the built sporting environment is replete with examples of architectural "repositories of history" (Bale, 1994), which consciously draw on particular structural and symbolic elements as a means of engaging the collective memory. Hellmuth, Obata, and Kassabaum Sports Facilities Group (HOK) is perhaps most renowned for advancing "retro" sport architecture, particularly the ballparks it has designed for numerous American baseball organizations (e.g., Oriole Park at Camden Yards in Baltimore, Jacobs Field in Cleveland, and Coors Field in Denver). A similar synthesis of faux historical authenticity and technological innovation dominates the interior design concept of the recently opened Manhattan Nike Town, a reproduction of a classic New York City school gymnasium. According to John Hoke, Nike Image Design Creative Director, "We looked to classical examples of historic buildings with contemporary interiors to reflect the contrasts of Nike's sports heritage and product innovation" (http://www.saigon.com/~nike/niketown.htm). Such examples of "high-tech nostalgia" (Epstein, 1996, p. A13) are pure architectural simulations: highly stylized and impressionistic renderings of traditional elements drawn from across historical periods and melded with state-of-the-art technology. As such, they graphically exemplify the historical artifice, depthlessness, and discontinuous demeanor of postmodern culture (Jameson, 1991; Kearney, 1989).

This concluding discussion offers what could be perceived as a disheartening vision of a contemporary sport culture dominated by an unquestioned adherence to the tenets of corporate capitalism (evidencing the demise of sporting evolution), and a concomitant emergence of a commercially motivated, essentially superficial, and politically neutered historicism (with the bland re-animation of historical sporting signifiers). In this contradictory moment, the practice of socio-cultural contextualization (of the type advanced most suggestively by C. Wright Mills' [1959] "sociological imagination" as outlined in the introduction to the book) is one of the few remaining avenues through which it may be possible to disrupt the creeping politico-economic inertia and cultural banality of contemporary sport. So, let us be wary of recent curricular drifts toward the banality of sport management and marketing, themselves corollaries of late capitalism's invasive influence. Rather, it becomes increasingly important to engage in rigorous and thoughtful critique of the hyper-commercial sporting cultures that transfix many of our lives. In other words, while as enthusiastic sport consumers we may be temporarily intoxicated by the intensity of a Dodgers' rally in the bottom of the ninth or a heroic feat by an American Olympian, we should not overlook the economic, technological, and political forces and relations that influence our understandings and experiences of contemporary sport. Whether we recognize it or not, the practice of sporting contextualization offers the possibility of nurturing a truly critical sporting and social consciousness, through which the consuming populace can begin to make sense of "the totality of its world." As the novelist E. M. Forster commanded, "Only connect! . . . Live in fragments no longer." In terms of cultural studies' preoccupation with the contextual and contextuality (with regard to the identification of particular forms and patterns of social existence and the amelioration of attendant forms of social injustice and inequality), it is important that we "give a better understanding of where 'we' are so that 'we' can get somewhere better" (Grossberg, 1992, p. 21). For, in both sporting and societal terms, it is difficult to accept that *this* (whether referring to late capitalist sport or late capitalist society in general) is as good as it gets.

REFERENCES

ABC. (1996, September 2). Nightline.

Albrow, M. (1996). *The global age: State and society beyond modernity.* Stanford: Stanford University Press.

Allen, J. (1992). Post-industrialism and post-Fordism. In S. Hall, D. Held, and A. McGrew (eds.), *Modernity and its futures* (pp. 168–204). Cambridge: Polity Press.

Allen, K. (1996). Advertising blitz to Introduce Woods to the world at large. *USA Today,* August 29, p. 11C.

Alms, R. (1994). Globe trotters: NBA takes a world view of marketing. *Dallas Morning News,* November 1, p. 1D.

Alt, J. (1983). Sport and cultural reification: From ritual to mass consumption. *Theory, Culture & Society,* 1(3), pp. 93–107.

Alter, J. (1996–1997). Thinking of family values. *Newsweek,* 30, pp. 32, 35.

Althusser, L. (1971). *Lenin and philosophy and other essays.* London: New Left Books.

Amin, A. (ed.) (1994). *Post-Fordism: A reader.* Oxford: Blackwell.

Anderson, D. (2001). Pro sports of the times: It's more program than pro. *The New York Times,* February 9, p. D1.

Andrews, D. L. (1996). The fact(s) of Michael Jordan's blackness: Excavating a floating racial signifier. *Sociology of Sport Journal,* 13(2), pp. 125–158.

Andrews, D. L. (1997). The [Trans]National Basketball Association: American commodity-sign culture and global localization. In A. Cvetovitch and D. Kellner (eds.), *Politics and cultural studies between the global and the local* (pp. 72–101). Boulder, CO: Westview Press.

Andrews, D. L. (1998). Feminizing Olympic reality: Preliminary dispatches from Baudrillard's Atlanta. *International Review for the Sociology of Sport,* 33(1), pp. 5–18.

Andrews, D. L. (1998). Excavating Michael Jordan: Notes on a critical pedagogy of sporting representation. In G. Rail (ed.), *Sport and postmodern times* (pp. 185–220). New York: SUNY Press.

Andrews, D. L. (1999). Dead or alive?: Sports history in the late capitalist moment. *Sporting Traditions: Journal of the Australian Society for Sports History,* 16(1), pp. 73–85.

Andrews, D. L. (2001). Sport. In R. Maxwell (ed.), *Culture works: The political economy of culture* (pp. 131–162). Minneapolis: University of Minnesota Press.

Andrews, D. L. (ed.) (2001). *Michael Jordan Inc.: Corporate sport, media culture, and late modern America*. Albany, NY: SUNY Press.

Andrews, D. L., Carrington, B., Jackson, S., and Mazur, Z. (1996). Jordanscapes: A preliminary analysis of the global popular. *Sociology of Sport Journal,* 13(4), pp. 428–457.

Andrews, D. L., and Jackson, S. J. (2001). Introduction: Sport celebrities, public culture, and private experience. In D. L. Andrews and S. J. Jackson (eds.), *Sport stars: The cultural politics of sport celebrity* (pp. 1–19). London: Routledge.

Andrews, D. L., Pitter, R., Zwick, D., and Ambrose, D. (1997). Soccer's racial frontier: Sport and the segregated suburbanization of contemporary America. In G. Armstrong and R. Giulianotti (eds.), *Entering the field: New perspectives on world football* (pp. 261–281). Oxford: Berg.

Anon. (1993). Soccer's last frontier. *The Economist,* December 4, p. 100.

Anon. (1996). Major League Soccer: Growing Stars. *The Economist,* April 13, p. 100.

Anon. (2000). Held to ransom. *Marketing Week,* March 9, p. 28.

Anon. (2001). XFL helps UPN ratings surge: Sunday game doubles typical viewership. *The Florida Times-Union,* February 6. p. E6.

Anon. (2001). 54 million watch XFL. *The New York Times,* February 7, p. D6.

Anon. (2002). The week that was. *Broadcasting and Cable,* March 18, p. 16.

Anon. (2002). NBA renews international TV deals. *NBA.com,* Available at: http://www.nba.com/news/international_tv_deals_renewed_021112.html.

Appadurai, A. (1990). Disjuncture and difference in the global cultural economy. *Theory, Culture & Society,* 7, pp. 295–310.

Archer, B. (1999). What the McDonald's ad says about you. *The Guardian,* June 18, p. 12

Arundel, J., and Roche, M. (1998). Media, sport and local identity: British rugby league and Sky TV. In M. Roche (ed.), *Sport, popular culture and identity* (vol. 5, pp. 57–91). Aachen: Meyer & Meyer Verlag.

Assael, S., and Mooneyham, M. (2002). *Sex, lies, and headlocks: The real story of Vince McMahon and the World Wrestling Federation*. New York: Crown.

The Associated Press (2001). XFL ratings falling fast, February 26.

Atkinson, M. (2002). Fifty million viewers can't be wrong: Professional wrestling, sports-entertainment, and mimesis. *Sociology of Sport Journal,* 19(1), pp. 47–66.

Augé, M. (1995). *Non-places: Introduction to an anthropology of supermodernity*. London: Verso.

Auletta, K. (1997). The next corporate order: American Keiretsu. *The New Yorker,* pp. 225–227.

Austrian, Z., & Rosentraub, M. (2002). Cities, sports and economicchange: A retrospective assessment. *Journal of Urban Affairs,* 24 (5), 549–563.

Baade, R., and Dye, R. (1988). An analysis of the economic rationale for public subsidies of sports stadiums. *Annals of Regional Science,* 22(2), pp. 37–47.

Baade, R., and Dye, R. (1990). The impact of stadiums and professional sports on metropolitan area development. *Growth and Change,* 21(2), pp. 1–14.

Baim, D. (1994). *The sports stadium as a municipal investment*. Westport, CT: Greenwood Press.

Bale, J. (1994). *Landscapes of modern sport*. London: Leicester University Press.

Bale, J. (1998). Virtual fandoms: Futurescapes of football. In A. Brown (ed.), *Fanatics: Power, identity and fandom in football* (pp. 265–278). London: Routledge.

Baltimore Orioles (1991). *1991 Media guide*. Baltimore, MD.

Baltimore Orioles (1992). *1992 Media guide*. Baltimore, MD.

Baltimore Orioles (2002). *Orioles information & record book 2002*. Baltimore, MD.

Barker, C. (1997). *Global television*. Oxford: Blackwell Publishers.

Barnett, S. (1990). *Games and sets: The changing face of sport on television*. London: British Film Institute.

Baudrillard, J. (1980). The implosion of meaning in the media and the implosion of the social in the masses. In K. Woodward (ed.), *The myths of information: Technology and postindustrial society*. Madison, WI: Coda Press.

Baudrillard, J. (1981). *For a critique of the political economy of the sign*. St. Louis: Telos.

Baudrillard, J. (1983). *Simulations*. New York: Semiotext(e).

Baudrillard, J. (1987). *Forget Foucault*. New York: Semiotext(e).

Baudrillard, J. (1988). *America*. London: Verso.

Baudrillard, J. (1993a). *Baudrillard live: Selected interviews,* M. Gane (ed.). London: Routledge.

Baudrillard, J. (1993b). *Symbolic exchange and death*. London: Sage.

Baudrillard, J. (1995). *The Gulf War did not take place*. Bloomington: Indiana University Press.

Becker, D. (1996). More women athletes head for Atlanta. *USA Today,* 18 January, p. 12C.

Belanger, A. (2000). Sport venues and the spectacularization of urban spaces in North America: The case of the Molson Centre in Montreal. *International Review for the Sociology of Sport,* 35 (3), pp. 379–398.

Bell, E., and Campbell, D. (1999). For the love of money. *The Observer,* May 23, p. 22.

Bellamy, R. V. (1998). The evolving television sports marketplace. In L. A. Wenner (ed.), *Mediasport* (pp. 73–87). London: Routledge.

Best, S., and Kellner, D. (1991). *Postmodern theory: Critical interrogations*. New York: Guilford Press.

Bianchini, F., and Schwengel, H. (1991). Re-imaging the City. In J. Corner and S. Harvey (eds.), *Enterprise and heritage: Crosscurrents of national culture* (pp. 212–34). London: Routledge.

Billings, A. C., Eastman, S. T., and Newton, G. D. (1998). Atlanta revisited: Prime-time promotion in the 1996 Summer Olympics. *Journal of Sport & Social Issues,* 22(1), pp. 65–78.

Binford, H. C. (1985). *The first suburbs: Residential communities on the Boston periphery 1815–1860*. Chicago: University of Chicago Press.

Birrell, S., and McDonald, M. G. (eds.) (2000). *Reading sport: Critical essays on power and representation*. Boston: Northeastern University Press.

Bisher, F. (2001). XFL sports radio: Ideal meld of subject, medium. *The Atlanta Journal and Constitution,* February 8, p. 3D.

Blake, A. (1996). *Body language: The meaning of modern sport*. London: Lawrence and Wishart.

Blount, R. (1979). Let's put life into the NBA. *New York Times,* February 5, p. C4.

Bogard, W. (1996). *The simulation of surveillance: Hypercontrol in telematic societies*. Cambridge: Cambridge University Press.

Bonitz, A. (2003). Bridging the Digital Divide: Building the Digital Harbor: A Smart Growth Economic Development Strategy for Baltimore. Available at: http://www.ci.baltimore.md.us/news/digitalharbor.

Borcila, A. (2000). Nationalizing the Olympics around and away from "vulnerable" bodies of women: The NBC coverage of the 1996 Olympics and some moments after. *Journal of Sport & Social Issues, 24*(2), pp. 118–147.

Bourdieu, p. (1978). Sport and social class. *Social Sience Information, 17*(6), pp. 819–840.

Bourdieu, P. (1984). *Distinction: A social critique of the judgment of taste*. Cambridge: Harvard University Press.

Bourdieu, P. (1986). The forms of capital. In J. G. Richardson (ed.), *Handbook of theory and research for the sociology of education* (pp. 241–258). Westport: Greenwood Press.

Bourdieu, P. (1990). Programme for a sociology of sport. In *In other words: Essays toward a reflexive sociology* (pp. 156–167). Stanford: Stanford University Press.

Bourdieu, P. (1993). *The field of cultural production*. New York: Columbia University Press.

Bourdieu, P. (1998). *Acts of resistance: Against the tyranny of the market*. New York: The New Press.

Bourdieu, p. (1978). Sport and social class. *Social Sience Information, 17*(6), pp. 819–840.

Boyd, T. (1997). The day the niggaz took over: Basketball, commodity culture, and black masculinity. In A. Baker and T. Boyd (eds.), *Out of bounds: Sports, media, and the politics of identity* (pp. 123–142). Bloomington: Indiana University Press.

Brady, D. (2000). One rock 'em, sock 'em company. *Business Week*, May 29, pp. 182.

Brah, A. (2002). Global mobilities, local predicaments: Globalization and the critical imagination. *Feminist Review, 70*, pp. 30–45.

Braudy, L. (1997). *The frenzy of renown: Fame and its history*. New York: Vintage.

Braverman, H. (1998). *Labor and monopoly capital: The degradation of work in the twentieth century* (25th ed.). New York: Monthly Review Press.

Broadcasting and Cable (2002). The week that was. March 18, p. 16.

Brookes, R. (2002). *Representing sport*. London: Arnold.

Broughton, D. (2002). Behind the numbers: How U.S. sports dollars are spent. *Street & Smith's Sports Business Journal*, March 11–17, pp. 30–39.

Bruck, C. (1997). The big hitter. *The New Yorker*, December 8, pp. 82–93.

Bryman, A. (1999). The Disneyization of society. *The Sociological Review, 47*(1), pp. 25–47.

Burwell, B. (1993). Pacers' victory could end ugly ball. *USA Today*, June 3, p. 3C.

Butsch, R. (ed.) (1990). *For fun and profit: The transformation of leisure into consumption*. Philadelphia: Temple University Press.

Cady, S. (1979). Basketball's image crisis. *The New York Times*, August 11, p. 15.

Cafardo, N. (2000). XFL will exert a wrestling hold on fans. *The Boston Globe*, April 30, p. C8.

Callinicos, A. (1983). *The revolutionary ideas of Marx*. London: Bookmarks.

Carlson, M. (1996). The soap opera games: Determined to make every event a tearjerker, NBC overplays the personal stories. *Time*, p. 48.

Carrington, B. (2000). Double consciousness and the black British athlete. In K. Owusu (ed.), *Black British culture and society* (pp. 133–156). London: Routledge.

Carrington, B. (2001). Postmodern blackness and the celebrity sports star: Ian Wright, "race" and English identity. In D. L. Andrews and S. J. Jackson (eds.), *Sport Stars: The cultural politics of sporting celebrity* (pp. 102–123). London: Routledge.

Carroll, J. M. (1999). *Red Grange and the rise of modern football*. Urbana: University of Illinois Press.

Carter, B. (1998). NFL is must-have TV: NBC is a have-not. *The New York Times,* January 14, pp. C1.

Carter, B. (2002). Fox puts gloves on faded fame and achieves ratings glory. *The New York Times,* March 15, pp. C1.

Cashmore, E. (2000). *Sports culture: An A-Z guide.* London: Routledge.

Cassy, J., and Finch, J. (1999). BSkyB linked to new Premiership buying spree. *The Guardian,* August 11.

Castells, M. (1983). Crisis planning and the quality of life: Managing the new historical relationships between space and society. *Environment and Planning D: Society and Space,* 1(1).

Castells, M. (1989). *The informational city: Information technology, economic restructuring and the urban-regional process.* Oxford: Blackwell.

Castells, M. (1996). *The rise of the network society.* Oxford: Blackwell.

Castle, G. (1991). Air to the throne. *Sport,* January, pp. 28–36.

Chadbourn, M. (1999). Why Lara Croft is too hot for the world to handle. *The Independent,* November 1, p. 14.

Chalkey, B., & Essex, S. (1999). Urban development through hosting international events: A history of the Olympic Games. *Planning Perspectives,* 14, pp. 369–394.

Chaplin, H. (1999). Past? Perfect! Nervous boomers take restoration cure. *American Demographics,* May, pp. 68–69.

Chen, K. H. (1987). The masses and the media: Baudrillard's implosive postmodernism. *Theory, Culture and Society,* 4(1), pp. 71–88.

Chisholm, A. (1999). Defending the nation: National bodies, U.S. borders, and the 1996 U.S. Olympic women's gymnastics team. *Journal of Sport & Social Issues,* 23(2), pp. 126–139.

Clarke, J. (1991). *New times and old enemies: Essays on cultural studies and America.* London: HarperCollins.

CNN Money. Statistical snapshot. Available at: www.money.com/best/bplive/details/2404000.html.

Cobbs, C. (1980). NBA and cocaine: Nothing to snort at. *Los Angeles Times,* August 19, p. C1.

Cole, C. L. (1996). American Jordan: P.L.A.Y., consensus, and punishment. *Sociology of Sport Journal,* 13(4), pp. 366–397.

Cole, C. L., and Andrews, D. L. (1996). "Look—It's NBA *ShowTime!*": Visions of race in the popular imaginary. In N. K. Denzin (ed.), *Cultural studies: A research volume* (vol. 1, pp. 141–181). Stamford, CT: JAI Press.

Cole, C. L., and Andrews, D. L. (2000). America's new son: Tiger Woods and America's multiculturalism. In N. K. Denzin (ed.), *Cultural studies: A research volume* (vol. 5, pp. 109–124). Stamford, CT: JAI Press.

Cole, C. L., and Denny, H. (1995). Visualizing deviance in post-Reagan America: Magic Johnson, AIDS, and the promiscuous world of professional sport. *Critical Sociology,* 20(3), pp. 123–147.

Comte, E. (1993). How high can David Stern jump? *Forbes,* June 7, pp. 42.

Connor, S. (1989). *Postmodernist culture: An introduction to theories of the contemporary.* Oxford: Basil Blackwell.

Conrad, P. (1998). Everybody's nightmare. *The Observer Review,* August 9, pp. 1–2.

Coughlin, S. (1997). Soccer: America's new, big kick. The world's sport comes of age in the United States. *Asheville Citizen-Times,* July 25, p. C1.

Crain, R. (1996). NBC's sappy profiles aid marketers. *Advertising Age,* 12 August, p. 15.

Critcher, C. (1986). Radical theorists of sport: The state of play. *Sociology of Sport Journal,* 3(4), pp. 333–343.

Danielson, M. (1997). *Home team: Professional sports and the American metropolis*. Princeton, NJ: Princeton University Press.

Davies, H. (1996). Rivals woo vital votes of the "soccer moms." *Daily Telegraph,* October 8, p. 14.

Dayan, D. and Katz, E. (1992). *Media events: The live broadcasting of history*. Cambridge, MA: Harvard University Press.

Dayton Daily News (2001). XFL on TV aims to be different. January 31, p. 8D.

Debord, G. (1990). *Comments on the society of the spectacle*. London: Verso.

Debord, G. (1994). *The Society of the Spectacle* (Nicholson-Smith, trans.). New York: Zone Books.

Delgado, F. (1997). Major league soccer: The return of the foreign sport. *Journal of Sport & Social Issues,* 21(3), pp. 285–297.

Denberg, J. (2003). Q&A with David Stern: Looking to expand into Europe. *The Atlanta Journal and Constitution,* February 7, p. 10D.

Denham, D. (2000). Modernism and postmodernism in the professional rugby league in England. *Sociology of Sport Journal,* 17(3), pp. 275–294.

Denzin, N. K. (1991). *Images of postmodern society: Social theory and contemporary cinema*. London: Sage.

Dirlik, A. (1996). The global in the local. In R. Wilson and W. Dissanayake (eds.), *Global local: Cultural production and the transnational imaginary* (pp. 21–45). Durham: Duke University Press.

Dizikes, J. (2000). *Yankee doodle dandy: The life and times of Tod Sloan*. New Haven, CT: Yale University Press.

Donnelly, P. (1996). Prolympism: Sport monoculture as crisis and opportunity. *Quest,* 48, pp. 25–42.

Downie, L., and Kaiser, R. G. (2002). *The news about the news: American journalism in peril*. New York: Knopf.

Doyle, B. (2001). No limit is theme for XFL: Sparks could fly in NBC debut. *Worchester Telegram & Gazette,* February 1, p. D1.

Du Gay, P., Hall, S., Janes, L., Mackay, H., and Negus, K. (1997). *Doing cultural studies: The story of the Sony Walkman*. London: Sage.

Duncan, M. C. (1990). Sports photographs and sexual difference: Images of women and men in the 1984 and 1988 Olympic Games. *Sociology of Sport Journal,* 7(1), pp. 22–43.

Duncan, N. G., and Duncan, J. S. (1997). Deep suburban irony: The perils of democracy in Westchester County, New York. In R. Silverstone (ed.), *Visions of suburbia* (pp. 161–179). London: Routledge.

Dunning, E. (1999). *Sport Matters: Sociological studies of sport, violence and civilization*. London: Routledge.

Dunning, E., and Sheard, K. (1979). *Barbarians, gentlemen and players: A sociological study of the development of rugby football*. New York: New York University Press.

Dyer, R. (1979). *Stars*. London: BFI Publishing.

Dyer, R. (1986). *Heavenly bodies: Film stars and society*. London: Macmillan.

Dyer, R. (1991). Charisma. In C. Gledhill (ed.), *Stardom: Industry of desire* (pp. 57–59). London: Routledge.

Dyer-Witheford, N. (1999). *Cyber-Marx: Cycles and circuits of struggles in high-technology capitalism*. Urbana: University of Illinois Press.

Dyson, M. E. (1993). Be like Mike: Michael Jordan and the pedagogy of desire. *Cultural Studies,* 7(1), pp. 64–72.

The Economist (1996). Sport and Television: Swifter, Higher, Stronger, Dearer. July 20, pp. 17–19.

Edwards, B. (1996). NBC to provide Olympics TV coverage for next 12 years. *Morning Edition*, National Public Radio, July 9.

Ehrenreich, B. (1989). *Fear of falling: The inner life of the middle class*. New York: Harper-Collins.

Eisenstadt, S. N. (ed.) (1968). *Max Weber on charisma & institution building*. Chicago: University of Chicago Press.

Eisinger, P. (2000). The politics of bread and circuses: Building the city for the visitor class. *Urban Affairs Review*, 35, pp. 316–333.

Eitzen, D. (1996). Classism in sport: The powerless bear the burden. *Journal of Sport & Social Issues*, 20, pp. 95–105.

Elliott, S. (2003). A super Sunday for football and Madison Avenue. *New York Times*, January 24, pp. C1, C4.

Epstein, E. (1996). Giants' Stadium architects sell high-tech nostalgia: Designs go for comfort, native flair. *San Francisco Chronicle*, March 18, p. A13.

Euchner, C. (1993). *Playing the field: Why sports teams move and cities fight to keep them*. Baltimore: Johns Hopkins University Press.

Ewen, S. (1976). *Captains of consciousness: Advertising and the social roots of the consumer culture*. New York: McGraw-Hill.

Fainstein, S. and Gladstone, D. (1999). Evaluating urban tourism. In S. Fainstein and D. Judd (eds.), *The tourist city* (pp. 21–34). New Haven: Yale University Press.

Fainstein, S. and Judd, D. (1999). Global forces, local strategies, and urban tourism. In S. Fainstein and D. Judd (eds.), *The tourist city* (pp. 1–20). New Haven: Yale.

Fairchild, C. (1999). Deterritorializing radio: Deregulation and the continuing triumph of the corporatist in the USA. *Media, Culture & Society*, 21(4), pp. 549–561.

Falcous, M. (1998). TV made it all a new game: Not again! Rugby league and the case of Super League in England. *Occasional Papers in Football Studies*, 1(1), pp. 4–21.

Falcous, M. and Silk, M. (2005). Manufacturing consent: Mediated sporting spectacle and the cultural politics of the war on terror. *International Journal of Media & Cultural Politics*, 1 (1), pp. 59–65.

Farhi, P. (1996). For NBC, Olympics are the golden days: Network sets records for viewership and profitability at games. *The Washington Post*, August 3, p. F1.

Featherstone, M. (1982). The body in consumer culture. *Theory, Culture & Society*, 1(2), pp. 18–33.

Featherstone, M. (1983). Consumer culture: An introduction. *Theory, Culture & Society*, 1(3), pp. 4–9.

Featherstone, M. (1991). *Consumer culture and postmodernism*. London: Sage.

Federal Bureau of Investigation. (2001). Uniform Crime Reports, November. Available at: http://www.morganquitno.com/metoorank.pdf.

Feder, A. M. (1995). A radiant smile from the lovely lady: Overdetermined femininity in ladies figure skating. In C. Baughman (ed.), *Women on ice: Feminist essays on the Tonya Harding/Nancy Kerrigan spectacle*. New York: Routledge.

Fendrich, H. (2001a). A new way of showing football on TV. *The Associated Press*, January 30.

Fendrich, H. (2001b). Shade of the USFL: XFL ratings slide 50 percent in week 2. *The Associated Press*, February 12.

Fendrich, H. (2001c). XFL ratings fall reveals problems. *The Associated Press,* February 12.

Fendrich, H. (2001d). XFL rating plummet again. *The Associated Press,* February 18.

Fetto, J. (2000). Patriot games: National pride swells in the heartland, but the rest of America isn't too far behind. *American Demographics,* July, pp. 48–49.

Fine, B., and Leopold, E. (1993). *The world of consumption.* London: Routledge.

Finnigin, D. (2002). Down but not out, WWE is using a rebranding effort to gain strength. *Brandweek,* June 3, pp. 43, 12.

Firat, A. F. (1995). Consumer culture or culture consumed? In J. A. Costa and G. J. Bamossy (eds.), *Marketing in a multicultural world: Ethnicity, nationalism, and cultural identity* (pp. 105–125). Thousand Oaks: Sage.

Fisher, E. (2001). X-rated XFL: New league hopes sex, violence equals success. *The Washington Times,* February 2, p. B1.

Fisher, E. (2003). Going global: Major league sports poised to expand to overseas markets. *The Washington Times,* January 5, p. A1.

Fishman, R. (1987). *Bourgeois utopias: The rise and fall of suburbia.* New York: Basic Books.

Fiske, J. (1987). *Television culture.* London: Routledge.

Fitzsimons, P. (1996). *The rugby war.* Sydney: HarperCollins.

The Florida Times-Union (2001). XFL helps UPN ratings surge: Sunday game doubles typical viewership. February 6, p. E6.

Forrest, B. (2002). *Long bomb: How the XFL became TV's biggest fiasco.* New York: Crown.

Fort, R. D. (1997). Direct democracy and the stadium mess. In R. G. Noll and A. S. Zimbalist (eds.), *Sports, jobs and Taxes: The economic impact of sports teams and stadiums* (pp. 146–177). Washington, DC: Brookings Institution Press.

Fox Entertainment Group. (2001). Annual Report 2001.

Friedman, M., and Andrews, D. (2002, November). Facadism: Theorizing urban spaces of sports consumption. Paper presented at the North American Society for the Sociology of Sport Conference, Indianapolis, Indiana.

Frow, J. (1997). *Time and commodity culture.* Oxford: Clarendon Press.

Fukuyama, F. (1989). The end of history? *The National Interest,* 16, pp. 3–18.

Galbraith, J. K. (1985). *The new industrial state.* Boston, MA: Houghton Mifflin.

Gano, R. (2000). Body slamming conventional football. *The Associated Press,* October 28, pp. 1–2.

Gans, H. J. (1967). *The Levittowners.* New York: Pantheon.

Gardner, P. (1996). *The simplest game: The intelligent fan's guide to the world of soccer.* New York: Macmillan.

Gartman, D. (1998). Postmodernism: Or, the cultural logic of post-Fordism. *Sociological Quarterly,* 39(1), pp. 119–137.

Gerbner, G. (1995). Television violence: The power and the peril. In G. Dines and J. M. Humez (eds.), *Gender, race, and class in media: A text-reader.* Thousand Oaks: Sage.

Gerdy, J. R. (2002). *Sports: The all-American addiction.* Jackson, MS: University of Mississippi Press.

Gereffi, G., and Korzeniewicz, M. (eds.) (1994). *Commodity chains and global capitalism.* Westport, CT: Greenwood Press.

Gershman, M. (1993). *Diamonds: The evolution of the ballpark from Elysian Fields to Camden Yards.* Boston: Houghton Mifflin.

Gilmore, J. H. (1998). Welcome to the experience economy. *Harvard Business Review,* July/August, p. 97.

Giroux, H. A. (1994). Animating youth: The Disneyfication of children's culture. *Socialist Review,* 24(3), pp. 23–55.

Gitlin, T. (1998). The culture of celebrity. *Dissent* (Summer), pp. 81–84.

Giulianotti, R. (1999). *Football: A sociology of the global game.* Cambridge: Polity Press.

Giulianotti, R. (2002). Supporters, followers, fans, and *flaneurs:* A taxonomy of spectator identities in football. *Journal of Sport & Social Issues,* 26(1), pp. 25–46.

Gledhill, C. (1991). *Stardom: Industry of desire.* London: Routledge.

Goldberger, P. (1989). A radical idea: Baseball as it used to be. *The New York Times,* November 12, p. H 39.

Goldman, R., and Papson, S. (1996). *Sign wars: The cluttered landscape of advertising.* Boulder: Westview Press.

Goodbody, J. (1996). NBC sets an Olympic broadcast record. *The Times,* August 7, p. 21.

Goodwin, M. (1993). The city as commodity: the contested spaces of urban development. In G. Kearns and C. Philo (eds.) *Selling places: The city as cultural capital, past and present* (pp. 145–162). Oxford: Pergamon.

Gottdiener, M. (2001). *The theming of America: American dreams, media fantasies, and themed environments* (Second ed.). Boulder, CO: Westview.

Gorz, A. (1989). *A critique of economic reason.* London: Verso.

Goss, J. (1995). We know who you are and we know where you live: The instrumental rationality of geodemographic systems. *Economic Geography,* 71(2), pp. 171–198.

Gottdiener, M., Collins, C., and Dickens, D. (1999). *Las Vegas: The social production of an all-American city.* Malden, MA: Blackwell.

Gratton, C., and Henry, I. (eds.) (2001). *Sport in the city: The role of sport in economic and social regeneration.* London: Routledge.

Gray, H. (1989). Television, black Americans, and the American dream. *Critical Studies in Mass Communication,* 6, pp. 376–386.

Grish, K. (1998). 7 on soccer: On the road to strong sales, soccer manufacturers navigate Fashion Avenue. *Sporting Goods Business,* April 15, pp. 31, 34.

Grossberg, L. (1992). *We gotta get out of this place: Popular conservatism and postmodern culture.* London: Routledge.

Grossberg, L. (1997a). *Bringing it all back home: Essays on cultural studies.* Durham: Duke University Press.

Grossberg, L. (1997b). Cultural studies, modern logics, and theories of globalisation. In A. McRobbie (ed.), *Back to reality? Social experience and cultural studies* (pp. 7–35). Manchester: Manchester University Press.

Grossberg, L., Wartella, E., and Whitney, D. C. (1998). *MediaMaking: Mass media in a popular culture.* Thousand Oaks, CA: Sage.

Gruneau, R. S. (1983). *Class, sports, and social development.* Amherst: University of Massachusetts Press.

Gunther, M. (1996). Get ready for the Oprah Olympics. *Fortune,* July 22, pp. 42–43.

Habermas, J. (1979). Conservatism and capitalist crisis. *New Left Review,* 115, pp. 73–84.

Hagstrom, R. G. (1998). *The NASCAR way: The business that drives the sport.* New York: John Wiley & Sons, Inc.

Haider, D. (1992). Place wars: New realities of the 1990s. *Economic Development Quarterly,* 6, pp. 127–34.

Hall, M. (2002). Taking the sport out of sports. *Street & Smith's Sports Business Journal,* August 19.

Hall, S. (1980). Encoding/decoding. In S. Hall (ed.), *Culture, media, language* (pp. 128–138). London: Hutchinson.

Hall, S. (1991). The local and the global: Globalization and ethnicity. In A. D. King (ed.), *Culture, globalization and the world-system* (pp. 19–39). London: Macmillan.

Hall, S. (1996). Introduction: Who needs "identity"? In S. Hall and P. du Gay (eds.), *Questions of cultural identity*. London: Sage.

Hall, S. (1998). The great moving nowhere show. *Marxism Today,* November/December, pp. 9–14.

Hamilton, B. W., and Kahn, P. (1997). Baltimore's Camden Yards ballparks. In R. G. Noll and A. S. Zimbalist (eds.), *Sports, jobs and taxes: The economic impact of sports teams and stadiums* (pp. 245–281). Washington, DC: Brookings Institution Press.

Hamilton, M. M. (1996). NASCAR's popularity fuels a powerful marketing engine. *The Washington Post,* May 26, pp. A01.

Hannerz, U. (1996). *Transnational connections : Culture, people, places.* London: Comedia.

Hannigan, J. (1998). *Fantasy city: Pleasure and profit in the postmodern metropolis.* London: Routledge.

Harpe, M. (1995, May 28). Soccer dollar limits blacks. *News & Record* (Greensboro, NC), p. C3.

Harper, W. A. (1994). *Grantland Rice and his heroes: The sportswriter as mythmaker in the 1920s.* Knoxville: University of Tennessee Press.

Harper, W. A. (1999). *How you played the game: The life of Grantland Rice.* Columbia: University of Missouri Press.

Harvey, D. (1985). The geopolitics of capitalism. In D. Gregory and J. Urry (eds.), *Social relations and social structures* (pp. 128–163). London: Macmillan.

Harvey, D. (1989). *The condition of postmodernity: An enquiry into the origins of cultural change.* Oxford: Blackwell.

Harvey, D. (1993). From space to place and back again: Reflections on the condition of postmodernity. In J. Bird (ed.), *Mapping the futures: Local cultures, global change* (pp. 3–29). London: Routledge.

Harvey, D. (2000). *Spaces of hope.* Berkeley, CA: University of California Press.

Harvey, D. (2001a). Reinventing geography: an interview with the editors of *New Left Review*. In D. Harvey (ed.), *Spaces of capital: Toward a critical geography* (pp. 3–26). Edinburgh: Edinburgh University Press.

Harvey, D. (2001b). From managerialism to entrepreneurialism: the transformation in urban governance in late capitalism. In D. Harvey (ed.), *Spaces of capital: Toward a critical geography* (pp. 345–368). Edinburgh: Edinburgh University Press.

Harvey, D. (2001c). A View from Federal Hill. In D. Harvey (ed.), *Spaces of Capital: Toward a Critical Geography* (pp. 128–157). Edinburgh: Edinburgh University Press.

Harvey, J., Law, A., and Cantelon, M. (2001). North American professional team sport franchise ownership patterns and global entertainment conglomerates. *Sociology of Sport Journal,* 18(4), pp. 435–457.

Hayes-Bautista, D. E., and Rodriguez, G. (1994). L.A. story: Los Angeles, CA, soccer and society. *The New Republic,* July 4, p. 19.

Healey, C. (1997). *From the ruins of colonialism: History as social memory.* Cambridge: Cambridge University Press.

Heath, T. (2000). Offering smash-mouth football, new league, a WWF in shoulder pads, targets young males. *The Washington Post,* November 24, p. D01.

Heath, T. (2001). XFL is set to deliver football a shot in the mouth. *The Washington Post,* February 2, pp. D01.

Heath, T., and Farhi, P. (1998). Murdoch adds Dodgers to media empire. *The Washington Post,* March 20, pp. A1.

Heisler, M. (1993). Uncommon marketing. *Los Angeles Times,* October 18, p. C1.

Held, D., McGrew, A., Goldblatt, D., and Perraton, J. (1999). *Global transformations: Politics, economics and culture.* Stanford, CA: Stanford University Press.

Held, D., and McGrew, A. (2000). The great globalization debate: An introduction. In D. Held and A. McGrew (eds.), *The global transformations reader: An introduction to the globalization debate* (pp. 1–45). Cambridge: Polity Press.

Hellmuth, Obata and Kassabaum, Inc. (1985). *Baltimore Stadium study.* Kansas City, MO.

Hellmuth, Obata and Kassabaum, Inc. (1987). *Preparation and evaluation of stadium concept alternatives and cost estimates for stadium development on the Camden Yard site and for renovation of Memorial Stadium, Volume 2: Architectural supplement.* Baltimore, MD: Peat Marwick.

Henderson, J. (2001). Thousands sign up to pay more. *The Observer,* August 12.

Herman, E., and McChesney, R. W. (1997). *The global media: The new missionaries of corporate capitalism.* London: Cassell.

Hersh, P. (1990). Soccer in U.S. at crossroads: World Cup seen as last resort to stir fan sport. *Chicago Tribune,* June 3, p. C1.

Hesmondhalgh, D. (2002). *The cultural industries.* London: Sage.

Higgins, R., and Tillery, R. (2003). Foreign or domestic? You choose. *The Commercial Appeal,* January 26, p. C12.

Higgs, C. T., Weiller, K. H., and Martin, S. B. (2003). Gender bias in the 1996 Olympic Games: A comparative analysis. *Journal of Sport & Social Issues,* 27(1), pp. 52–64.

Hiltzik, M. A. (1997). Playing by his own rules. *Los Angeles Times,* August 25.

Hirst, P., & Thompson, G. (1999). *Globalization in question* (Second ed.). Cambridge: Polity Press.

History Channel (2002). Bodyslam! The history of professional wrestling.

Hitchens. (1998). Goodbye to all that: Why Americans are not taught history. *Harper's,* November, p. 37.

HNTB, and Touche Ross and Co. (1986). *New stadium site evaluation for Maryland Special Advisory Commission on Professional Sports and the Economy.* Baltimore, MD.

Hobsbawm, E. J. (1990). *Nations and nationalism since 1870: Programme, myth, reality.* Cambridge: Cambridge University Press.

Hobsbawm, E. (1998). The big picture: The death of neo-liberalism. *Marxism Today,* November/December, pp. 4–8.

Hobsbawm, E., and Ranger, T. (eds.) (1983). *The invention of tradition.* Cambridge: Cambridge University Press.

Hogan, J. (2003). Staging the nation: Gendered and ethnicized discourses of national identity in Olympic opening ceremonies. *Journal of Sport & Social Issues,* 27(2), pp. 100–123.

Holcomb, B. (1999). Marketing cities for tourism. In S. Fainstein and D. Judd (eds.), *The tourist city* (pp. 54–70). New Haven: Yale University Press.

Holleb, D. B. (1975). The direction of urban change. In H. S. Perloff (ed.), *Agenda for the new urban era* (pp. 11–43). Chicago: American Society of Planning Officials.

Holliman, J. (1931). *American sports (1785–1835).* Durham, NC: Seeman Press.

Hornung, M. N. (1994). 3 billion people can't be wrong. *Chicago Sun-Times,* June 17, p. 39.

Horovitz, B. (1999). IMG's "Team Ali" has single mission. *USA Today,* June 8, p. 2A.

Howell, J., and Ingham, A. (2001). From social problem to personal issue: The language of lifestyles. *Cultural Studies,* 15(2), pp. 326–351.

Hruska, B. (1996). What NBC has Planned: High Tech and High Drama. *TV Guide,* July 20, pp. 8–10.

Hubbard, P. (1996). Urban design and city regeneration: Social representations of entrepreneurial landscapes. *Urban Studies,* 33 (8), pp. 1441–1461.

Hula, R. (1990). The Two Baltimores. In D. Judd and M. Parkinson (eds.), *Leadership and Urban Regeneration: Cities in North America and Europe* (pp. 191–215). Newbury Park, CA: Sage.

Hunter, S. (2000). Border-bending creative. *Boards Magazine,* March 1. http://www.boards mag.com/articles/magazine/20000301/ideas.html.

Hutchins, B. (1996). Rugby wars: The changing face of football. *Sporting Traditions,* 13(1), pp. 151–162.

Hutchins, B. (1998). Global processes and the Rugby Union World Cup. *Occasional Papers in Football Studies,* 1(2), pp. 34–54.

Impoco, J. (1996). Live from Atlanta: NBC goes for women viewers and platinum ratings. *U.S. News and World Report,* July 15, p. 36.

Ingham, A. G. (1985). From public issue to personal trouble: Well-being and the fiscal crisis of the state. *Sociology of Sport Journal,* 2(1), pp. 43–55.

International Movie Database (2002). USA box office charts archive, November 12. Available at http://www.imdb.com/Charts/usboxarchive.

Isidore, C. (2002). Ready to pay for some football? NBA TV deal shows that big games, like Super Bowl, are headed to pay TV. Available at: http://money.cnn.com/2002/01/25/companies/column_sportsbiz.

Jackson, K. T. (1985). *Crabgrass frontier: The suburbanization of the United States.* New York: Oxford University Press.

Jackson, S. J., and Andrews, D. L. (1999). Between and beyond the global and the local: American popular sporting culture in New Zealand. *International Review for the Sociology of Sport,* 34(1), pp. 31–42.

Jameson, F. (1991). *Postmodernism, or, the cultural logic of late capitalism.* Durham: Duke University Press.

Jameson, F. (1998). *The cultural turn: Selected writings on the postmodern, 1983–1998.* London: Verso.

Jarvie, G., and Maguire, J. A. (1994). *Sport and leisure in social thought.* London: Routledge.

Jary, D. (1999). The McDonaldization of sport and leisure. In B. Smart (ed.), *Resisting McDonaldization* (pp. 116–134). London: Sage.

Jeffords, S. (1994). *Hard bodies: Hollywood masculinity in the Reagan era.* New Brunswick, NJ: Rutgers University Press.

Jenkins, B. (2000). XFL has a chance if it's anti-NFL. *San Francisco Chronicle,* December 19, p. 1.

Jensen-Verbeke, M. (1989). Inner cities and urban tourism in the Netherlands: New challenges for local authorities. In P. Branham, I. Henry, H. Mommas, and H. Van Der Poel (eds.), *Leisure and urban processes: Cultural studies of leisure policy in Western European cities.* London: Routledge.

Jhally, S. (1989). Cultural studies and the sports/media complex. In L. A. Wenner (ed.), *Media, sports, and society* (pp. 70–93). Newbury Park: Sage.

Jhally, S., and Lewis, J. (1992). *Enlightened racism: The Cosby Show, audiences, & the myth of the American Dream.* Boulder, CO: Westview.

Johns Hopkins Institute for Policy Studies. (2000). Baltimore in transition: How do we move from decline to revival? Available at: http://www.jhu.edu/~ips/newsroom/ transition.pdf.

Johnson, A. (1986). Economic and policy implications of hosting sports franchises: Lessons from Baltimore. *Urban Affairs Quarterly,* 21(3), pp. 411–433.

Johnson, L., and Roediger, D. (1997). Hertz, don't it? Becoming colorless and staying black in the crossover of O. J. Simpson. In T. Morrison and C. Brodsky Lacour (eds.), *Birth of a nation'hood: Gaze, script, and spectacle in the O. J. Simpson case* (pp. 197–239). New York: Pantheon Books.

Johnson, R. (1987). What is cultural studies anyway? *Social Text,* 6(1), pp. 38–79.

Jones, R., Murrel, A. J., and Jackson, J. (1999). Pretty versus powerful in the sports pages: Print media coverage of U.S. women's Olympic gold medal winning teams. *Journal of Sport & Social Issues,* 23(2), pp. 183–192.

Jose, C. (1994). *The United States and World Cup soccer competition: An encyclopedic history of the United States in international competition.* Metuchen, NJ: The Scarecrow Press.

Judd, D. (1999). Constructing the tourist bubble. In S. Fainstein and D. Judd (eds.), *The tourist city* (pp. 35–53). New Haven: Yale University Press.

Kantor, P. (1995). *The dependent city revisited: The political economy of urban development and social policy.* Boulder, CO: Westview Press.

Kaplan, D. (2003). Forecast: Venue financing tougher in '03. *Street & Smith's Sports Business Journal,* 5(37), January 6, pp. 1, 25.

Katz, D. (1994). *Just do it: The Nike spirit in the corporate world.* New York: Random House.

Kearney, R. (1989). *The wake of the imagination: Toward a postmodern culture.* Minneapolis, MN: University of Minnesota Press.

Keating, W. D. (1996). Cleveland: The "Comeback City": The politics of redevelopment and sports stadiums amidst urban decline. In Lauria, M. (ed.), *Reconstructing urban regime theory: Regulating urban politics in a global economy* (pp. 189–205). Thousand Oaks, CA: Sage.

Kelley, R. D. G. (1997). *Yo' mama's disfunktional!: Fighting the culture wars in urban America.* Boston: Beacon Press.

Kellner, D. (1992). *The Persian Gulf TV war.* Boulder, CO: Westview.

Kellner, D. (1995). *Media culture: Cultural studies, identity and politics between the modern and the postmodern.* London: Routledge.

Kellner, D. (2002). *Media spectacle.* London: Routledge.

Kelner, S. (1996). *To Jerusalem and back.* London: Macmillan.

Kiersh, E. (1992). Mr. Robinson vs. Air Jordan: The marketing battle for Olympic gold. *Los Angeles Times Magazine,* March 22, p. 28.

Kirkpatrick, C. (1987). In an orbit all his own. *Sports Illustrated,* November 9, pp. 82–98.

Klein, N. (1999). *No Logo: Taking aim at brand bullies.* New York: Picador.

Kleinberg, B. (1995). *Urban America in transformation: Perspectives on urban policy and development.* Thousand Oaks, CA: Sage.

Knisley, M. (1996). Rock solid. *The Sporting News,* December 30, pp. S5–S7.

Knisley, M. (1998). All Rupert, all the time. *The Sporting News,* December 14, p. 16.

Lafrance, M. R. (1998). Colonizing the feminine: Nike's intersections of postfeminism and hyperconsumption. In G. Rail (Ed.), *Sport and postmodern times* (pp. 117–142). New York: SUNY Press.

Langman, L. (1991). From pathos to panic: American national character meets the future. In P. Wexler (ed.), *Critical theory now* (pp. 165–241). London: Falmer Press.

Lasch, C. (1979). *The culture of narcissism: American life in an age of diminishing expectations*. New York: W. W. Norton.

Lears, J. (1994). *Fables of abundance: A cultural history of advertising in America*. New York: Basic Books.

Lefton, T., and Warner, B. (2001). He's got global game. *The Industry Standard*, February, p. 19.

Lemann, N. (1989). Stressed out in suburbia: A generation after the postwar boom, life in the suburbs has changed, even if our picture of it hasn't. *The Atlantic*, November, p. 34.

Leslie, D. A. (1995). Global scan: The globalization of advertising agencies, concepts, and campaigns. *Economic Geography*, 71,(4), pp. 402–426.

Levin, G. (1996a). Peacock prancing proudly at return on Olympics. *Variety*, July 29, p. 21.

Levin, G. (1996b). Peacock web basks in Olympian glory. *Variety*, August 5–11, p. 25.

Lewis, M. (1996). Just buy it. *The New York Times Magazine*, June 23, p. 20.

Levine, M. (1999). Tourism, urban redevelopment, and the "world-class" city: The cases of Baltimore and Montreal. In Andrew, C., P. Armstrong and A. Lapierre (eds.), *World-Class cities: Can Canada play?* (pp. 421–450). Ottawa: University of Ottawa.

Linder & Associates, Inc (2002). *Baltimore believe—progress report: Phase 1*. New York: Author.

Lipsitz, G. (1984). Sports stadia and urban development: A tale of three cities. *Policy Studies Review*, 10 (2/3), pp. 117–129.

Lipsyte, R. (1996a, August 4). Little girls in a staged spectacle for big bucks? That's sportainment! *The New York Times*, August 4, p. 28.

Lipsyte, R. (1996b, September 8). Woods suits golf's needs perfectly. *The New York Times*, September 8, p. 11.

Lowes, M. (2002). *Indy dreams and urban nightmares: Speed merchants, spectacle, and the struggle over public space in the world-class city*. Toronto: University of Toronto Press.

Lucas, J. A., and Smith, R. A. (1978). *Saga of American sport*. Philadelphia: Lea & Febiger.

Luke, T. (1996). Identity, meaning and globalization: Detraditionalization in postmodern space-time compression. In P. Heelas, S. Lash, and P. Morris (eds.), *Detraditionalization: Critical reflections of authority and identity* (pp. 109–133). Cambridge: Blackwell Publishers.

Luke, T. (1999). Simulated sovereignty, telematic territoriality: The political economy of cyberspace. In M. Featherstone and S. Lash (eds.), *Spaces of culture: City-nation-world*. (27–48) London: Sage.

Lury, C. (1996). *Consumer culture*. Cambridge: Polity Press.

Lury, C. and Warde, A. (1997). Investments in the imaginary consumer: Conjectures regarding power, knowledge and advertising. In M. Nava, A. Blake, I. MacRury and B. Richards (eds.), *Buy this book: Studies in advertising and consumption* (pp. 87–102). London: Routledge.

Lusted, D. (1991). The glut of the personality. In C. Gledhill (ed.), *Stardom: Industry of desire* (pp. 251–258). London: Routledge.

Lyon, D. (1994). *The electronic eye: The rise of the surveillance society*. Oxford, England: Polity Press.

MacFarquhar, N. (1996). What's a soccer mom anyway? *The New York Times*, October 20, pp. E1, E6.

Maguire, J. A. (1993). Globalization, sport development, and the media/sport complex. *Sport Science Review*, 2(1), pp. 29–47.

Maguire, J. A. (1999). *Global sport: Identities, societies, civilization*. Cambridge: Polity Press.

Maguire, J. A. (2000). Sport and globalization. In J. Coakley and E. Dunning (eds.), *Handbook of sports studies* (pp. 356–369). London: Sage.

Mandel, E. (1999). *Late capitalism* (6th ed.). London: Verso Classics.

Manly, H. (2001). Reputations on the line. *The Boston Globe,* February 2, p. E8.

Marantz, S. (1997). The power of air. *The Sporting News,* December 24, pp. 12–20.

Marketing Week (2000a). Held to ransom. March 9, p. 28.

Marketplace. (2004, February 13). Shifting gears: Has America become the NASCAR nation? *National Public Radio.*

Markovits, A. S., and Hellerman, S. L. (1995). Soccer in America: A story of marginalization. *Entertainment & Sports Law Review,* 13(1/2), pp. 225–255.

Markovits, A. S., and Hellerman, S. L. (2001). *Offside: Soccer and American exceptionalism.* Princeton: Princeton University Press.

Marshall, P. D. (1997). *Celebrity and power: Fame in contemporary culture.* Minneapolis: University of Minnesota Press.

Marx, K. (1977a). The Eighteenth Brumaire of Louis Bonaparte. In D. McLellan (ed.), *Karl Marx: Selected writings* (pp. 300–325). Oxford: Oxford University Press.

Marx, K. (1977b). Grundrisse. In D. McLellan (ed.), *Karl Marx: Selected writings* (pp. 345–387). Oxford: Oxford University Press.

Maryland Stadium Authority. (1987). *Request of the Maryland Stadium Authority to final competitors for the design and planning contract for the State of Maryland's twin stadium project.* Baltimore, MD.

Maryland Stadium Authority. (1992). *Maryland Stadium Authority 1992 Annual Report.* Baltimore, MD.

Maryland Stadium Authority. (1993). *Maryland Stadium Authority 1993 Annual Report.* Baltimore, MD.

Maryland State Lottery (2002). Maryland State Lottery Results. Available at: http://www.maryland-state-lottery-results.com/.

Mason, D. S. (2002). "Get the puck outta here!": Media transnationalism and Canadian identity. *Journal of Sport & Social Issues,* 26(1), pp. 140–166.

McAvoy, K. (2001). Baseball gets the bucks. *Broadcasting and Cable,* April 2, p. 26.

McCallum, J. and O'Brien, R. (1996). Women's games. *Sports Illustrated,* August 12, p. 17.

McChesney, R. W. (1997). *Corporate media and the threat to democracy.* New York: Seven Stories Press.

McKay, J., and Miller, T. (1991). From old boys to men and women of the corporation: The Americanization and commodification of Australian sport. *Sociology of Sport Journal,* 8(1), pp. 86–94.

McKay, J., and Rowe, D. (1997). Field of soaps: Rupert v. Kerry as masculine melodrama. *Social Text,* 50, pp. 69–86.

McNulty, R. (2001). No one should be shocked by dismal XFL debut. *The Denver Post,* February 4, p. C6.

Mercer, K. (1994). *Welcome to the jungle: New positions in black cultural studies.* London: Routledge.

Merrifield, A. (1993). The struggle over place: Redeveloping American Can in southeast Baltimore. *Transactions of the Institute of British Geographers,* 18, pp. 102–121.

Meyers, B. (1998). Nike tees up to try again: Woods brand gets new look. *USA Today,* September 18, pp. 1B–2B.

Miles, S. (1998). *Consumerism: As a way of life.* London: Sage.

Miliband, R. (1983). Dialectics. In T. Bottomore (ed.), *A dictionary of Marxist thought* (pp. 122–129). Cambridge: Harvard University Press.

Miller, J. E. (1990). *The baseball business: Pursuing pennants and profits in Baltimore*. Chapel Hill, NC: University of North Carolina Press.

Miller, S. (1999). Taking sports to the next level: Start with teams, add arenas, media and you've got a sports empire. *Street & Smith's Sports Business Journal*, August 23–29, pp. 23, 32.

Miller, T. (2001). *Sportsex*. Philadelphia: Temple University Press.

Miller, T., Lawrence, G., McKay, J., and Rowe, D. (2001). *Globalization and sport: Playing the world*. London: Sage.

Miller, T., and McHoul, A. (1998). *Popular culture and everyday life*. London: Sage.

Milliken, R. (1996). Sports is Murdoch's "battering ram" for pay TV. *The Independent*, October 16, pp. 28.

Mills, C. W. (1959). *The sociological imagination*. London: Oxford University Press.

Mollenkopf, J., and Castells, M. (1991). *Dual City: Restructuring New York*. New York: Russell Sage Foundation.

Moore, D. (1992). A new world for the NBA in the 90s. *Dallas Morning News*, November 6, p. 1B.

Moore, D. (1994). Transition game: League no longer flourishing, but foundation remains strong. *Dallas Morning News*, November 3, p. 1B.

Moran, M. (1979, February 5). Status of pro basketball worrying player's group. *New York Times*, p. C4.

Morgan, M. (2001). Stepping into the void: XFL opens its first season with fans in mind. *The Commercial Appeal*, February 3, p. D1.

Morley, D. (1992). *Television, audiences and cultural studies*. London: Routledge.

Morley, D., and Robins, K. (1995). *Spaces of identity: Global media, electronic landscapes and cultural boundaries*. London: Routledge.

Mormino, G. R. (1982). The playing fields of St. Louis: Italian immigrants and sport, 1925–1941. *Journal of Sport History*, 9, pp. 5–16.

Morton Hoffman and Company. (1964). *Economic and market analysis, Inner Harbor area, Baltimore, Maryland*. Baltimore, MD.

Mullen, L. (2002). Losses make Fox wary of sports deals. *Street & Smith's Sports Business Journal*, 1, p. 33.

Mullen, M. (1999). The pre-history of cable television: An overview and analysis. *Historical Journal of Film, Radio and Television*, 19(1), pp. 39–56.

Murdoch, R. (1996). *News Corporation annual report: Chief executive's review*. Adelaide, Australia.

Murdoch, R. (1998). *News Corporation annual report: Chief executive's review*. Adelaide, Australia.

Murray, R. (1990). Fordism and post-fordism. In S. Hall and M. Jacques (eds.), *New times: The changing face of politics in the 1990s* (pp. 38–53). London: Verso.

Naughton, J. (1992). *Taking to the air: The rise of Michael Jordan*. New York: Warner Books.

NBA.com (2002). NBA renews international TV deals. Available at: http://www.nba.com/news/international_tv_deals_renewed_021112.html.

Negus, K. (1997). The production of culture. In P. D. Gay (ed.), *Production of culture/cultures of production* (pp. 67–118). London: The Open University.

Nelson, D. D. (1998). *National manhood: Capitalist citizenship and the imagined fraternity of white men*. Durham, NC. Duke University Press.

The New York Times (1996). NBC's Time Warp. August 2, p. A26.

The New York Times (2001). 54 million watch XFL. February 7, p. D6.

News Corporation (2002). *Earnings release for the quarter ended December 31, 2001*. Adelaide, Australia.

News Corporation (2004a). *News Corporation annual report*. Adelaide, Australia.

News Corporation (2004b). *News Corporation full financial report*. Adelaide, Australia.

Nibert, D. (2000). *Hitting the lottery jackpot: Government and the taxing of dreams*. New York: Monthly Review Press.

Nikefootball.com. The Geoforce. http://www.nikefootball.com/english/front/index.html.

Nixon, H. L. (1984). *Sport and the American dream*. New York: Leisure Press.

Noll, R. G., and Zimbalist, A. S. (1997). Build the stadium—Create the jobs! In R. G. Noll and A. S. Zimbalist (eds.), *Sports, jobs and taxes: The economic impact of sports teams and stadiums* (pp. 1–54). Washington, DC: Brookings Institution Press.

Norris, C. (1992). *Uncritical theory: Postmodernism, intellectuals, and the Gulf War*. Amherst: University of Massachusetts Press.

Office of National Drug Control Policy (2002). *Baltimore, Maryland: Profile of drug indicators*. Rockville, MD: ONDCP Clearinghouse.

Ohmae, K. (1990). *The borderless world*. New York: HarperBusiness.

O'Malley, M. (2000). Leadership in the New Economy. Speech Delivered to the Democratic Leadership Council, July 14, 2001. Available at: Mayoral Speeches, http://www.ci.baltimore.md.us/mayor/speeches/sp000714.html.

O'Riordan, B. (2002). Good times may be over for professional sports. *Australian Financial Review*, February 16, p. 3.

Page, C. (1996). *Showing my color: Impolite essays on race and identity*. New York: HarperCollins.

Patton, P. (1986). The selling of Michael Jordan. *The New York Times Magazine*, November 9, pp. 48–58.

Patton, P. (1995). Introduction. In J. Baudrillard (ed.), *The Gulf War did not take place*. Bloomington: Indiana University Press.

Pelissero, J., Henschen, B., and Sidlow, E. (1991). Urban regimes, sports stadiums, and the politics of economic development agendas in Chicago. *Policy Studies Review*, 10 (2/3), pp. 117–129.

Perez, A. (1997). Soccer looks: Soccer fashion. *Sporting Goods Business*, March 24, pp. 30, 44.

Perry, N. (1994). *The dominion of signs: Television, advertising, and other New Zealand fictions*. Auckland: Auckland University Press.

Pesky, G. (1993a). The changing face of the game. *Sporting Goods Business*, March, p. 32.

Pesky, G. (1993b). On the attack: The growth of soccer in the United States. *Sporting Goods Business*, April, p. 31.

Peterson, I. (1996). Leading Olympic advertiser? NBC. *The New York Times*, August 6, p. D7.

Pierce, C. P. (1995). Master of the universe. *GQ*, April, pp. 180–187.

Pluto, T. (1991). *Loose balls: The short, wild life of the American Basketball Association—As told by the players, coaches, and movers and shakers who made it happen*. New York: Simon and Schuster.

Post, T. (1994). Feet of the future. *Newsweek Special Issue*, Spring, pp. 60–65.

Poster, M. (1990). *The mode of information: Poststructuralism and social context*. Chicago: University of Chicago Press.

Poster, M. (1995). *The second media age*. Cambridge: Polity Press.

Postman, N. (1985). *Amusing ourselves to death: Public discourse in the age of show business*. New York: Penguin Books.

Potter, J. (1997). Woods widens game's appeal: Role model encourages minorities. *USA Today*, January 15, p. 3C.

Powdermaker, H. (1950). *Hollywood—The dream factory: An anthropologist looks at the movie-makers*. Boston: Little, Brown and Company.

Prendergrast, M. (1998). *For God, country and Coca-Cola: The unauthorized history of the great American soft drink and the company that makes it*. New York: Touchstone Books.

Quick, S. P. (1991). What a catch! The establishment of cricket on Australian commercial television. *Media Information Australia*, 61, August, pp. 81–85.

Quirk J. P., and Fort, R. D. (1992). *Pay dirt: The business of professional team sports*. Princeton, NJ: Princeton University Press.

Rader, B. G. (1984). *In its own image: How television has transformed sports*. New York: The Free Press.

Rader, B. G. (1983). Compensatory sport heroes: Ruth, Grange and Dempsey. *Journal of Popular Culture*, 16(4), pp. 11–22.

Rae, S. (1999). *W. G. Grace: A life*. London: Faber & Faber.

Rail, G. (1991). Postmodernity and mediated sport: The medium is the model (author's translation of Technologie post-moderne et culture: Un regard sur le sport mediatise). In F. Landry, M. Landry, and M. Yerles (eds.) *Sport . . . The third millennium*. Les Sainte-Foy: Presses de L'Université Laval.

Ratings for XFL plummet (2001). *The Associated Press*, February 12.

Ratnesar, R. (2000). Changing stripes: Just as with his golf game, Tiger has had to adjust his life to meet the demands of celebrity. *Time*, August 14, pp. 62–66.

Real, M. R. (1989). Super Bowl football versus World Cup soccer: A cultural-structural comparison. In L. A. Wenner (ed.), *Media, sports, and society* (pp. 180–203). Newbury Park: Sage.

Real, M. R. (1998). MediaSport: Technology and the commodification of postmodern sport. In L. A. Wenner (ed.), *Mediasport* (pp. 14–26). London: Routledge.

Reeves, J. (2000). WWF chair McMahon promises "smash mouth" action in XFL. *The Associated Press*, August 2.

Reeves, J. L., and Campbell, R. (1994). *Cracked coverage: Television news, the anti-cocaine crusade, and the Reagan legacy*. Durham: Duke University Press.

Reich (1991). *The work of nations: Preparing ourselves for twenty-first-century capitalism*. New York: Knopf.

Rein, I., Kotler, P., and Stoller, M. (1997). *High visibility: The making and marketing of professionals into celebrities*. Chicago: NTC Business Books.

Reisman, D., and Denny, R. (1951). Football in America: A study in culture diffusion. *American Quarterly*, 3, pp. 309–325.

Remnick, D. (1996). Inside-Out: The NBC strategy that made the games a hit. *The New Yorker*, 5 August, pp. 26–28.

Rich, W. (ed.) (2000). *The economics and politics of sports facilities*. Westport, CT: Quorum Books.

Richards, J. (1994). *Facadism*. London: Routledge.

Richmond, P. (1993). *Ballpark: Camden Yards and the building of an American dream*. New York: Simon & Schuster.

Rider, J. (2000). Don't dismiss McMahon's new football league so fast WWF owner's marketing strategies will come into play. *The Sunday Gazette Mail*, February 6, p. 8D.

Riess, S. A. (1991). *City games: The evolution of American urban society and the rise of sports*. Urbana: University of Illinois Press.

Riess, S. A. (1998). Historical perspectives on sport and public policy. *Review of Policy Research*, 15, pp. 3–15.

Rigby, S. H. (1998). *Marxism and history: A critical introduction* (Second ed.). Manchester: Manchester University Press.

Rinehart, R. E. (1998). *Players all: Performances in contemporary sport*. Bloomington: Indiana University Press.

Ritzer, G. (1988). *Contemporary sociological theory*. New York: McGraw-Hill.

Ritzer, G. (1998). *The McDonaldization thesis: Explorations and extensions*. London: Sage.

Ritzer, G. (1999). *Enchanting a disenchanted world: Revolutionizing the means of consumption*. Thousand Oaks, CA: Pine Forge Press.

Ritzer, G. and Stillman, T. (2001). The postmodern ballpark as a leisure setting: Enchantment and simulated De-McDonaldization. *Leisure Sciences*, 23, pp. 99–113.

Robbins-Mullin, J. (2001, February 10). Sex meets violence: Welcome to the XFL. *Pittsburgh Post-Gazette*, p. B3.

Robins, K. (1990). Global local times. In J. Anderson and M. Ricci (eds.), *Society and social science: A reader* (pp. 196–205). Milton Keynes: Open University.

Robins, K. (1991). Tradition and translation: National culture in its global context. In J. Corner and S. Harvey (eds.), *Enterprise and heritage: Crosscurrents of national culture* (pp. 21–44). London: Routledge.

Robins, K. (1997). What in the world's going on? In P. D. Gay (ed.), *Production of culture/cultures of production* (pp. 11–66). London: The Open University.

Roche, M. (2000). *Mega-events and modernity: Olympics, expos and the growth of global culture*. London: Routledge.

Rodriguez, J. (2001). Three cheers for the XFL. *The Gazette*, February 17, p. G1.

Rofe, J. (1999). The 800-pound gorilla keeps growing: Fox discovers that buying sports properties is cheaper than renting—and it heads off the competition. *Street & Smith's Sports Business Journal*, August 23–29, p. 24.

Rojek, C., and Turner, B. S. (1993). *Forget Baudrillard?* London: Routledge.

Rosentraub, M (1999). *Major league losers: The real cost of sports and who's paying for it* (Second ed.). New York: Basic Books.

Rowe, D. (1995). *Popular cultures: Rock music, sport and the politics of pleasure*. London: Sage.

Rowe, D. (1996). The global love-match: Sport and television. *Media, Culture & Society*, 18(4), pp. 565–582.

Rowe, D. (1997). Rugby league in Australia: The Super League saga. *Journal of Sport & Social Issues*, 21(2), pp. 221–226.

Rowe, D. (1999). *Sport, culture and the media: The unruly trinity*. Buckingham: Open University Press.

Rowe, D., and McGuirk, P. (1999). Drunk for three weeks: Sporting success and the city image. *International Review for the Sociology of Sport*, 34 (2), pp. 125–142.

Rowe, D., and McKay, J. (1999). Field of soaps: Rupert v. Kerry as masculine melodrama. In R. Martin and T. Miller (eds.), *SportCult* (pp. 191–210). Minneapolis: University of Minnesota Press.

Rowe, D., and Stevenson, D. (1994). Provincial paradox: Urban tourism and city imaging outside the metropolis: Australia and New Zealand. *Journal of Sociology*, 30, pp. 178–93.

Ruibal, S. (1999). NBC's Gravity Games an alternative to NFL. *USA Today*, October 1, p. 12C.

Rushin, S. (1994). Chapter one: The titan of television. *Sports Illustrated*, August 16, pp. 35–41.

Russakof, D. (1998). Okay, soccer moms and dads: Time out! Leagues try to rein in competitive parents. *The Washington Post*, August 25, p. A1.

Ryan, J. (1995). *Little girls in pretty boxes: The making and breaking of elite gymnasts and figure skaters*. New York: Warner Books.

Safire, W. (1996). Soccer moms. *The New York Times Magazine*, 27 October, pp. 30, 32.

Sage, G. H. (1990). *Power and ideology in American sport: A critical perspective*. Champaign: Human Kinetics.

Sage, G. H. (1998). *Power and ideology in American sport: A critical perspective* (Second ed.). Champaign: Human Kinetics.

Sakamoto, B. (1986). Jordan's glamour fills league arenas. *Chicago Tribune*, December 16, p. D10.

Sandomir, R. (1992). NBC's games show: Live connection and cable jeopardy. *The New York Times*, July 19, p. 11A.

Sandomir, R. (1996a). NBC's money shots prove it: They love a parade. *The New York Times*, July 19, p. 14B.

Sandomir, R. (1996b). Olympic moments, but hours later on TV. *The New York Times*, July 25, p. A1.

Sassen, S. (1991). *The global city: New York, London, Tokyo*. New Jersey: Princeton University Press.

Sassen, S. (2001). *The global city: New York, London, Tokyo* (Second ed.). New Jersey: Princeton University Press.

Sassen, S. and Roost, F. (1999). The city: Strategic site for the global entertainment industry. In S. Fainstein and D. Judd (eds.), *The tourist city* (pp. 143–154). New Haven, CT: Yale University Press.

Savage, M., and Warde, A. (1993). *Urban sociology, capitalism and modernity*. London: Macmillan.

Schimmel, K. (2001). Sport matters: Urban regime theory and urban regeneration in the late-capitalist era. In C. Gratton, and I. Henry (eds.) *Sport in the city: The role of sport in economic and social regeneration* (pp. 259–277). London: Routledge.

Schimmel, K., Ingham, A., and Howell, J. (1993). Professional team sport and the American City: Urban politics and franchise relocation. In A. G. Ingham and J. W. Loy (eds.), *Sport in Social development: Traditions, transitions, and transformations* (pp. 211–244). Champaign, IL: Human Kinetics.

Schlesinger, A. (1963). *The politics of hope*. Boston: Houghton Mifflin.

Schor, J. B. (1998). *The overspent American: Upscaling, downshifting and the new consumer*. New York: Basic Books.

Schrof, J. M. (1995, June 19). American women: Getting their kicks. *Science & Society*, June 19, pp. 118, 59.

Schulian, J. (1996). Protecting the investment: NBC's opening-night coverage was as commercial as the games themselves. *Sports Illustrated*, July 29, p. 112.

Schlosser, J. (2001). Revved up for NASCAR. *Broadcasting and Cable*, February 12, p. 18.

Schmidt, R. (2001). Murdoch reaches for the sky. *Brill's Content*, June, 74–79, pp. 126–129.

Schwartz, D. (1998). *Contesting the Super Bowl*. New York: Routledge.

Segal, M. D. (1994). The First Amendment and cable television: Turner Broadcasting System, Inc. v. FCC. *Harvard Journal of Law and Public Policy*, 18(3), pp. 916–928.

Shapiro, L. (1996). In rating the TV coverage, It's a thin line between love and hate. *The Washington Post*, August 6, p. E6.

Shawcross, W. (1997). *Murdoch: The making of a media empire*. New York: Touchstone Books.

Shropshire, K. L. (1995). *The sports franchise game: Cities in pursuit of sports franchises, events, stadiums, and arenas*. Philadelphia: University of Pennsylvania Press.

Silk, M. L. (2002). *"Bangsa Malaysia"*: Global sport, the city and the media refurbishment of local identities. *Media, Culture & Society,* 24(6), pp. 775–794.

Silk, M. (2004). A tale of two cities: Spaces of consumption and the façade of cultural development. *Journal of Sport and Social Issues,* 28(4), pp. 349–378.

Silk, M. and Amis, J. (2005). Bursting the tourist bubble: Sport and the spectacularization of urban space. *Sport in Society* 8(2), pp. 280–301.

Silk, M. and Falcous, M. One Day in September / One Week in February: Mobilizing American (Sporting) Nationalisms. *Sociology of Sport Journal,* 22 (4), pp. 447–471.

Silverstone, R. (1997). Introduction. In R. Silverstone (ed.), *Visions of suburbia* (pp. 1–25). London New York: Routledge.

Slater, D. (1997). *Consumer culture and modernity.* Cambridge: Polity Press.

Sloane, A. (1999, December 11). Echo of Europe. *The New Zealand Herald.*

Smith, A. (2001). Sporting a new image? Sport-based regeneration strategies as a means of enhancing the image of the city tourist destination. In C. Gratton and I. Henry (eds.) *Sport in the city: The role of sport in economic and social regeneration* (pp. 127–148). London: Routledge.

Smith, A. D. (1991). *National identity.* London: Penguin.

Smith, A. M. (1994). *New right discourse on race and sexuality.* Cambridge: Cambridge University Press.

Smith, J., and Ingham, A. G. (2003). On the waterfront: Retrospectives on the relations between sport and community. *Sociology of Sport Journal,* 20(4), pp. 252–274.

Smith, J. W., and Clurman, A. (1997). *Rocking the ages: The Yankelovich report on generational marketing.* New York: HarperBusiness.

Smith, V. and Siegel, F. (2001). Can Mayor O'Malley save ailing Baltimore. *City Journal,* Available at: http://www.city-journal.org/html/11_1_can_mayor_omalley.html.

Soccer Industry Council of America (1997). *Soccer in the U.S.A.: An overview of the American soccer market.* N. Palm Beach, FL: Soccer Industry Council of America.

Soccer Industry Council of America (1998). *National Soccer Participation Survey.* N. Palm Beach, FL: Soccer Industry Council of America.

Sporting Goods Manufacturers Association (1998). State of the Industry Report.

Stark, S. (2002). U.S. losing basketball grip. *Montreal Gazette,* November 25, p. C8.

Stark, S. D. (1997). *Glued to the set: The 60 television shows and events that made us who we are today.* New York: Delta.

State of Maryland (1985). Report of the Special Advisory Commission on Professional Sports and the Economy. Annapolis, MD.

Staudohar, P.D. (1989). *The sports industry and collective bargaining.* Ithaca: ILR Press, Cornell University.

Steinbrecher, H. (1996). Getting in on soccer: The hottest sport to reach international markets. Paper presented at Marketing with Sports Entities, February 26–27, Swissotel, Atlanta, GA.

Stevens, K., and Winheld, M. (1996). Fans flocking to catch Tiger at brink of fame. *USA Today,* September 19, p. 16C.

Stevenson, D. (1997). Olympic Arts: Sydney 2000 and the Cultural Olympiad. *International Review for the Sociology of Sport,* 32, pp. 227–38.

Stewart, L. (2000). NBC gives XFL the backing it needs. *The Los Angeles Times,* March 31, p. D8.

Stodghill, R. (1997). Tiger, Inc. *Business Week,* April 28, pp. 32–37.

Stoeltje, M. F. (1999). In your face. *The Houston Chronicle,* October 17, p. 1.

Stotlar, D. K. (2000). Vertical integration in sport. *Journal of Sport Management*, 14(1), pp. 1–7.

Strasser, J. B., and Becklund, L. (1991). *Swoosh: The unauthorized story of Nike and the men who played there*. New York: Harcourt Brace Jovanovich.

Strategic Management Committee (1991). *The Renaissance continues: A 20 year strategy for downtown Baltimore*. Baltimore, MD.

Struna, N. (1996). *People of Prowess: Sport, Leisure and Labor in early Anglo-America*. Urbana: University of Illinois Press.

Sugden, J. (1994). USA and the World Cup: American nativism and the rejection of the people's game. In J. Sugden and A. Tomlinson (eds.), *Hosts and champions: Soccer cultures, national identities and the USA World Cup* (pp. 219–252). Aldershot: Arena.

Sugden, J., and Tomlinson, A. (1994). Soccer culture, national identity and the World Cup. In J. Sugden and A. Tomlinson (eds.), *Hosts and champions: Soccer cultures, national identities and the USA World Cup* (pp. 3–12). Aldershot: Arena.

Sunderland, L. E. (1998). Deal could mean bonanza of $500M to U.S. Soccer: Venture with IMG, Nike seen shoring foundations. *Baltimore Sun*, April 22, p. 3E.

Swift, E. M. (1991a). From corned beef to caviar. *Sports Illustrated*, June 3, pp. 74–90.

Swift, E. M. (1991b). Reach out and touch someone: Some black superstars cash in big on an ability to shed their racial identity. *Sports Illustrated*, August 5, pp. 54–58.

Sydney Morning Herald (2000, December 23). Murdoch's end game, December 23, pp. 13.

Thomas, G. S. (1998). *The United States of suburbia: How the suburbs took control of America and what they plan to do with it*. New York: Prometheus Books.

Thurow, R. (1996). The Olympics: Lord of the rings. *The Wall Street Journal*, July 19, p. 14.

Toch, T. (1994). Football? In short pants? No helmets? *Science & Society*, 166, June 13, pp. 76, 78.

Todd, J. (2000). XFL latest threat to future of the CFL: The Vince McMahon NBC league is everything a sports league should not be. *The Vancouver Sun*, November 7, p. F6.

Tomlinson, A. (1999). *The game's up: Essays in the cultural analysis of sport, leisure and popular culture* (vol. 15). Aldershot: Ashgate.

Tomlinson, J. (1999). *Globalization and culture*. Cambridge: Polity Press.

Tomlinson, A. (2002). Theorising spectacle: Beyond Debord. In J. Sugden & A. Tomlinson (Eds.). *Power Games: A critical sociology of sport* (pp. 44–60). London: Routledge.

Trujillo, N. (1995). Machines, missiles, and men: Images of the male body on ABC's Monday Night Football. *Sociology of Sport Journal*, 12(4), pp. 403–423.

Turner, R., and Rosentraub, M. (2002). Tourism, sports and the centrality of cities. *Journal of Urban Affairs*, 24(5), pp. 487–492.

Unger, H. (1996). Goodwill Games offers $5 million in prize money: Turner also cuts number of sports for '98 event. *Atlanta Journal and Constitution*, September 25, p. 1E.

United States Census Bureau (2001). The 2000 Census. Available at: http://factfinder.census. gov/bf/_lang = en_vt_name = DEC_2000_SF3_U_DP3_geo_id = 16000US2404000 .html.

Urquhart, J., and Crossman, J. (1999). The Globe and Mail coverage of the Winter Olympic games: A cold place for women athletes. *Journal of Sport & Social Issues*, 23(2), pp. 193–202.

USA Today (1996). Goodwill Games changes gear. September 25, p. 2C.

Van Rooij, M. (2000). Stadium fever. In Provoost, M. (ed.), *The stadium: The architecture of mass sport*. Rotterdam: NAI Publishers.

Voisin, A. (1991, December 3). NBA takes active role in dealing with AIDS issue. *Atlanta-Constitution*, p. December 3, F1.

Wade, D. (2001). McMahon's football not all bad. *The Commercial Appeal,* February 5, p. D4.

Wagg, S. (1995). The business of America: Reflections on World Cup '94. In S. Wagg (ed.), *Giving the game away: Football, politics and culture on five continents* (pp. 179–200). Leicester: Leicester University Press.

Wagner, P. (1996). *The construction of urban tourism space: Baltimore's Inner Harbor, 1964– 1990.* Unpublished master's thesis, University of Maryland, College Park.

Walker, S. (1997). Defending the sabbath from soccer. *The Christian Science Monitor,* Oct. 16, p. 1.

Walsh, A., and Brown, A. (1999). *Not for sale! United for United: Manchester United, Murdoch and the defeat of BskyB.* Edinburgh: Mainstream Publishing.

Walsh, A. J., and Giulianotti, R. (2001). This sporting mammon: A normative critique of the commodification of sport. *Journal of the Philosophy of Sport,* XXVIII, pp. 53–77.

Webley, I. A. (1986). Professional wrestling: The world of Roland Barthes revisited. *Semiotica,* 58(1/2), pp. 59–81.

Weingarten, M. (2002). Site by site, NBA takes on the world. *The New York Times,* November 14, p. G2.

Weir, T. (1993). Basketball's appeal is international. *USA Today,* June 18, p. 1B.

Wenner, L. A. (1994). The Dream Team, communicative dirt, and the marketing of synergy: USA basketball and cross-merchandising in television commercials. *Journal of Sport & Social Issues,* 18(1), pp. 27–47.

Wenner, L. A. (ed.) (1998). *Mediasport.* London: Routledge.

Wernick, A. (1991). *Promotional culture: Advertising, ideology and symbolic expression.* London: Sage.

Westhead, R. (2001). XFL TV ratings a real concern: League forced to give away free advertising. *The Gazette,* February 22, p. D7.

Whannel, G. (1992). *Fields in vision: Television sport and cultural transformation.* London: Routledge.

Whannel, G. (1998). Individual stars and collective identities in media sport. In M. Roche (ed.), *Sport, popular culture and identity* (pp. 23–36). Aachen: Meyer & Meyer Verlag.

Whitney, C. (1898). American football. In F. G. Aflalo (ed.), *The encyclopaedia of sport* (pp. 422–425). London: Richard Clay and Sons.

Whitson, D. (1994). The embodiment of gender: Discipline, domination, and empowerment. In S. Birrell and C. L. Cole (eds.), *Women, sport, and culture.* Champaign, IL: Human Kinetics.

Whitson, D., and Macintosh, D. (1993). Becoming a world-class city: Hallmark events and sports franchises in the growth strategies of Western Canadian cities. *Sociology of Sport Journal,* 10, (3) pp. 221–240.

Whitson, D., and Macintosh, D. (1996). The global circus: International sport, tourism, and the marketing of cities. *Journal of Sport & Social Issues,* 20(3), pp. 278–295.

Whyte, W. H. (1956). *The organization man.* New York: Simon & Schuster.

Waitt, G. (1999). Playing games with Sydney: Marketing Sydney for the 2000 Olympics. *Urban Studies,* 36, (7) pp. 1055–1077.

Wideman, J. E. (1990). Michael Jordan leaps the great divide. *Esquire,* November, pp. 140– 145, 210–216.

Wilbon, M. (2003). A talent show out of this world. *The Washington Post,* February 9, p. D1.

Wilcox, R. and Andrews, D. L. (2003). Sport in the city: Cultural, economic and political portraits. In R. Wilcox, D. L. Andrews, R. Pitter, and R. Irwin (eds.) (2003). *Sporting dystopias: The making and meanings of urban sport cultures* (pp. 1–16). New York: SUNY Press.

Williams, G. (1991). *1905 and all that: Essays on rugby football, sport and Welsh society*. Llandysul: Gomer Press.

Williams, J. (1994). The local and the global in English soccer and the rise of satellite television. *Sociology of Sport Journal*, 11(4), pp. 376–397.

Williams, R. (1981). The analysis of culture. In T. Bennett, G. Martin, C. Mercer and J. Woollacott (eds.), *Culture, ideology and social process* (pp. 43–52). Milton Keynes: The Open University.

Williams, S. (1996). Tiger a ratings master, too: His Grand Slam triumph is most-watched TV golf ever. *Daily News*, April 15, p. 87.

Willis, S. (1991). *A primer for daily life*. London: Routledge.

Wilson, B. (1997). "Good blacks" and "bad blacks": Media constructions of African-American athletes in Canadian basketball. *International Review for the Sociology of Sport*, 32(2), pp. 177–189.

Wilson, W. J. (1997). *When work disappears: The world of the new urban poor*. New York: Vintage Books.

Winner, C. P. (1998). U.S. soccer needs infusion of heart. *USA Today*, June 15, p. 1A.

Wise, M. (2004). NBC's Ebersol puts his game face on, comes up a winner. *The Washington Post*, August 28, C1.

Woods, J. (1992). Lost in the wilder shores of reality. *The Guardian*, 27 February, p. 23.

Wright, G. (1983). *Building the dream: A social history of housing in America*. Cambridge, MA: MIT Press.

Yu, H. (1996). Perspective on ethnicity: How Tiger Woods lost his stripes. *Los Angeles Times*, December 2, p. 4M.

Zaleski, J., Gold, S. F., Rotella, M., Andriani, L., and Scharf, M. (2002). Review: Sex, lies, and headlocks. *Publishers Weekly*, 249, May 6, pp. 44.

Zipay, S. (1996). Atlanta Olympics: Media-absurdity dominates coverage. *Newsday*, July 30, p. A60.

Zimbalist, A. S. (1998). The economy of stadiums, teams and cities. *Policy Studies Review*, 15(1), pp. 17–29.

Zukin, S. (1991). *Landscapes of power: From Detroit to Disney World*. Berkeley: University of California Press.

Zukin, S. (1998). Urban lifestyles: Diversity and standardisation in spaces of consumption. *Urban Studies*, 35(5–6), pp. 825–839.

Zwick, D., and Andrews, D. L. (1999). The suburban soccer field: Sport and America's culture of privilege. In G. Armstrong and R. Giulianotti (eds.), *Football cultures and identities* (pp. 211–222). London: Macmillan.

INDEX

Toby Miller
General Editor

Popular Culture and Everyday Life is the new place for critical books in cultural studies. The series stresses multiple theoretical, political, and methodological approaches to commodity culture and lived experience by borrowing from sociological, anthropological, and textual disciplines. Each volume develops a critical understanding of a key topic in the area through a combination of thorough literature review, original research, and a student-reader orientation. The series consists of three types of books: single-authored monographs, readers of existing classic essays, and new companion volumes of papers on central topics. Fields to be covered include: fashion, sport, shopping, therapy, religion, food and drink, youth, music, cultural policy, popular literature, performance, education, queer theory, race, gender, and class.

For additional information about this series or for the submission of manuscripts, please contact:

> Toby Miller
> Department of Cinema Studies
> New York University
> 721 Broadway, Room 600
> New York, New York 10003

To order other books in this series, please contact our Customer Service Department:

> (800) 770-LANG (within the U.S.)
> (212) 647-7706 (outside the U.S.)
> (212) 647-7707 FAX

Or browse online by series: www.peterlangusa.com